The Throwaway Boy

I didn't understand why my husband cried himself to
sleep every night – then the truth came out...

ALIX CHAPEL

JOHN BLAKE

Published by John Blake Publishing Ltd
3 Bramber Court, 2 Bramber Road,
London W14 9PB, England

www.johnblakebooks.com

www.facebook.com/johnblakebooks 🔘
twitter.com/jblakebooks 🔘

First published in paperback in 2008
This edition published in 2017

ISBN: 978 1 78606 255 0

British Library Cataloguing-in-Publication Data:

A catalogue record for this book is available from the British Library.

Design by www.envydesign.co.uk

Printed in Great Britain by CPI Group (UK) Ltd

1 3 5 7 9 10 8 6 4 2

Papers used by John Blake Publishing are natural, recyclable products made from wood
grown in sustainable forests. The manufacturing processes conform to the environmental
regulations of the country of origin.

Every attempt has been made to contact the relevant copyright-holders, but some were
unobtainable. We would be grateful if the appropriate people could contact us.

To love a thing means wanting it to live
Confucius

AUTHOR'S NOTE

All the family names have been changed to protect the privacy and dignity of my husband (except the dog – who couldn't be anything other than 'our Ben'). Our friends in Canada, who are mentioned in the book, have all chosen for me to use their real names. All other names, in both Canada and the UK, have been changed. I have also changed the names of the abusers – but not to protect their privacy or dignity.

Some place names in the UK have been changed. Also please note that the flashback experiences are written based on what both my husband and I remember of those times and our interpretation of those events as seen from that age.

The order of some events have been changed and some details have been added or changed in order, once again, to protect my husband's privacy and for editing purposes. Any details of abuse are taken from either my husband's police statement or from discussions with him and are exactly as my husband remembers them.

There's one thing I know for sure
We started with minds and hearts so pure
There's something that happens on the way
And turns all the colours back to grey

And you wish and you hope
When you're climbing the slope
That the closure you find
Will leave it behind
And the space that you seek
When you're reaching the peak
Will reveal peace of mind
When the stars are aligned

We shine like stars in the wintertime
You're not a throwaway boy
You can see it now

'Billy's Song' by James K

ACKNOWLEDGEMENTS

I will start by thanking everyone at John Blake Publishing. Particularly John Blake and Steve Burdett, but especially Elena Tsangarides… for reading the manuscript… believing in it… and passing it on to John.

Also, I'd like to thank the people who made my childhood what it was. The 'before' people… My family: Mum, Dad & sisters; Uncle Hal, Auntie Helen, Catherine and Neale; Uncle Clinton; maternal and paternal grandparents… you're not all still here, but you'll still know of my gratitude. And of course my most special friends: Samantha Temple, Deanna Tognela, Leanne Hamilton, Gail Johnson, Krista Hitch (and all of their families!). And not forgetting my best teachers: Barry Robbins and Dave Dunnett. My husband didn't have people like them in his childhood, so most importantly I want to thank The Divine Power that granted him such an exquisite mind and blessed him with such a resilient psyche – both specifically for him and instrumental in the same way that the above people were for me.

Some of those aforementioned people were also significant 'during' people, along with and especially 'The Jeffrey Five', Tracey MacGowan, Marjorie & Bruce Johnson, Katrina Kearley, and all of my 'Baby Buntings' – in particular, A Thomson, P Inches, M Hartnell, S Johnson, the Mollenhaur sisters, J & T Eason and L Crisp (and all their parents!).

So it stands to reason then that next I want to thank our 'after' people. Again, some important ones have already been named, but must include new friends: Christine Schwabe; my darts girls and, in particular, Lesley and Jo; and finally the special members of the exclusive B.B. book club; Samantha Jeffrey – for everything! (before, during and after). And Erin Simpson – for sharing my love of books and writing, for training Our Boy Ben and for seeing that he was a prince among dogs.

That done, I must give a big thank you to my sister 'Kate' and D. Brown. We wouldn't have been able to make 'the move' if it hadn't been for both of their support. Our life is better because of it. To my brother-in-law, aka James K, you have done so much; it is difficult to know where to start! I will forever be in your debt.

I would also like to thank everyone who allowed me to quote their lyrics in the book and to include their songs on the *NAPAC Un-muted* CD. Particularly, the family of Dirk McCray as well as all the members of Lahayna – especially Matt Edun and their manager Paul Cannon.

On 'Billy's' behalf, thanks to all his new friends from the village. You don't all know it, but you have been instrumental in his recovery, which in turn has impacted upon both of our lives. Clearly, some people we were simply meant to meet, and none more so than one particular family (who somehow knew exactly the way to support us in their own unique, quiet – yet exactly the right – way). So, thank you to them – for everything, but especially for providing Billy with the best therapist ever!

Now, special thanks to Keith and Catherine Roberts, and Helen Patton – for ensuring our life in the Northeast is still filled with family support and love. Which naturally leads to heartfelt recognition, and all our best love and gratitude going to Daniel, Susannah and Rosie-Rose – all three of you help to fill the void. Immeasurably. XO

Family and friends covered, I now simply must continue. I personally want to thank all the Operations across the UK that carried out the Historical Abuse Investigations, in particular, 'Liam' & 'Mark'. Thank you both for your professionalism and dedication. At least some paedophiles were brought to justice! Thank you to George Bennett and the Tees, Esk and Wear Valleys NHS Trust, for providing one of the highest levels of mental-health care in the whole country.

ACKNOWLEDGEMENTS

Huge gratitude must also go to Ady Davies. You were amazing, made the biggest difference... and we miss you. Thank you. Thank you.

Lastly, but certainly NOT least, a huge thank you to NAPAC, for all that you do for survivors all over the UK. Especially Helen Munt (for all your help with the CD, as well as everything else!). And to Peter Saunders, NAPAC'S Founder/Chief Executive... what can I say? The biggest thank you isn't enough! I will close by saying, to both of you, bless your heart.

CONTENTS

PREFACE

County Durham, England
December 2005

When I'm reminded of something, or if I'm remembering somewhere my husband, Billy, and I went or something we did during the 20 years we've been together, I automatically categorise it as either 'before', 'during' or 'after'. Even now, when I think of 'before', my tummy turns over. It doesn't matter how lovely the memory is, I still get that feeling because I know what is to come.

The 'during' phase, for me, starts with my husband's mental breakdown. The memories from the years that follow are clouded in a sort of haze. It was like a bad dream. It was so awful for so long that now it is as if I lost those years of my life.

I can't believe it all started in 1997 – a decade has passed since then. What makes me feel even worse is that for my husband it all started over thirty-five years ago.

The period of 'after' is the same for both of us – basically, after the truth came out. However, Billy's 'before' and 'during' are vastly different. Perhaps most poignant is that he doesn't have many 'before' memories. He was so young when the bad took over that, for him, all his life from an early age has been in the 'during' phase.

My childhood was a stark contrast. I grew up in Canada, where my parents emigrated in the mid-1960s, and led a happy and normal life. While I was squabbling with my sisters over Barbie dolls, Billy, growing up in Wales, was experiencing what no child should have to go through. I sometimes feel guilty for what I had, but I also know that my childhood helped to make me who I am, which has enabled me to be there for Billy.

By the time Billy was in his early twenties, he was a master at being able to push the memories away. His mind had done a remarkable job of protecting him. Sadly, it had had lots of practice. He learned to avoid things that made him remember his past. He spent the whole of his twenties pretending he was just like everyone else and adapting to living with the feelings of worthlessness and guilt that never left his head. He felt ashamed and dirty all the time. He hated himself, but hid it well, and worked hard at doing so. I met that boy hiding in a man's body in 1985. He fell in love with me, and I fell in love with him. But deep down he didn't think he deserved my love. The chip on his shoulder was fast becoming a chunk and his demons were constantly lurking below the surface.

PART I

CHIPS AND CHUNKS

INTRODUCTION

(Before)

Two years after our marriage in 1989, we made the decision to move to Canada. I recall being very surprised to discover how keen Billy had been to leave Wales. In fact, he was the one who first brought the subject up. I hadn't ever mentioned moving because I just assumed Billy would never want to. I didn't question his enthusiasm – I simply accepted it.

Looking back, I suppose there were signs, although I can't actually remember when I first started noticing the pattern of Billy's behaviour. It was evident, quite early on – certainly before we moved to Canada – that he would withdraw from time to time and become quite moody. I didn't link all the episodes together, at least not until much later. I now know all those times he was quiet and reclusive he was having flashbacks – but, back then, I had no idea.

1

HOME AND AWAY

Chasing the dream
You find its promise spent

I was the kind of child who fastidiously arranged her toys in order of colour, size or babyishness. Teddies lived on the top shelf of my rustic wooden bookcase; dolls on the middle shelf; books, placed tallest to shortest, on the bottom two. Thought had to be given to what things went where and attention paid to the level of accessibility for the things most played with. I have always contemplated organisation and believed in order – every aspect of my life has been a result of forward planning. A reliable infrastructure was required and was achieved very early on – perhaps even in infancy, if that is possible.

Over time, the items put under such disciplined scrutiny changed. Evolving from an arranged assortment of simplistic girlish treasures and an ordered array of adolescent accoutrements came finally the methodical accumulation of the essential household items of adulthood. Photo albums filled with a careful chronology of snapshots replaced the teddies. Novels, positioned alphabetically, replaced the picture books, which expanded over time from two shelves to two whole bookcases. Cotton vests changed to silky bras, Ladybird pants changed to La Senza knickers – different dressers, in different homes, in different countries, still housed my underwear in the top drawer. The organisation of kitchen cupboards, linen closets and wardrobes took over. The items were different but still everything had a place. Every thing, from rogue elastic bands to surplus carrier bags; gardening tools to camping equipment; summer clothes to Christmas decorations.

Over the years many people have teased me about my obsessive inclination towards order. One particular day in December 1994, the method I implemented for the storage of our Christmas decorations had been the cause of such playful ridicule. I had asked Billy to go down to the basement to retrieve the box labelled 'Mantelpiece', as I wanted to make a start on decorating the house. 'It's in the utility room in the cupboard by the dryer,' I called out as he made his way down the stairs. 'Right-hand side of the top shelf…' I shouted down as an afterthought.

Two minutes later, I heard him laughing as he clumped back up the stairs. 'You are the ultimate queen of organisation,' he said as he entered the living room. For some reason, he always found it hilarious that I knew where everything was, not to mention the fact that I labelled everything. By the time I brought up the box labelled 'Tree Baubles', he was relentlessly taking the piss. I didn't know any other way.

Unearthing the boxes of Christmas decorations always brought feelings of nostalgia and excitement. That year in particular, it didn't seem possible that Christmas was upon us – time had flown by as it was wont to do when one has been busy and not noticing. We had finally managed to buy our first house and had recently moved in. We had moved to Canada in 1992 and, after two years, had finally saved up enough for the deposit on our own place.

'It's our first Christmas in our new house, babes!' I excitedly said to Billy when all the boxes had been brought upstairs. I was so looking forward to decorating the house ready for the festive season. 'What's the matter? Aren't you excited?' I asked when I got no response – the laughter over the boxes already forgotten.

'What? Yeah, yeah… whatever,' Billy replied.

God, I thought to myself, he never gets excited about anything! I took a deep breath and exhaled at length to stop myself from saying something foul to Billy. It is important to be supportive, I reminded myself, and I knew there was no point in getting irritated over his lack of enthusiasm. I was exasperated but I wasn't going to let him dampen my excitement. I had long since given up asking why he never got excited. I was excited enough for both of us. I wanted to start making our own traditions, especially since we'd soon have a baby of our own.

I pictured our child growing up enjoying the kind of Christmases that I had experienced as a child. I hoped and prayed 1995 would be the year we would finally be blessed. We had been trying to get pregnant for six years at that point and had undergone countless tests. I had elected to try fertility drugs and had been on them for the past year. All I'd got from them, though, was a weight gain of 40lb, but I didn't care. I would rather have been an overweight mum than skinny and childless.

After many laparoscopies, the last one having been in September of that year, we were assured by my gynaecologist that there was nothing wrong and to be patient. I had been experiencing quite a lot of pelvic pain but believed my gynaecologist's diagnosis. I had no reason not to fully trust him and, although I was impatient, I was sure it would all work out in the end. I continued to believe it wasn't a matter of *if* we had a baby, it was *when*. I had always thought positively – long before it was popular – and this was no exception.

I remember I had said to him, 'Look, Billy, it's the fairy you made for our tree when we were living in Southampton! We were so skint that year, remember? We only had £5 to spend on each other!' I suppose I was still trying to get him involved.

'I bought you Turkish Delight,' Billy said, finally responding to me.

'Yeah, and I got you a box of Maltesers,' I remembered and smiled. 'Would you have thought then that nine years later we would own our own home and be living in Canada?' I asked, wanting to keep the verbal exchange going.

'No chance!' Billy replied. 'We've come a long way, love... I couldn't have done it without you.'

'I didn't think you would ever leave Britain,' I added speculatively.

'I don't know why! I'm glad to be shot of the place... there's nothing there for me now,' Billy snapped back, already grumpy again.

'That's a bit harsh, Billy,' I gently chided – always the peacekeeper.

Billy suddenly got up and gruffly announced that he was taking the dog for a walk.

'All right, love,' was what I said, although I was actually thinking, Shit… moody bastard!

When he returned, he was in a better mood .We decided to leave the decorating until the next day, get a pizza delivered, and watch the video I had picked up from Blockbusters. Billy lit the fire and, with our dog Ben sprawled on the floor by our feet, we cuddled up together on the couch.

The next day, again I tried in vain to get Billy involved with the decorating. In the end, he was so distracted I just carried on by myself. He was looking at the television but I knew he wasn't watching the programme. He did that now and again and, as always, when I asked him what he was thinking about, he just replied with a vague answer. What made his behaviour even more confusing was that there was never any pattern to it. I wished he would talk to me more but at least I was sure that he wasn't in a bad mood because of something I had said or done. It wasn't about *us*, I was certain of that. I reassured myself that Billy could snap out of his mood as quickly as it came and convinced myself not to be too overly concerned about it.

After finishing the mantelpiece, I started on the tree. Rummaging through the remaining boxes, I came across a misplaced, ornamental ceramic tree that I had made in kindergarten. The mere sight of it every Christmas transported me back, reminding me how the whole class had made those festive decorations. We had each been given a lump of clay that we kneaded and formed into a cone shape. Then we were told to pinch the sides all over to give the appearance of small branches. After that was completed, the caretaker came to our classroom to show us how to paint them and told us that he would take them all down to the basement and bake them in the kiln. He stressed that it was very important not to get any paint on the bottom of our trees as it could cause them to get too hot and they could explode. I remember I concentrated so hard, determined to only brush the paint on the sides.

I had been horrified when some paint did smudge on the bottom. I tried desperately to wipe it off, but without success. In fact, I most likely made it worse. I was scared, but said nothing. I just put my tree on the tray with the rest of them.

That night I worried so much I felt sick. I lay in bed sucking my thumb, imagining my tree getting too hot and exploding. I couldn't bring myself to tell Mummy or Daddy. The next morning, as we walked to school, I was terribly nervous. As we rounded the corner, I felt sure I was going to be faced with total devastation, the school reduced to a pile of rubble. When I knew the school would be in view, I was too scared to look. I had been expecting Mummy and my sister, Kate, to gasp, but, when they continued talking, I dared to look. I had been so glad to see the school intact.

When I reached my classroom and saw all the trees on a tray on the teacher's desk, the sense of relief had been immense. I remember that feeling. As an adult, standing in my living room, I saw the tiny speck of paint on the bottom of the tree and immediately realised what a silly worry-wart I had been, especially since it had all been for nothing. Undoubtedly, loads of other trees would also have had paint on the bottom.

Obviously, I was already a head-dweller and showed obsessive-compulsive tendencies even at that young age. I often wonder if that obsessive part of my personality is inherited. I can see a definite link with Dad's side of the family. My sisters and I, Dad, Grandma – we all have OCD to varying degrees, but the fact that it manifested itself in different ways with each of us suggests against it being learned behaviour. We are all very particular and we all have fixations, but not with regard to the same things, although, admittedly, there are similarities. None of us has the hand-washing issue that is so associated with OCD, and some 'obsessions' are actually rather funny. I always laugh at Kate when we are sharing M&Ms, for example; she has to have an even amount to eat, so, if her share totals an odd number, she throws one away; I will only eat one colour at a time, even though I know they all taste the same. Obviously, we are as bad as each other.

I love having mementos from my childhood, like the ceramic tree, around me. Still clutching the tree, I began thinking, as I often had in the years since Billy and I first met, how strange it was that he literally had nothing from his childhood. Well, except two old battered pictures from when he was about three years old. He wouldn't even have had those if I hadn't asked to have them from his mum. Maybe it was just a guy thing.

I especially loved those little pictures of him; he looked so cute and innocent. I had the best one framed and put it on my bedside table. On Billy's bedside table I put a picture of me at the same age. The day I put them in our bedroom, Billy commented on the photo of me but he couldn't even bring himself to look at his photo.

Deciding to stop decorating for the day, I placed the ornament on the coffee table just as Billy's voice broke through my thoughts, asking if I wanted to take Ben out. I thought it was a great idea and ran to get Ben's lead. As soon as Ben heard the jingle of his lead, he came barrelling into the kitchen and started bounding round and round me. He was a Collie cross, and the most gorgeous dog I had ever seen. He had the same colouring as Lassie and, although we didn't know what he was crossed with, we thought it was something like a Lab as he had their size and shape.

We had got him as a tiny pup seven years earlier, when we'd lived in Cardiff. We both loved Ben with all our heart. He filled the baby void so completely we couldn't possibly imagine life without him. Both Billy and I adored him with equal measure. But Ben, he adored Billy. I wasn't jealous. You just had to look at them together to know that nobody could compete with that. Billy and Ben... Ben and Billy. They were inseparable. They were the reason dogs were referred to as 'man's best friend'. That, he most certainly was.

I always kind of thought that Billy's love for him was different – strange almost. Billy seemed to get something from Ben that I have never witnessed before, and stronger than any other master–dog relationship I had ever seen. And, actually, there was a certain something that passed between them that was almost human. When we had decided to move to Canada, it was never a question of whether he would come with us – it was more a question of how we would make it work.

That afternoon we decided to take Ben to Willows Beach. I loved it there especially because it was a place that held such lovely memories of my childhood; I had played there such a lot as a child. When I lived in Britain, it was the one thing I missed most about Victoria.

It was a clear day, so I hoped we would be able to see Mount Baker in the distance. The only downside with taking Ben to the beach in the winter was that we had to keep him on the lead. He loved the water so much and would be straight in given half the chance. Other dogs swam in the winter, but I worried that it would be too cold and might not be good for him – obviously, overprotective as well as obsessive!

All too soon, the weekend was over and it was Monday morning, and back to work. I ran my own children's nursery and Billy worked as a care-giver at a day-centre for mentally and physically disabled adults.

When we had first arrived in Canada, Billy got a construction job. It was what he had always done. After a while, his back was starting to cause him a lot of pain. Eventually, he was diagnosed with arthritis of the spine and advised to change his job. At first, he thought he would be fine and continued his construction job, but it soon became evident that he would have to try something new. After a lot of assurances that we would manage just fine, I convinced him to leave construction, rest his back for a while and see what transpired.

He had only been out of work for a few weeks when a friend suggested he try volunteering at a local day-centre for mentally and physically disabled adults. At first, Billy was sure that he couldn't do it – 'People like me don't get jobs like that,' he had said. I was used to his lack of confidence but I was really sure he would be great at it. I asked what he meant by 'people like me', and told him he mustn't sell himself short all the time. I knew he liked the idea and I finally talked him into giving it a try.

I was so proud of him. He did so well that, within a few months, he was offered a part-time position and then, a few months after that, he landed himself a full-time job. He came home bursting with enthusiasm and said that, for the first time ever, he actually looked forward to going to work. He also said, after the first few days, that he thought people went to work because they had to, not because they wanted to. I found that, in particular, very sad and was so grateful that he had been given the chance to prove to himself what he was capable of. I was convinced he had found his calling.

I had trained as a nursery nurse in Britain and, when I returned to Canada, I opened my own nursery. Like Billy, I, too, loved my job but I was also really looking forward to our Christmas break that year. As it happened, that was nothing unusual. We only had one more week of work and I couldn't wait. The week flew by and, before we knew it, it was the weekend again. Billy and I spent the whole week before Christmas enjoying our new home and getting ready for our visitors.

Billy loved cooking and baking and was really good at it, so I quite happily let him take over with the food preparations and I stuck to decorating. On Christmas Eve, my parents, my younger sister, Naomi, and her husband, and my youngest sister, Sophie, all came over for dinner. My older sister, Kate, was living in England and, although she had been home for Christmas the year before, that year she couldn't get the time off work.

I wanted to start a new tradition so I got small, fun presents for everyone to open on Christmas Eve at our house. I decided I would do it every year from then on. I got Billy a selection pack of chocolates. Mum and Dad had gone to Britain that autumn, as they had done every year to visit family, and I got them to bring one back so I could give it to Billy. We couldn't get them in Canada and I thought it was something Billy might have had as a child. British chocolate had always been the best so I knew he would enjoy it.

He seemed surprised when he opened it. He laughed at the bars of chocolate he hadn't seen in ages and said he couldn't wait to eat them. Next, Sophie opened hers. As she was ripping off her wrapping paper, I glanced over at Billy. He seemed distracted again. I called out to him but, wherever he was, he didn't hear me. With everyone there and all that was going on, no one seemed to notice… but I did.

*   *   *

Cardiff

He sat looking at the Christmas tree. The sound of children playing outside could be heard through the closed window. He didn't want to play. He just wanted to stay sitting in the big chair. He could feel the tears prickling his eyes. He swallowed hard, trying to get rid of the lump in his throat. He was confused and didn't understand what he had done to deserve being brought to that place.

Shortly after he had arrived, a lady came to get him and showed him where he would be sleeping. He thought she must have made a mistake because surely he wouldn't be staying overnight. He desperately wanted to go home. When he got up enough courage to ask the lady when he could go home, she told him, in a matter-of-fact tone, he couldn't.

He knew some lads from the estate who had been taken into care so he figured that that was what was happening to him. It was just his luck to be taken away so close to Christmas. It wasn't as though he would miss much, though. Father Christmas always seemed to miss their house. Billy thought it was because, with the street being so dark, he couldn't see the houses. The street lamps were smashed. They had always been smashed – well, at least for as long as he could remember. Father Christmas didn't leave any toys at the other houses either, so he felt sure it wasn't because he had been naughty. Anyway, there was no way he would find them that year. Not only were the street lamps broken, but their house was in total darkness as well. Billy's mam, Hannah, hadn't been able to afford to put any coins in the electric meter for ages. When there had been a choice between paying for gas or 'lecky', gas always won. Of course, sometimes they had neither. Billy didn't mind all that, though, he just wanted to be with his family.

In the children's home that Christmas, Billy was given a toy gun, but he would have given it up in a flash if it meant he could go home. He still didn't understand why he had been taken away from his mam, brothers and sisters, but he figured it must have had something to do with his father. He thought of him and his anger once again surfaced, as it always did – but then even more so. He was upset and confused by his leaving and hated to see his mam so unhappy.

He was a very sensitive and 'knowing' little boy, more so than his two older siblings, and even more so than his twin. Perhaps that was why he was the one who was acting up. The others, oblivious to their mother's struggle, just carried on, while Billy, taking it all in and becoming increasingly angry, frustrated and completely helpless, rebelled. Even though Hannah's plight was nothing to do with him, he felt responsible.

There was no doubt that things had gone downhill since his father had left, especially financially, although life hadn't been that great before. Hannah bore the brunt of her husband's ways and sheltered her three youngest children from a great deal. He was a violent man who drank too much and was very selfish. His money was spent on himself – and his wardrobe full of suits – while the children often went without.

By the time he walked out on them, Hannah was worn ragged. She was devastated that her husband had left, and still loved him, despite his treatment of them. She had been used to just getting by, always having to try to stretch what little money he gave her but, on her own, there often just wasn't any money at all.

Everything suffered as a result that first year. All the children were undernourished, but even so they grew out of their clothes and, of course, there was no money to buy new ones. Then, as a result of not eating properly, Billy wasn't able to concentrate and was getting behind with his schoolwork. That was particularly hard as Billy's twin, Jon, was also in the same class and he wasn't having difficulty, which bothered Billy all the more. Gradually, he began to dread going to school and started playing truant. His mam was so fraught that, to begin with, she hadn't noticed – and then, when she did, it was just another one of those things that she didn't discipline him over. She was too tired and caught up with getting through her own day and looking after Billy's little sister, Lauren. Eventually, Billy was taken into care and, even though he had been through some bad experiences before being taken away, he entered the children's home a naive, sensitive, vulnerable little boy. He cried himself to sleep every night but then, after a while, he stopped, already becoming hardened by the experiences of his first few weeks.

In the beginning, before he started running away from the children's home and lost the privilege, Billy was allowed back home to his family. He hated being in the children's home but found the times back with his family equally as upsetting. He felt like an outsider and hated not feeling part of the family. He began to think that it must be his fault, especially since he had been the only one taken away. He would get himself so worked up that all the feelings of frustration, anger and bitterness would spiral out of control. It happened every time he was home. He would get there and all his good intentions of behaving properly would go out the window when faced with the situation at home. He felt so misunderstood.

He didn't mean to be naughty, he just couldn't control his feelings and vented them without thinking of the consequences. He would misbehave, get into trouble and, inevitably, his social worker would find out and he would be sent straight back to the children's home. Ironically, even though the time spent at home was so hard – emotionally as well as physically – he spent the whole time he was away pining to go back. He built home up so much in his mind while he was away, imagining how it was going to be, setting himself up for disappointment and upset every time, but never getting to the point where he didn't want to go home.

Billy had apparently been made a ward of the court so the local authority could do a better job of caring for him than his mother could. Ironically, the opposite was true. It was hard enough for any child to be taken into care, even when they were being rescued from bad parents, but, when the experience in care was far worse than what he would have endured if he had remained with his family, it was tragic and inexcusable. At seven, when other boys were playing cowboys and Indians and marbles, Billy was becoming accustomed to a life without love or protection.

In those first few months, coping with life in and out of the homes, Billy was under the illusion that was as bad as things could get. He had been through such a lot of turmoil and it had been far from easy, but it couldn't have occurred to him that, compared to what lay ahead, life then was actually not that bad.

★   ★   ★

Later, when everybody had gone home, I gingerly asked Billy if anything was wrong.

'No, love, I'm just tired,' he replied.

'Billy, you seemed miles away. What were you thinking about?'

'Nowt!' Billy's voice was laced with anger and the fall into dialect seemed evidence of his mood.

'Well, I know something is bothering you. Why won't you tell me?' I pleaded.

After a few moments of silence, when I feared his mood could have gone either way, Billy, in a quiet, subdued voice, just told me that the selection pack had made him feel sad.

'Why? Did it make you homesick?' I asked.

Billy sighed. 'No, love… I never got a selection pack when I was a lad. I don't even know if they were around then. Most of the time we just got an apple and a manky orange in an old sock. Although I do remember getting a toy gun one year.'

'From your mum?' I asked.

'No,' he mumbled and quickly changed the subject. Billy's memories could flood in like a high tide at times but, like sea water, they usually retreated before he could properly grasp them – not that he particularly wanted to.

That night, lying in bed, I felt so sorry for the 'little' Billy. I knew he hadn't had a childhood like mine and that they were really poor, and I knew he had spent time in children's homes, but I didn't realise just how much his childhood had obviously affected him. I felt guilty for all my reminiscing.

* * *

Victoria, British Columbia

'Come on, Alix, get your coat on please. Don't forget your hat and mittens, they're on the kitchen table.'

Mummy was busy getting Sophie and Naomi dressed in their all-in-one winter snowsuits. It was cold but it hadn't snowed. We were ever hopeful for a white Christmas. There was still time – Christmas was still two weeks away. That night, we were getting ready to walk around to the fire hall. We loved to look at all the lights that decorated the whole station.

Every Christmas, as we walked to the fire hall along the path past Bowker Creek, up over the wooden bridge, I'd get Mummy to repeat the 'hola pola' story. As we approached the bridge, Mummy smiled at me. I guess she knew I was going to ask her but, before I could, she held my hand and started to laugh and then said, 'It was the Christmas before you turned two, Alix. You were just learning to talk and could only say a few words. For days on end, all you would keep repeating, over and over again, was "hola pola… hola pola…" We couldn't figure out what you were trying to say. "What do you want, darling?" Daddy would ask. Over and over you would repeat, "hola pola… hola pola…" Then one day we were driving towards the fire hall when you started shouting "hola pola… hola pola…" and pointing to the lights. We all screamed and clapped our hands… we'd finally figured it out!'

I loved to hear that story. Mummy said she never did figure out how I got 'hola pola' from 'fire-hall lights'. I tried to remember being two, but I couldn't. I could remember when I was five and crying when I had to go to kindergarten. I could also remember when I was about four; we had been at Cook Street Park waiting to pick Mummy up from her tennis lesson, and I fell and cut the bottom of my foot on the roundabout. But, no matter how hard I tried, I couldn't remember much before that.

'Where was I when Alix was two?' Naomi asked.

'You were in Mummy's tummy, darling… you hadn't been born yet,' Mummy answered patiently. Naomi always asked those sorts of questions.

'Where was Kate?'

'With us, she was five,' Mummy replied.

Satisfied with her answer, Naomi ran ahead to catch up with Kate. When we rounded the corner, we all simultaneously exclaimed, 'Wow!' The lights were better than ever! I liked Rudolph's red nose the best. We didn't stay long. We were all feeling the cold, even with our hats, mittens and big winter coats.

Christmas time for our family was full of tradition. No sooner was Hallowe'en over than the preparations would start. I loved coming home from school and smelling the festive aromas of Christmas baking wafting out of the kitchen window as we ran down the driveway. While we were at school, Mummy would make her Christmas cake, Christmas pudding and mince tarts. Then, when we were at home, we would take turns helping her with the shortbread, gingerbread and sugar cookies. My favourite to make was always the sugar cookies because, not only did we use Christmas tree and star cookie cutters to make the shapes, but we also decorated them with icing and sprinkles. When it came to eating them, though, my all-time favourite was the shortbread.

We would usually go, with Daddy, to get the Christmas tree on the first weekend in December. Then we would listen to Christmas carols on the record player while we all helped to decorate it. We always made decorations at school and I would spend lots of time finding the best branches for mine to hang from. Lastly, when all the decorating was done, Daddy would lift Sophie up, because she was the youngest, for her to reach over and put the angel on the top.

Also, at the beginning of December, two big parcels would arrive. One was filled with presents from Grandma and Grandpa in Northern Ireland, and the other was from Grama and Granda in England. We were never allowed to open them before Christmas Day but it was exciting just seeing them sitting under the tree, our anticipation building with each passing day.

Every year, on the nights leading up to Christmas, we loved to watch the Christmas specials on the television. After a hot bath, two at a time, we would get into our nighties and dressing gowns and settle in front of the fire and watch the specials. We knew all the words and would sing along to 'Rudolf the Red-Nosed Reindeer' and 'Frosty the Snowman'. They were great but I liked watching The Grinch the most. We all thought Sophie looked just like Cindy-Lou Who.

On the weekend before Christmas, we would go to Simpson Sears to see Santa. There was no way I was going to sit on his knee, though. Well, at least not unless Kate came with me. I preferred to write a letter to Santa, and send it to the North Pole, rather than asking him in person.

The year before, when I was six, I had really wanted an Easy Bake Oven. We had started letters to Santa in school, then I brought it home and worked on it for hours to make sure it was my best printing. I always wondered if Santa had received it, although he must have because I got the Easy Bake Oven. Unless, of course, Kate told him. I worried that the letter would get lost on its long journey and pictured my letter floating out of the mailbag on the postal train, like the one on 'Frosty the Snowman'. Even if I had sat on Santa's knee, though, there was no way I would ever have asked him about the letters. I never did get up the nerve actually to speak to him.

On Christmas Eve, we always watched something more grown up on television. The Railway Children always seemed to be on and I thought it was great. It always reminded me of being at Grama and Granda's house in England.

By the time Christmas morning arrived, my sisters and I were bursting with excitement. The minute we woke up, we would all congregate in Kate's room. We were never allowed to go down to see if Santa had been before 8.00am, and certainly not without Mummy and Daddy. We always woke up, at the latest, by 7.00am, so we had an hour, at least, to get even more excited. On the dot of 8.00am, we would all assemble on the landing, itching to go down the stairs. Daddy would count, '1… 2… 3…' and we would be off, charging down the stairs. We all opened our stockings at the same time and then, when everyone was finished, Kate would have the job of handing out the presents from under the tree one by one.

I was thrilled when it was my turn. I got a Mrs Beasley doll.

*   *   *

I was having trouble falling asleep. I felt bad that the selection pack hadn't had the desired effect but I was glad it got him to open up a bit – at least that was something. I wondered who had given him the toy gun. I felt he was holding back but I didn't want to push him. I hoped he didn't think I was silly making such a big deal over Christmas. His lack of enthusiasm made sense – he most likely just wanted to forget his Christmas memories and there I was shoving Christmas down his throat. I reassured myself that all I could do was to make sure that all his future Christmases would be better.

2

DRIVEN TO
DISTRACTION

Do you lie awake
Your mind a meeting place
Where others seem to congregate
And half the time
You don't know who they are

'Turn the Light on Love' by Dirk McCray

I love 'looking after', organising and fixing. I think some people, including Billy, interpret that as a kind of control-freakery or appalling bossiness, but it isn't meant that way. Well, in truth, I may want to be in control, but not of other people – just myself. At no other time are my organisational skills executed to their full potential than when preparing for a holiday. On the days leading up to any trip, I am in my element – organising, planning, preparing. I have refined my routine to such an extent, and have put it into practice on so many occasions, I now have it down to a fine art. I pride myself on remembering everything and being prepared for every eventuality, within the confines of the minimum amount of luggage, of course. It is just something I have always done.

When we lived in Canada, we camped a lot. Preparing for camping trips always posed the biggest challenge, due to the fact that many more things had to be considered, but I was in no way put off by the challenge. In fact, if I'm honest, I would have to admit that I relished the extra planning. Billy always teased me when I got my camping lists out. We joked about it but I suspected that he found the whole procedure slightly irritating. I was conscious of the fact that Billy sometimes felt that I took charge too much, so I tried to involve him in as much as I could bear to relinquish. We used to laugh about the fact that friends of ours always argued before a trip because the wife expected the husband to do it all. For Billy, chance would have been a fine thing, and I suspect that he would have preferred it more that way.

I was so caught up in doing it my right way I even took charge of the unpacking and setting up at the campsites when we arrived. What I knew, that Billy didn't, was that my 'right' way didn't mean that I thought Billy's way was wrong. My meticulous planning was really only meticulous to me. For all I knew, what I considered to be meticulous may not have been by someone else's standards. But that's my point – it was, and still is, my own right way. Not necessarily *the* right way.

Ironically, Billy is a perfectionist; he would have set up perfectly, but he would have set up *later*, and I couldn't wait. So, Billy's personality type ensured he didn't speak up and mine ensured I took charge. I was aware that if I took charge too much, without consulting Billy, he would start to think that I did it all because I thought he wasn't capable and I had enough insight to tell him I did it all because I wanted to, but I made the mistake of assuming he understood what I was saying. Intellectually, maybe, he did, but that didn't stop him from feeling inferior. I really didn't see the ramifications of that.

August of 1996 was the first time we went on a trip to the USA. I had been when I was a child and was looking forward to introducing Billy to some of the places I'd visited with my parents and sisters. Usually, we just camped on the Island but that holiday was our first proper road trip. I wanted Billy to get excited about the trip, so I suggested we plan our route together. I also thought if I asked for his input into the preparations he would feel a part of it all and begin to look forward to the trip more.

With that in mind, I asked him if we should pack up the 4Runner on the Friday night after work. I also added that we could then just get up and go for the first ferry. However, it was a question that I didn't really require an answer to. Truthfully, I think I asked it just so that I could say that I *had* consulted him.

When Billy firmly stated that he didn't want the gear to stay in the vehicle overnight I was taken aback, and my shocked expression must have shown that. I remember that I had been confused; it hadn't occurred to me that he wouldn't agree to packing up on the Friday night. I thought the worst I would have had to put up with was his input into where things should go, not putting it off until the next day – the day we were leaving! I was horrified at the mere suggestion.

I noticed Billy's expression had changed. He actually looked angrily at me. 'We'd look well if it all got pinched!' he snapped.

'What do you mean? You're so paranoid… it won't get stolen!' I said, trying so hard not to sound whiny.

'For fuck's sake, do what ya wanna do!'

'Billy, don't be ridiculous! We're meant to be looking forward to our trip… why are you being like this?' For the first time the process of packing was going wrong and I began to feel a slight panic at the thought of chaos.

'Forget it!'

'No, I want to know when we are packing! I'm not leaving it to the last minute, running around like a chicken with its head cut off and then rushing to catch the ferry!' I wanted to save the situation, to stop his mood, and I tried frantically to think, at the same time as speaking, what he could be getting so upset about.

'What's the big deal? I'll put it all in in the morning, before you get up. I don't mind getting up early,' Billy replied.

'But I want to put it all in a certain place.'

'Christ! I am capable of doing it, you know!'

I could see he was getting it all wrong and it only made me more frustrated. 'I know you are, for Christ's sake! I didn't say you weren't!' I was beyond exasperated. 'I just figured out a way that it all fits and there are some things I need easy access to!' I was praying he would see what I meant.

'Like what?' Billy asked, equally as exasperated.

'Well, the cooler for one. Also, if each thing has a specific place it will be easier to pack up the next time. How about we leave the clothes out until Saturday morning and we put the camping equipment in on Friday night?' I compromised, saying anything, trying to defuse the situation.

'Aye, OK… I should be used to your organising by now,' he said resignedly. 'I guess being unorganised is a guy thing,' he joked in a cod Canadian accent. Panic over. The switch had been tripped and peace was restored.

'No,' I laughed. 'There are just disorganised people and organised people – it doesn't matter what gender they are. Anyway, I know my organising drives you up the wall, but it's just the way I am. I know I can be a bit obsessive about it.'

I knew I sounded light-hearted but the lingering notion that, even though his mood had improved, he still didn't really understand what I meant niggled in the back of my mind. I really couldn't even consider throwing all the stuff into the back of the 4Runner without any thought as to where things should go. I found the mere suggestion absurd.

'Actually, I like how you organise things and don't leave them to the last minute. It makes me feel safe,' Billy added quietly.

At that point, the wind had been sucked out of my sails. Not for one minute had I imagined that was how he actually felt. I didn't know what else to say. He had always been prone to getting worked up occasionally over the smallest of things. He would over-react and would often be paranoid about things going wrong – like the stuff getting stolen out of the 4Runner. It never lasted long, though, and then he would be OK again. It didn't happen often but, over the years, I had adapted to handling those moods without even realising it and, unbeknownst to me at the time, had learned ways to defuse the situation.

I often wonder what would have happened if I had a different personality and what impact that would have had on our relationship. I know what Billy's buttons are but I choose not to push them, which can't help but calm things down. I don't yell, so Billy doesn't yell. The quote 'If you don't run you can't be chased' often comes to mind.

At the time, I was so shocked that Billy actually said he liked my organising that it didn't register that he had said it made him feel safe. It wasn't until later that night, when I was lying in bed, that I thought about what he had actually said. When Billy came to bed I asked him what he meant. He simply said that his childhood had been chaotic at the best of times, and it was nice to have a life that was predictable for a change, something he could rely on. He kissed me goodnight and turned over, but I was aware that he wasn't asleep. I lay awake also, thinking how ironic it was that, actually, we both really just wanted to avoid chaos, even if it was for different reasons. And it made me feel closer to him. I started going over what I had to do the next day and, as I started to drift off to sleep, I was aware that Billy was still awake. I couldn't help but wonder what he was thinking about.

★   ★   ★

South Wales

Billy knew he needed to keep out of sight. He couldn't risk being seen by anyone. Lying under the hedge was uncomfortable but he had hidden in worse places. That time it was summer and the light nights proved to be a challenge. At least in the winter, when it could get dark as early as 4.00pm, he could cover more ground by walking as soon as it got dark. It was much harder to remain inconspicuous in the summer. He would just have to stay out of sight until nightfall.

He knew that once he got to the loft he would be fine. The problem was getting there. He was terrified of being seen, so was very diligent about hiding during the day and only venturing out in the daylight if there was no alternative. If he had been bigger, it would not have been such a problem, but he had always been small for his age. He wished he were older, big enough to be on his own without anyone noticing.

Although he wanted to come across as tough and hard, in reality he was vulnerable and sensitive-looking, which, along with his size, made him appear even younger than his eight years. As it was, if someone saw him roaming around on his own, in the middle of nowhere, undoubtedly his or her attention would be drawn, even if it was just to say hello to him; certainly not worth the risk. He didn't want to speak to anyone anyway but, more importantly, he didn't want anyone to remember seeing him.

Sometimes, from his hiding places, he was able to watch children playing. In those days, children played out at a young age, their parents oblivious to the dangers, seemingly unaware. Sadly, Billy was all too aware of the evil that was out there. Experience told him to trust no one, especially adults. Billy was drawn to watch any children he came across, probably intrigued by their carefree ability to run around and play, but would frequently become anxious, as if he was expecting something bad to happen to them. He was wary when adults were around and earnestly watched their movements, but he also had an uncanny ability of pinpointing the bullies. It only took a few seconds of observation before the children's body language warned him of potential danger. He was constantly on guard and felt somehow responsible for these nameless children, conscientiously 'taking on' the misplaced role of protector. The children were completely unaware that they had their own guardian angel watching out for them – which was fortunate, considering they were probably not, actually, in any danger at all and would most surely have thought Billy strange.

Other than the usual bullying that goes on within groups of children, Billy didn't witness anything untoward, at least nothing that required him to take any action – which was just as well, as he couldn't have done much and wouldn't have wanted to draw attention to himself in any case. As was usual, he didn't think that far ahead; he just took it upon himself to 'look out' for them. If nothing else, it kept him occupied while he lay in wait. He needed to stay awake, which was quite difficult when he was constantly exhausted, so having something to do helped. It had been so long since he had experienced a good night's sleep – years, in fact. He had to be alert at all times. The dangers were different, depending on where he was, but he was always afraid to let his guard down.

He felt like he had been under the hedge for hours but he knew it couldn't, actually, have been more than one or two at the most. He had made his escape during a day out at the seaside, slipping away when no one was watching. He had never been on a proper holiday and the day out was the only chance he would get to go to the seaside that year, but he didn't care. He would rather grab the chance to sneak away.

He had stolen some coppers and jumped on a bus heading out of town. He passed through a village and, on the outskirts, got off with a load of older lads, thinking he would be less likely to be noticed in a group. The older boys were too engrossed in talking about their plans for the weekend even to notice Billy. He had no idea where he was but he knew he had to get out of sight for the time being and then make his way back to Cardiff when darkness fell; hence the hedge. It was as good a place as any, but he was starting to get stiff and was wondering what the time was.

Not long after, he spotted a girl coming down the lane that ran alongside the *hedge. She seemed to be rushing. From his camouflaged vantage point, Billy also saw a group of bigger girls approaching her from behind. They were all wearing school uniforms and were clearly on their way home, which gave him an idea of the time. It was a warm afternoon and all the girls had their coats off, swinging them around as they sauntered down the lane. They were being quite raucous, despite their slow gait. The little girl, obviously hearing them, quickly turned around. Billy could see her perfectly. She was almost right beside him. His heart started to pound when he recognised the look in her eyes; she was frightened.*

In an instant Billy's senses were pricked. He knew the little girl was in trouble before anything had even happened. Her pace quickened but the girls caught up to her in no time. They were a few yards past Billy by this time but he was under no illusion as to what was transpiring. They were clearly taunting the little girl and starting to get physical. Although Billy couldn't hear exactly what they were saying, their intention was as plain as day. The little girl wet herself, right there in front of her tormentors. Billy felt sick with empathy. Perhaps he was over-reacting, but he could feel his temper rising. He gave way to it and, in an instant, he sprang from under the hedge, yelling for them to leave her alone.

The bullies were startled and ran away in such a hurry one of them dropped her coat. Billy yelled after them, hurling swear words, the like of which they probably had never heard before. When he turned around, the little girl had gone, but she, too, left in such a hurry she had dropped her schoolbag. Picking up the coat and bag, he hurried after her. Once she was in sight, he kept his distance and continued following her. She turned into a street, ran up to a house and in through the front door.

From behind a parked car, Billy mentally took note of the house number, then retraced his steps and, once again, hid under the hedge, knowing he needed to remain hidden until darkness fell. While lying in wait, he pulled the two items to himself for closer inspection. The coat, clearly, belonged to a girl, but he knew he would be glad of the warmth later, so resourcefully concluded that he could turn the coat inside out to hide the colour.

With no intention of keeping the schoolbag, he figured it wouldn't hurt to have a look inside it. He unzipped the flap and pulled it open, revealing schoolbooks, a bag of crisps, a bag of sweets and a few coppers. He zipped the bag back up again, laid his head upon it and waited, cramped and uncomfortable.

Finally, after several hours, he determined that it was dark enough to start his journey. The coat was already proving to be a godsend as it was much colder in the twilight. After safely depositing the schoolbag, completely intact, on the doorstep he had noted earlier, he started his trek.

His belly felt hollow and empty. He hadn't eaten since breakfast, but experience told him that, if he waited long enough, the grumbles would stop, leaving just a familiar emptiness. He was used to going for days without food, not just on the run, but in the homes as well, but he realised that he would need to keep his strength up. Travelling on foot would take it out of him so he decided he would steal a bottle of milk off a float in the morning if he was lucky enough to come across one.

He loved being out in the night. The quietness and the darkness made him feel safe. He knew he wouldn't be seen easily and he also could hear anyone approaching much better than in the daytime, which gave him an added advantage of ensuring he had plenty of time to dive for cover if the need arose. He particularly loved it when he came across the nocturnal animals. They always seemed to sense he wasn't a threat and would come right up to him to check him out, sometimes even following him on his journey. It was only at these times that he felt, just a little bit, less lonely. And, inevitably, when they parted company, Billy always felt like he'd lost a friend. He gave each and every animal, large and small, all of himself. He had no one else to give it to. He felt, too, that he got the same back from them, which ensured his relationships with all his animal family were fatefully spirit building.

He was much more experienced on that journey. He ran away that often he had lost count of the number of times, and the length of time before he was apprehended was getting longer each time due to all the tricks he was learning. It didn't even matter how severe the punishment was when he did go back; he would keep running away; and getting caned for being away for just one night was worth it. At least at those times he knew why he was getting beaten. There were many other occasions when he didn't even know what he had done to bring it on. The more abuse he received, the more he expected it, until eventually he believed he must deserve it.

He got used to the beatings and developed ways to escape mentally while the torture was being inflicted. After months of it, he had toughened up so much that he refused to cry, vowing not to give his abusers the satisfaction. It wasn't the physical beatings that he was running away from, though, and, no matter how much he was punished for running away and how many privileges he lost, he would keep trying to escape.

Usually, by the time he had made it back to his mam's, he was in desperate need of food and a warm, dry place to sleep. He made the mistake the first time he actually made it that far – it was only across town, but was a huge distance for a seven-year-old boy – of going straight to his mam's house. He wanted so much for her to protect him and look after him. Of course, she couldn't, but he didn't understand why. Owing to the fact that he had been taken into the care of the local authority, she was obliged to inform them if Billy ever turned up. So it was, when he appeared on her doorstep that first time, she did what she had no choice but to do.

When his social worker came to take him back, he was devastated. Not only was he being returned to hell, but he was also being betrayed by his own mother. He thought, if she loved him, she would help him but, of course, it was not as simple as that. Billy knew why he was running away and what he was running away from – his mother didn't. He had tried to tell her but he could not find the words. She sensed that something was not quite right but, when she enquired, she was told that he was just unruly and was rebelling against discipline. It never dawned on her not to trust them; they were people in authority, which to her meant that they must be telling the truth. She had been brought up to respect such people and she didn't have enough self-worth or confidence to question them. It never occurred to her, in her wildest dreams, that anything sinister was going on.

Each time he was caught and taken back, he started thinking what he would do differently the next time. Sadly, every time he ran away, he was still drawn to his old neighbourhood, but he knew he couldn't let his family know, so he would hide in a huge tree in the field across from their house and watch the goings-on with a sort of morbid curiosity. Feeling hopeless and depressed, he would climb to the very top of the tree, taking an alarming risk, almost hoping that he would fall. He would sit precariously on a branch, barely holding on, without any thought for his safety, and watch. It hurt him deeply to see his brothers and sisters but he couldn't stop himself.

He didn't understand why they were allowed to be at home and he wasn't. He knew he kept getting into trouble, but that was only because he kept running away; and he had to run away, he just had to. He felt jealous and bitter. He knew they often went without food and life was tough for them all, but at least they didn't have to endure what he did.

Sometimes he would sleep in the garden sheds of some of the neighbours; sometimes he would sneak into the sheds at the allotments; and sometimes he would sleep in empty council houses that had been boarded up to keep people out, although Billy always managed to get in somehow.

Most of the time and, indeed, the best idea of all, he broke into his mam's, when she was out, and went up into the loft. It was especially good in the winter, as he was able to keep fairly warm. He was very resourceful for such a young boy and could usually come up with some solution to make things better for himself. The first time he tried to get up there he had had a bit of a job but he could soon hoist himself up without too much difficulty and, as long as his mam didn't move the chair that he used to get up there, it would remain a good plan. He was careful not to move around when anybody was home and it proved to be an excellent solution. Billy felt clever to have come up with it.

The longest he was up there was for a few weeks, coming down when the coast was clear to go to the toilet and occasionally to get a change of clothes from his twin brother, Jon. He kept the dirty clothes from the children's home hidden in the loft but, when he changed in and out of his brother's clothes, he would just throw the dirty ones on the bedroom floor as Jon did. He was sure his mam wouldn't notice but, even so, he was careful not to change too often.

The only problem with being in the loft was the lack of food. He couldn't bring himself to take food from his mam and siblings; he knew they had very little as it was, but he daren't go out of the house during daylight hours, so he had to risk getting down in the night when he was sure that everyone in the house would be asleep. Hearing the men leaving the pub after last orders, he knew that he only needed to wait a while longer before the coast was bound to be clear outside as well, then he would cautiously make his move, silently slipping down and out through the kitchen door. He would then steal food from wherever he could.

He loved it when he actually got enough food to enable him to leave some on the side for his family. It gave him such a thrill to think of them all wondering where the food had come from. He usually got back up into the loft without any problems, but once, in the middle of winter, he had to wait out the back for ages until his mam went back to bed after she had got up to make a cup of tea.

Luckily, whenever he'd been caught, it had happened when he'd been out of the house. He would not say where he had been sleeping, so for a long time he was able to continue with the loft plan, heading there every time he managed an escape.

This latest journey was proving to be more difficult, though, as it was the first time he had been taken outside the city of Cardiff itself. He had always paid close attention when they took him to the homes, but he got totally confused when faced with having to find his way from the seaside. However, the opportunity to make a break for it had been too good to pass up. He walked all of the first night but he wasn't even sure if he had gone in the right direction. He never did make it to the loft that time. He managed to elude capture for over a week but was eventually picked up by police after getting caught by a gardener, stealing vegetables from his allotment.

★   ★   ★

The next morning, Billy looked really tired. I suspected he hadn't had a very good night's sleep. I suggested the possibility of getting off work early but he thought he shouldn't. He figured that, since he was about to have three weeks' holiday, the least he could do was to put in a full day before we left.

I was excited as I drove to work. We both really needed a holiday; the whole year had been very stressful as I had been diagnosed with endometriosis, a painful and sometimes chronic condition that involved the production of uterine cells outside the womb itself. It had been misdiagnosed for years and was at a severe stage, requiring extensive major surgery. It was the cause of all the pain I had been experiencing and was, in all likelihood, the reason for my infertility.

I had the surgery over my Christmas break, which was convenient as I only missed a few days of work. During the week that I was in hospital, Billy came straight in after work to visit. He always used humour to lighten hard times and this was no exception. He was constantly making me laugh and I would plead with him to stop as my stitches hurt so much. I shared my room with three elderly women and, since Billy was always there when our evening meals came, he would attentively go to each lady and help to open their meals or get them drinks. Propped up in my bed, I watched him help those people he didn't know and marvelled at his compassion and gentle manner.

It wasn't until a few days after the surgery that my gynaecologist finally made it in to see me. He told me, in a matter-of-fact tone, that he had to remove my right tube and ovary and that the left tube was unattached to its ovary – adding, without even a hint of compassion, that I would never conceive naturally. For the first time in my life, I tasted unfairness – a strange, metallic bitterness. Then, with its tartness, came the realisation that the shape of things that I had trusted and thought to be certain could be twisted beyond recognition, as well as the knowledge that I wouldn't be able to stop it.

I was completely unprepared for that news, so was left feeling terribly shocked and totally devastated. He had explained beforehand that he wouldn't be able to predict the extent of the damage before he opened me up, which I understood, but I guess my denial stopped me from truly understanding the possibility of permanent infertility. He continued by telling us that the only way we would achieve a pregnancy was through in vitro fertilisation (IVF). I remember thinking, A test tube baby... I can do that. It was still fairly uncommon back then but I knew in the first second that I wanted to try it. I also needed something to hang on to – an expensive grain of hope though it was.

Billy was harder to convince. He thought it would be too upsetting if it didn't work, and it would be too hard on me. I just wanted the chance – I would simply have done anything. Billy made sure I knew that there were other options that he was happy to pursue, like adoption. I wasn't ruling that out, I just really felt that IVF was the right thing to do. I had my heart set on it and, actually, I was optimistic. I suppose I was just making a hopeless, yet deliberate, attempt at cutting down the odds of failure – as if positive thinking might miraculously influence the outcome. Billy wasn't as optimistic but, then, he never was, so that didn't particularly bother me. In the end, Billy didn't object, even though it was going to cost $10,000 – money we didn't have.

I knew Billy had agreed to go ahead with it for me. If the decision had been solely up to him, I don't think he would have gone through with it; I'm sure he would have wanted to avoid the potential of disappointment and heartbreak. You see, I knew, even then, that he was an avoider. For me, it was about weighing the level of heartbreak. I was sure the anguish of an unsuccessful outcome would have been less devastating than giving up and not doing all we could. I remember someone said to me that it was a lot of money to pay for something that wasn't guaranteed – which I thought was a typical response from someone who had children.

I fully understood that we only had about a 30 per cent chance of achieving a pregnancy – I felt, though, that we were paying for the opportunity to become pregnant and I thought that that chance was worth every single cent of $10,000.

As soon as I had recovered from the surgery, I was put on the waiting list for IVF. We knew we would have to go into debt to cover the cost, so we both planned to take on extra work over the weekends and to cut our outgoings by eliminating any unnecessary spending. When the time came, I was excited, scared and very nervous all at the same time.

A lot of organising and planning went into making it all possible, especially with regard to our work. I had to find a substitute for the nursery so, when my mum volunteered, I was extremely grateful. It was the perfect solution as the children already knew her and I was confident that they would all be in good hands.

Also, as all the treatment was to take place in Vancouver, we had to figure out where we were going to stay and how we were going to afford to be there for a month. Again, we were very fortunate because we were invited to stay with Bruce and Marjorie Johnson who were the parents of an old schoolfriend, Gail. They lived in Vancouver and were happy to help. I hadn't seen Gail for years, as she had moved to Alberta, but her brother Eric got in touch with me the year before when he and his wife were looking for care for their son. I was thrilled to have him attend my nursery and it was then, through Eric, that his parents found out about us needing to stay in Vancouver.

I was grateful beyond words and, with that arranged, I believed that I had thought of everything. I knew that it probably wouldn't work the first time we tried and I was mentally prepared for that. What I wasn't prepared for was the whole thing being cancelled before it ever really got started. My first ultrasound, before egg retrieval, showed a mass near my remaining ovary, so I needed another surgical procedure before they could proceed any further with the IVF.

I was absolutely devastated. It didn't seem anything like the made-for-TV dramas – the ones with the fairytale endings. It wasn't exciting or romantic or inspirational. It was just disappointing and headache-inducing and so, so hard.

Somehow, we got through it. Even though, at the back of my mind, I knew I had to face another operation, the prospect of going on holiday took my mind off it somewhat. Again, figuring out who would look after Ben, finding cover for the nursery and then ensuring both were fully briefed about their responsibilities took a lot of time to organise, and was a welcome diversion – subconsciously using the planning and arranging as a habitual gesture of reassurance that I was still in control.

Driving to work that morning, the day before our trip, I felt satisfied that I had everything in order and, with all the preparations taken care of, I found that I could really start to experience that lovely anticipatory excitement that always builds on the days leading up to a holiday. Some of my best memories from childhood were of that excitement. That train of thought soon had me forgetting about the events of the past year and brought, instead, memories of holidays past.

★　　★　　★

California

'Are we there yet?' I asked expectantly.

'Not yet, darling, we still have quite a drive ahead of us.'

I was lying in the back of our orange Volkswagen van, looking out of the window, watching the changing scenery and listening to the sound of Tony Orlando and Dawn as 'Tie a Yellow Ribbon' played on the radio. The smell of Daddy's Pall Mall cigarettes wafted back. I was eight years old. We were on our annual, summer camping trip and that year we were driving further than we ever had. My sisters and I had known for days that we were going on a trip but we didn't know where. Kate had seen Mummy with the holiday checklist, then I noticed that our sleeping bags, after being pulled out of their winter storage and washed, had been hung on the line in the backyard to dry in the summer breeze.

That night, Daddy announced at the dinner table that we were going to Disneyland. My sisters and I were thrilled. Sophie, who was then four years old, not knowing what all the fuss was about, was swept up in our excitement and was soon shrieking in as high-pitched a shriek as us, if not higher. We were told we could bring two favourite things, but no more, because Daddy would need to be able to pack everything we'd need for two weeks in the van. I put a lot of thought into what I would take, and finally decided on my pet rock and my 'Holly Hobbie' doll.

The days leading up to our trips were always full of anticipation. I'd sit on the driveway, watching Daddy pack everything into the van. He always put the things in the van in the same order and everything always went in the same place. He routinely put the clothes in first. My clothes always went in a little box under the back seat. The bedding went in last. All the sleeping bags were folded and piled on top of each other in the very back, behind the back seat. That created a 'bed' level with the back window, where we took turns lying and looking out of the window. That was my favourite place to be when on the road. Sometimes, Naomi and Sophie fell asleep on the back seat and, as Kate liked to sit in the front between Mummy and Daddy helping to navigate, I'd get to stay in the back longer.

Exploring the campsite when we first arrived was the best part. My favourite sites were the ones with lots of trees. Sometimes, the trees were so dense you couldn't even see the other campers in the neighbouring sites.

'I just saw a California licence plate!' Kate had announced from the front. 'First one to five is the winner!'

Kate's voice jolted me out of my trance. 'OK, I'll look out the back and you look out the front,' I grudgingly replied.

I didn't really want to play. I preferred to lie with my own thoughts. I'd lie for ages thinking about things and retreating to my own little world while being mesmerised by the passing traffic and the soothing sound of Elton John, The Carpenters or Helen Reddy playing on the radio. I was the quiet one and was quite happy to be by myself. When I wasn't thinking, I would read. I always took a few books on holiday, thankful that books didn't count as one of our allotted items.

The previous Christmas Grandma and Granda had sent me, from England, another Enid Blyton book, which I had kept for our summer holiday. It was one of the Famous Five series appropriately titled Five Go Off in a

Caravan. *I had already read two of her books and couldn't wait to start another adventure. I would immerse myself into their world, feeling as though I was there with them. Page after page, I became more and more engrossed and was always sorry to get to the end. Often, Mummy and Daddy would have to repeat themselves over and over to get my attention. I also had two Nancy Drew books to take, so I had been well prepared.*

Kate ended up winning the licence-plate game but I didn't care, as I hadn't been paying attention anyway.

The only thing I didn't like about camping was when we had to go out at night, into the darkness, to go to the toilet. I imagined there were bears lurking about, ready to pounce on us if we left the van. Even though Mummy or Daddy would come with me, I often just waited until morning to go. Sometimes, I would lie in bed, listening to the night noises, and get really scared. Then the morning would come and I would look around at the harmless surroundings and feel silly for being so frightened. Gone were all the dark shadows and mysterious shapes, only half-seen in the moonlight, to be replaced with tree stumps and picnic tables by day.

We eventually got to California after two days of driving. Daddy explained that California was a big state and that Disneyland was down at the bottom. We started to see lots of palm trees the further south we drove. Big open trucks filled with tomatoes hurtled past us. Often they would fall off, leaving horrible-looking red splatters along the road, baking in the hot sun. On and on we drove, through a sort of desert that Daddy said was the Sacramento Valley. We saw row upon row of orange trees filled with the delicious-looking fruit. Daddy told us that the part of California where Disneyland was was called Orange County. I thought that was a perfect name.

On the third day, we finally got there. We set up camp and went to bed early, willing the next day to come quickly. I hardly slept at all that night. I tried, without success, to imagine what it was going to be like. When the day finally dawned, we were eager to go.

It was agony having to wait for Daddy to get his wallet in order. Every morning, he would get out the day's money and put it in the front of his wallet. He budgeted a certain amount for each day. Some days, if he was under budget, the left-over money would go to the back part of his wallet for 'extras'. He never went over budget. We had watched him do this on every trip we had ever been on, so at eight I knew more about the importance of budgeting than the *average adult. He also wrote a log of the mileage, where and when he bought gas, and the amount paid. Normally, Kate and I enjoyed watching him get organised, but that morning we were itching to get on our way.*

We eventually got there and found it to be everything we had hoped it would be and more. We went on loads of rides, including The Pirates of the Caribbean and the Matterhorn. We ate huge pickles and pretzels and even bigger ice creams. We were exhausted by the time we returned to the campsite.

We also went to Mexico for a day trip. We drove down to San Diego, stayed overnight in a campsite and then drove from there early the next morning. We waited in the queue at the border, sweltering in the sun, our bare legs sticking to the seats. We all had the windows rolled down but it wasn't helping. There was no breeze and the air hung heavy and hot. We were all getting uncomfortable but, luckily, it didn't take too long.

I didn't know what I was expecting Mexico to be like, but it wasn't that. We drove to a place called Tijuana. I didn't like it. There were too many people and the buildings were all grotty. Children with dirty, ripped clothing were wandering the streets. A lady stopped Mummy and asked her something I didn't quite hear. She was holding a baby that was wrapped in a dirty shawl. It had a runny nose and it just stared at me. That look left me feeling very uncomfortable. I felt scared and a bit sick, but not really sick, there was just a funny feeling in my tummy. That feeling stuck with me all day. Mummy asked me if I was OK, as I was so quiet − even quieter than normal. I shook my head up and down in response, with my thumb stuck in my mouth. I couldn't say what was wrong because I didn't know.

Later that night, as I was lying in bed, I asked Kate why the people we saw were so dirty.

'Oh, they are just poor,' she had flippantly replied.

'Why?' I asked again.

'I dunno… go to sleep!' she snapped.

I didn't ask her any more questions that night but my mind was still working overtime. I wondered where they were at that precise moment and hoped they were as cosy as I was. I wondered if the baby I had seen was a boy or a girl and what its name was. I finally drifted off to sleep but I tossed and turned all night, haunted by the eyes of the little baby.

The rest of the trip was full of new places and adventures and, before we knew it, we were on the ferry back home to Vancouver Island. I still thought about Mexico and the people we had seen. I even noticed, for the first time, people in the other places we visited along our route home, and even in our own city, who made me have that same unsettled feeling. Why hadn't I ever noticed them before? I wondered. They didn't seem to be as poor as the people in Mexico, but they still appeared to be living through hard times.

When the opportunity arose, I asked Mummy why the people we had seen were like that. She tried to explain, as best she could, saying that the people we saw didn't have jobs and were very poor. Some didn't even have homes. I was horrified. She talked for a long time but most of it I didn't really understand. I couldn't imagine not having my own bedroom, let alone not living in our house. It was the first time I realised that not every one lived like us.

★   ★   ★

My reflective mood stayed with me all through that morning. It was a lovely sunny day so the nursery children and I walked down to the beach for a picnic lunch. As I sat watching the children playing in the sand, I thought about my memories of that distant camping holiday. I realised that the Mexico day trip was actually a pivotal juncture in my childhood. Being exposed to the poverty there really was the first time I had noticed and understood – well, as much as an eight-year-old can, and definitely enough to make me feel uncomfortable – that life would always have the potential of being tough. I accepted that most children probably would have noticed the poverty but I really didn't think many would have been as affected as I had been. Kate, being three years older, certainly hadn't seemed either to notice or care.

I recognised that it had been a blessing that I had had that experience – without it, my advantaged childhood could have actually left me too sheltered. Of course, there had always been evidence of poverty in our city as well as, to a certain extent, in my day-to-day life, but before Tijuana I hadn't noticed. Nor had I noticed that one or two kids at school didn't have a packed lunch anywhere near as nice as the rest of us; or that those same kids wore coats with sleeves that were just that bit too short. Granted, I would have been excused for not recognising such subtle indications but I guess the shock of Tijuana packed a big enough punch to have brought even the smallest things to my attention and to have left such an impression. It made me think that being exposed to some bad stuff in childhood might actually be a good thing. Too perfect a childhood could leave one unprepared for the harsh reality of the real world – or lacking in the ability even to contemplate the possibility.

The next day, we left, as planned, on the first ferry out of Swartz Bay. The trip ended up being great. We drove down through Washington State and into Oregon. The interstate was huge in parts, with five lanes of traffic filled with shiny, big, expensive sport utility vehicles zooming along. The further south we drove, the warmer the air became until getting out of the 4Runner felt like entering an oven.

For Billy, it was like another world. We continued into California, down through LA and across to Palm Springs, where we spent a week with my best friend from childhood, Samantha. She lived there with her husband, John, and their two small boys, Connor and Rhys. It was incredibly hot there – so hot, in fact, that we couldn't be outside during the day unless we were in their pool. Neither Billy nor I had ever experienced that kind of temperature before.

In the evening, once the sun had dipped behind the surrounding mountain, we enjoyed sitting outside on their patio, drinking ice-cold fruity cocktails, while John prepared delicious steaks on the barbecue. It was so different from our life in Victoria that it was the perfect place to forget my health problems. Watching Connor and Rhys playing in the pool, seeing their toys strewn around the house, hearing their laughter and even sometimes their cries, of course I was reminded of what we didn't have, but it was so evident that Samantha cherished her children. I could never have begrudged her having them and I was genuinely happy for her.

The week spent with them flew by. On the road again, we drove up the coast along the 101, stopping at campsites along the way. I remember vividly the way the world looked to me on that drive north – the sky made bleak by the clouds gathering overhead, the temperature dropping – and how suited the weather was to the feeling in my soul and the thoughts in my head.

3

MAY NOT LAST
FOR EVER

I wake up early every morning
With thoughts running through my head
Just don't know where I am heading to
But I know right now that I'm here.

'Right Tonight', by James K

There's something about driving that attracts me, I just don't quite know what it is. I don't have to be the driver – although, I have to say, I do love being behind the wheel. Whatever the weather, whatever the view… I just love driving. I've even been known to take longer routes, going out of my way, just to steal a bit longer; a bit more thinking space; a bit more me time.

For as long as I can remember, I've been the same. I even went through a phase, when I was very young, of wanting one day to marry a long distance lorry driver just so that I could go along for the ride. I thought that sounded like some kind of heaven. I don't recall my parents saying anything to put me off that idea although I suspect they were relieved when I decided I'd rather marry Ricky Ricardo.

Travelling through fantastic scenery, while listening to music on a beautiful sunny day, is my kind of wonderful. Driving along the Oregon Coast on our way to California, with Sheryl Crow playing on the radio, was one such time.

It was the summer of 1997 and we were escaping our everyday life

– and my health problems – and were once again seeking solace with best friends, just as we had done the previous year.

In fact, the whole of 1997 had been like a mirror image of the one before. I had had another operation over the Christmas holiday and we went through another IVF cycle. The Johnsons again kindly offered to have us stay with them. A godsend really, not only because it saved us the expense of hotel accommodation but also because it gave me the comfort and support of a home away from home, especially during the times when Billy had to stay in Victoria for work.

We got through the whole treatment that time but we weren't successful in achieving a pregnancy. I was so devastated I didn't even cry. I felt like it was too awful to cry. Bitterness was setting in.

Looking back at that time, I think I was on autopilot. Work was bittersweet. It was therapeutic to have all the little ones around me but I was constantly reminded of what I longed for. On a daily basis, I was faced with reminders. I was bombarded with overworked mums complaining to me about how hard their lives were. I lost count of the number of times I heard the sleepless-nights complaint. I was having sleepless nights as well, only I wasn't sharing them with a child – I was just wishing I was. At any one time, at least one of the mums was pregnant with their second or third child and it was hard to watch them getting bigger and bigger. I even had to endure some showing me their ultrasound scans.

I wasn't minimising their complaints or denying them their excitement; it was just so very hard to be a part of. And, typically, it wasn't just the obvious things that hurt, it was also the little things that jumped out of nowhere and stung me. Once, as I was changing a little girl, I just froze, while holding a tiny white sock with ladybirds embroidered delicately around the ankle, wondering if I'd ever get to buy socks. The little girl's chattering interrupted my brooding and, like so many other times, I swallowed the lump in my throat and carried on. As always, though, Billy made it bearable. He could still make me laugh and it helped us get by.

As the miles went by, we either sang along in unison, accompanying the radio, chatted together or sat in companionable silence. After a few days of driving, camping along the way, we found that the temptations of a comfy bed and a long bath were too much to bear so we booked into a hotel. Later that afternoon, we were lounging in our room after a swim in the pool, and we could hear the television on in the background as we chatted and looked at our map deciding our route for the next day. We were aware of the voices on the television but neither one of us was actually concentrating on what was being said. Suddenly, I found myself dropping the map, my body reacting to a newsflash before my brain had a chance to realise what I had heard.

'What? Lady Diana has been killed?! That can't be right… Billy, look!'

Billy was bending over to retrieve the map and hadn't picked up what had been said.

'The Americans must have it wrong,' he said confidently.

'It looks pretty official to me.'

We both watched in disbelief, then, slowly, as more information trickled through, we realised it was tragically true. I shall never forget where we were and what we were doing that day; it was definitely one of those 'moments'.

We were at my friend Samantha's house by the time the funeral was held on Saturday, 6 September. She and I stayed up to watch the live coverage on the television which, because of the time difference, aired at 3.00am. Although Billy thought it was a terribly sad thing to have happened, he didn't think much beyond that and certainly wouldn't have even entertained the idea of staying up to watch the coverage. I knew he thought I was a bit of a freak to be so affected by it all, but I was used to his feelings towards the Royal Family, so I wasn't at all surprised at his lack of interest. He believes that the Royal Family are a drain on society, an opinion I absolutely and totally disagree with, but I had long since given up debating the subject. He would ramble on about how much money they waste and how they live so extravagantly – often quoting various ridiculous articles about the amount one of them spent on their laundry or something equally as silly. I would often reply that I wouldn't want their lives for double the money, as they have no life of their own and no freedom, but I couldn't ever get my point across and I certainly couldn't *make* him change his opinion, so I gave up. He never could come up with anything to justify his point of view and I often thought it rather curious that he had such convictions.

To my comment of 'The monarchy is what makes Britain Britain', he would reply, ' Piss off! A pint and a steak and kidney pie, that makes Britain Britain!' We definitely had to agree to disagree!

Of course, Billy isn't the only one; lots of people have a less than magnanimous view of the monarchy. Some may have valid points to back up their opinions, but I rather think that a lot of them have some sort of chip on their shoulders. I was sure that that was the case with Billy. In fact, I often teased him that he must have had a sore shoulder after all the years of carrying it around and eventually started nicknaming him 'chunk' as the chip was so big. In the end, I just put his unsavoury attitude towards members of the Royal Family down to one of his many grudges; residue from a childhood that I didn't understand.

As it turned out, that was not the only incident during our trip that brought Billy's stronger feelings to the fore. The second incident happened while we were driving through quite an isolated area a few days later. It was extremely hot so the windows were rolled all the way down, which created loads of wind but minimal temperature reduction. Again, we were singing along to the radio, this time Sarah McLachlan's voice, singing her song 'Angel', mingled with ours. It was hardly much of a surprise, but I found the lyrics eerily representative of the events of the previous week.

Not long after, needing a break, we decided to pull over into a lay-by and get a cold drink out of the cooler in an effort to satisfy our unquenchable thirst. We hadn't been there long when I noticed an approaching police car. I watched it through the rear-view mirror as it pulled in behind us.

'What the fuck does he want?' Billy snapped.

I looked at him totally flabbergasted, although I should have been used to such outbursts. I didn't have a chance to say anything before the policeman walked up to the driver's side window. 'Afternoon, folks,' he said. 'Everything all right?'

'Yes, we're fine thanks,' I replied. 'We're just having a break.'

'Good for you. It's mighty hot, ain't it? Y'all have a nice day now, ya hear.' He tipped his hat and walked back to his car, then tooted his horn as he drove away.

'Nosy bastard,' Billy snarled.

Here we go again, I thought. 'He was just checking we were all right. We could have been experiencing car trouble or something… he was just being nice!' I pleaded.

'Regular arse-licker… Aye!' he shouted bad-temperedly. If anyone had seen his face they would have thought he was very, very angry. The look he had in his eyes was so dark at times. I had become used to it over the years.

Very early on in our relationship, when his temper was raised over something that wasn't down to me, I would experience the oddest feeling. My skin would become cold and prickly, but inside I felt warm. It was like I was getting comforted, as if someone was saying, 'Don't worry, he's not mad at *you*.' I don't know why, but it was the only way I could really feel properly comforted by another person – except Billy, of course. I suppose the first time I can remember it happening was quite early on in childhood, and then, once I had experienced that, nothing else compared. It happened so much after I met Billy – I guess a testament to how often he got angry – but it never happened when he was genuinely mad at me. And, if he was mad at me, he never got that dark look in his eyes.

That episode with the policeman certainly wasn't the first time I had noticed the harshness of Billy's tone but, gradually, over time, he had been sounding worse and it was becoming more noticeable. I couldn't pinpoint when his voice started sounding so dead and his eyes started looking so blank. Maybe I had been blinded by whatever people get blinded by. His unlikeable and confusing mannerisms used to stop by from time to time over the years, I had noticed, but lately they seemed to have taken up residence – like unpleasant relatives that insisted on visiting and outstaying their welcome.

In any case, on this occasion, he was really getting on my nerves. Mainly because, by my sticking up for the policeman, when Billy ranted about him for no reason, he thought I was not agreeing with him just to be awkward. I didn't know what planet Billy came from but, to me, to think that the policeman was being anything other than nice and considerate was completely ludicrous.

It was at those times that I wondered who Billy really was. I felt like I knew him so well, then that side of him would rear its ugly head, as if to reprimand me, and let me know just how much I didn't really understand him. He was like Jekyll and Hyde. Granted, he didn't behave like that all the time, but it happened enough over the years that I began to know when it was best for me just to bite my tongue. After all, I knew nothing I could say would ever change his steadfast, unreasonable view.

So many of his attitudes were alien to me, and his sweeping generalisation of the police, or anyone in a position of authority for that matter, never ceased to amaze and confuse me. He was never actually rude to their faces, which I was grateful for, at least not unless they were rude first. I wouldn't have been able to sit by and listen to him vocalising his misplaced thoughts or behaving rudely towards someone. Actually, we wouldn't even be together if he behaved that way. As it was, he would just get so filled with bitterness and would rant and rave about someone solely based on what they did for a living. It was almost like he was an inverted snob, but it had nothing to do with how posh they were. It was all very confusing.

Sometimes, when I thought he wouldn't like someone, he did, which only served to confuse me more. I was sure there was some rhyme or reason behind Billy's unconformable attitudes, something that might somehow justify or explain them, but, whatever it was, I couldn't figure it out. The majority of the time, I thought he was being absurd, but I knew anything I said in the person's defence only seemed to fuel him, so I soon just kept my mouth shut, or at least tried my best to. Luckily, it never happened in relation to people I knew, unless it was true, of course, and then I agreed with him, so I never found myself in a position where I felt like I had to stick up for them.

Actually, Billy had always liked my cousin's absolutely lovely, friendly and funny husband, who is a police officer in England, so I guessed that, by actually knowing the people, whatever misapprehension he may have had would be wiped away – proving that the majority of his views weren't warranted. Again, I just put it down to another one of his idiosyncrasies that I figured must be related to his childhood.

Before I knew it, Billy was joking about the policeman's accent and all was OK again. After a while, I decided I just couldn't let him continue to have such a tainted view, and felt I had to say something. I could not agree with him simply to keep the peace – if I did so, I would be signing our death warrant, if only because, if I suppressed too many of my own beliefs, I ran the risk of resenting Billy later on.

'Why do you hate all policemen?' I asked.

Billy wouldn't answer, so I just continued talking, but he interrupted me and told me, in no uncertain terms, just to drop it.

★ ★ ★

Cardiff

'Oi, you! Stop!' the policeman shouted.

'Piss off. You'll never catch me, ya fat bastard!' Billy yelled back. He ran until his chest burned and his legs felt heavy. He was proud that he could always outrun the coppers.

As a designated delinquent, Billy figured he might as well act like one. He had been branded as such for so many years he believed that was all he could be. He was constantly in trouble and had soon turned into a self-proclaimed 'hard boy'. He even pretended to be proud of that image. The grudge he was carrying around was getting bigger and bigger as time went by. The events of the past years had almost succeeded in generating a non-existent faith, but not entirely. Somewhere, deep inside his psyche, Billy had a grain of self-preservation. A little something that gave him an inner strength. Billy didn't know it was there and certainly no one else paid close enough attention to realise anything at all about the real Billy. To them, he was just a bad lad, but it was there all the same.

He had incredible courage, but, if anyone had suggested such a thing, he wouldn't have believed them. He wasn't used to compliments, having never received any; either that, or he would have thought that being courageous was something bad.

By the time he was thirteen, he was consumed with feelings of hopelessness. He tried desperately to marshal his unruly emotions back into line, if, in his chaotic short life, they ever were truly in line – but he couldn't. He found the situation in the homes added to this. He felt sure that was just how life was going to be for him and had become resigned to the fact that nobody would ever hear his desperate cries for help. He saw no way out and, somewhere along the line, had stopped hoping. He convinced himself he didn't care about *anyone or anything. His yearning had been replaced with despondency. There was still, and probably always would be, a deep-rooted vulnerability, but his behaviour and antics made it hard for anybody to recognise it, even though they should have.*

He was filled with anger and still vented his feelings inappropriately, as he had done ever since he was first taken into care, but his behaviour was becoming more and more destructive. He was spiralling out of control and no one seemed to care – least of all Billy.

The desire to abscond was just as high on his priority list as it had been right from the start but, over the years, it had taken on the form of a sort of game – albeit, to Billy, it was about survival. He took pride in outsmarting the people in charge and thrived on out-running the police or anyone else who attempted to chase him. A lot of the time, he ran away to get away from the situation in the homes; at other times, he ran away because he missed his family. Sometimes, it was just something he could have control over.

He was sent to a number of different children's homes in an effort to put an end to his running away, but it never occurred to anybody to figure out why he was running away. Eventually, he was sent to an approved school but he continued to get into trouble. He knew that this development was a step up to the big league. He had heard boys bragging about lads they knew, or their older siblings, who had been sent to such a place, as if it was an achievement, or something to be proud of. Billy didn't have such a misguided view. His misbehaviour wasn't a conscious thing – nor was he being naughty for the sake of appearing 'cool' among his peers. He was just in trouble – as much in his being as in his actions.

Billy didn't think much about where he might end up if he continued to break the rules – he didn't think much about anything. He was in survival mode, full stop – it was as simple as that. It was just unfortunate that what he was doing as a means of survival was continuing to get him into trouble.

Billy didn't think it was cool to get sent to approved school, although he might have given that impression to the other children. He actually was very scared and apprehensive. Most of the time, he was relieved to be moved on, but it was also very scary, as he didn't know where he'd be sent. He had had so many bad experiences that he had given up hope that the next place would be any better. Mostly, it was a case of 'better the devil you know'.

He didn't mix well with other children as a rule. He tended to get bullied quite a lot, probably due to the fact that he was always so withdrawn. He did want to fit in, though, so he kept himself to himself during the first few weeks, watching the other boys and figuring out what he needed to do, or not do, in order to avoid attention. He liked it best when he could just blend into the woodwork, under everyone's radar. If the other boys didn't pay him any attention, positive or negative, that was an added bonus. The main thing was to do whatever he could to ensure that he wasn't noticed by any of the adults. He wasn't usually naughty in the first few weeks at a new place; he was trying so hard not to stand out, anxious to not draw attention to himself, that he daren't put a foot out of line.

The very first thing he did when he got to yet another home was to negotiate an escape route. In the beginning, it had been quite easy getting away, sometimes simply walking out through the front door but, over the years, his reputation preceded him, forcing him to come up with elaborate plans that were fast becoming feats of ingenuity of which Houdini would have been proud. He was so agile and nimble and could manoeuvre and squeeze himself through such tiny, awkward openings that often his escapes needed to be seen to be believed.

He started to notice, after a while, that the boys who seemed the most confident, the ones who were bullish and vocalised their grievances, were often the ones who didn't seem to attract the attention from the adults – at least, not the kind of attention that he was trying to avoid. Yes, they got into trouble but that didn't worry Billy, he could handle the telling off, the verbal abuse and even the caning. These boys could often be heard taunting other children, sometimes even the adults, or slinging complaints around – 'I'm not eating that crap' or 'This tastes like shite'. Every home had them. They were the ones who talked at night after lights out but they were never the ones to get taken from their beds at night.

It was strange – Billy never did anything wrong in those days, but he was always the one to get punished in that terrible way. He couldn't help but feel he must have deserved it, but he couldn't figure out what he'd done wrong. He felt the only thing he could do was to start behaving like those other boys. Maybe being quiet and trying to remain unnoticed was the very thing that was making him more of a target?

He couldn't work out why, but he just knew that the loud-mouthed lads didn't have the trouble he did. Part of him still believed it was his fault that bad things always seemed to happen to him but, after a while, when running away didn't get him anywhere, he decided that he may as well give up on his 'blending-in' strategy.

That new approach – going against his natural instinct and becoming bolder – coincided with his first placement at an approved school. It certainly hadn't been easy at all, especially being somewhere different, but he adapted, as he always did, when faced with something new. In many ways, that new behaviour benefited Billy. The other kids didn't bully him and, best of all, he didn't have to endure anything untoward, at least not in the way that he had before. He became a little bit more confident – just enough to make a difference. He was, for the first time, mixing with the other boys and was proud to be accepted by the tough lads. He was still escaping, although probably more out of habit than necessity at that point, and often would not actually run away but, instead, sneak back in after roaming around for a few hours.

Those escapades always happened during the night. Billy was a poor sleeper and had been for quite a few years. This was partly due to his being a worrier, lying in bed, in the dark, when his mind would refuse to shut off. But mostly it was because of a pattern he had got into, a pattern bred from the nightmare of his years in care. A pattern bred from never feeling safe.

He would often seek out companions on those nocturnal outings, although not of the human sort. Ever since he had first realised that the animals made him feel special and loved, he had looked forward to seeing them. He'd slip into farmyards where the only ones awake were the animals. Amazingly, the dogs wouldn't bark; instead, they would approach him and, although some were initially a bit wary, they all ended up wagging their tails and allowing him to make a fuss of them. It was with these straightforward, undemanding creatures that Billy learned about love and trust – and where his natural, gentle manner had a chance to flourish. How incredibly touching, yet ironic, that he developed these human emotions from animals and how amazing that the human spirit can manifest situations that not only give it what it needs but also give it a chance to express its own abilities. Billy would often creep into the barns, especially in the winter when he was desperate to keep warm, and curl up in the hay, often nodding off and then waking to find lambs, calves, cats or dogs nestled beside him.

The only drawback with that new plan was that, by hanging about with the naughty boys, he was slowly introduced to more dubious pastimes. Before long, he was mixed up in activities that ensured he lived up to everyone's expectations. They were also illegal.

*For quite some time, he had been getting away with criminal activity –
stealing motorcycles or cars and joyriding through the lanes. Not getting caught
fuelled the bravado and he thought he had it all figured out. He was still
getting into trouble and being sent to the dreaded, cold, dark place, where the
naughtiest boys would be locked in solitary confinement, but he didn't mind
such punishment; he knew that on those occasions he had deserved it and, in
a strange way, he felt he was in control.*

*It didn't last long, though; inevitably, he was caught stealing a car and was
sent to a detention centre. One of the biggest differences there was that it was
a secure and locked institution. If he had thought that being sent to approved
school was a step up to the big league, then the detention centre was an entire
staircase.*

★   ★   ★

'Are we friends again?' I teased, trying to lighten the mood.

Billy had been quiet for ages. I knew he was miles away, back to a time
of bad memories. I knew the signs. Billy was beginning to realise that he
hadn't forgotten his past. Not really. His memory wasn't failing him, he
had just been protected from remembering. Things were coming back
and he knew enough to know that that wasn't a good thing.

'Do you fancy a coffee?' Billy asked, by way of an apology, as he
pulled into a gas station.

'Yeah, I do. Shall I run in and get some?' I answered light-heartedly,
by way of saying, 'Apology accepted.'

'I could kill for a proper cup of tea but, as Americans can't do tea,
I guess a coffee will have to do,' he joked.

I jumped out of the 4Runner and ran into the shop as Billy filled
up on gas. While I was waiting to pay, I watched Billy through the
window. He had finished filling up and was washing all the baked-on
dead bugs off the windscreen. At the next pump, a motorcycle pulled
up. A leather-clad Hell's Angel type got off the bike and proceeded to
fill up. He was a big, burly man. His black, sleeveless leather vest
allowed full view of his tattooed arms. Even from a distance, I could
see a silver earring peeking out from just under his skullcap.

I looked on in amazement, as Billy appeared to be speaking to him.
Sure enough, a smile appeared on the biker's face, totally transforming

it. They continued talking. To a passer-by, they would have seemed to be well acquainted, albeit mismatched – Billy in his Gap T-shirt, Roots shorts and Nike flip-flops, and the biker in his leathers. As I walked towards them, they were saying their goodbyes with their right hands raised up to shoulder height in a buddy-like clench, patting each other on the upper arm with their left hands.

'Take care, mate,' I heard Billy say.

'Yeah, you, too, man. Catch ya later,' the biker replied as he walked off to pay for his gas.

As I handed Billy his coffee, I jokingly asked, 'Who's your home-boy?'

'He's a nice bloke. I was admiring his bike and we got talking… What's so funny?' he asked when I continued to grin.

'Nothing, love… you are just so cute. I would never have even looked at him, let alone spoken to him. He looked totally scary.'

'You shouldn't judge a book by its cover, Alix,' Billy added reprovingly.

'What? Look who's talking! What about that policeman? You judged him just based on his uniform,' I countered.

'Coppers are different,' he snapped.

'Yeah, whatever. Shall I put a CD on?' I asked, hoping to change the subject.

'Do what you wanna do,' he answered moodily.

Within minutes, Billy was singing along to the song, his mood already forgotten. My mind wandered as I looked out at the passing scenery.

★   ★   ★

Victoria

'Bye, Mummy, have a nice time,' I called from the basement.

'When is Samantha coming over?' she asked as she stopped at the top of the stairs.

'She's not. She has to go out with her mum.'

'Oh dear, that's too bad. Won't you be bored when the girls go to bed?'

'No, it's OK. I'm going to watch Fantasy Island and Love Boat.'

'OK, darling, we won't be late. I've already told Naomi and Sophie they can stay up until 9.00pm. Make sure they go to bed then… I don't want Sophie watching Love Boat.'

'Oh, Mummy, there isn't anything bad in Love Boat,' I laughed.

I was still rolling my eyes as Mum and Dad left. They had only just started letting me babysit. Kate used to, but lately she complained about it so much that it was decided that at sixteen she was allowed to go out with her friends and I, being thirteen, could then be left in charge of Naomi and Sophie.

The three of us watched television until 9.00pm and then they went up to bed. I settled on the couch to watch my programmes. The TV room was in the basement of our house. At one end of the room, the stairs went up into the kitchen and at the other end was a door out to the back yard. I wasn't nervous as a rule, but I did always make sure that the door was locked whenever I was downstairs on my own.

As I watched the programme, I glanced over at the door just as I heard a noise outside on the patio. I could feel my heart pounding in my chest. I couldn't take my eyes off the door handle. After a few moments, I began to question what I had heard – like you do. It sounded like the crunching sound that was made when someone walked over the crushed rock on the patio, but I wasn't completely sure.

I convinced myself I had imagined the noise and immediately felt foolish for getting myself all freaked out. I glanced over at the door to prove to myself that I wasn't scared. The hairs on the back of my neck stood on end and my breath caught in my throat. I wanted to get up and put the light on, but I couldn't get up the courage actually to move. I was rigid with fear, and was straining my eyes to get a proper view of the doorknob through the darkness, when I thought that I saw the handle turn, but I couldn't be sure. I told myself that my eyes must be playing tricks, then suddenly I thought that, if someone was out there, whoever it was probably thought no one was in; I did have all the lights out after all. I reasoned that perhaps I could scare him off if I let him know I was there, but there was no way I was going to manage to put the light on as the switch was right by the door.

So I decided, after tense deliberation, to put the volume up on the TV and then run upstairs and wake up Naomi. She was younger than me, by almost two years, but in many ways tougher. She certainly wasn't a wimp and I knew she wouldn't panic. I almost wet my knickers when I noticed the doorknob definitely turn. Here goes, I thought, now or never.

I put up the volume and then flew to the stairs. I went so fast that my feet barely touched the floor. I didn't want to scare Naomi, but I was so frightened

I burst into her room. She was obviously startled and, as I wasn't making much sense, she kept saying, 'What… what… what?' over and over. I took a deep breath and managed to explain what had happened.

'OK, OK, OK…' she said. 'Let's try not to wake up Sophie, she will get too scared. Let's just go together to the kitchen and phone the police.'

So that is what we did. Within seconds, a patrol car pulled into the driveway and a lovely, friendly police officer stayed in the living room with us while the other one checked outside. I was totally embarrassed, worrying that I had imagined it all, but the policeman said that, even if it was all a mistake, phoning them had been the right thing to do. The other officer then confirmed there was evidence that someone had been trying the door. He reassured us that whoever it was had obviously run away and that he was sure they wouldn't come back. As Mum and Dad were due home soon, the policemen said they would wait outside until they came home just to ensure we felt safe.

When they eventually arrived home, the policemen filled them in on the night's events. Listening from the kitchen, I heard one of the officers telling Dad that there had been a break-in on the next street the previous night and that they would have a patrol car check the area thoroughly throughout the night. Dad then thanked them for their assistance and they assured him they were only too happy to help.

About a week later, a police car drove past Naomi and me as we walked to school. It was the same two policemen that had come to the house. They honked and waved at us. I was thoroughly mortified but, at the same time, I thought it was very cool that they had remembered us.

We never did find out who it was who had tried to break in, but the incident didn't make me more nervous. In fact, it had the opposite effect. From then on, I always felt complete trust in our neighbourhood police force and had faith in them. Of course, we had visits from the police and firemen many times in school and we knew that they deserved our respect — we were brought up to feel that way. We had been taught that they were there to 'serve and protect' and we knew that dedication needed to be honoured, but all the same it meant more when we had personal experience of that service, even though, thankfully, it had been a minor incident.

★   ★   ★

I couldn't help smiling to myself when I remembered my childhood experiences. It was obvious that Billy's negative attitude was a world apart from mine. I knew that in Britain a lot of children often grew up without a sense of respect for the police but Billy's lack of regard for them seemed to go much deeper than that.

I smiled, too, thinking about the nursery children. Whenever we were out on a walk and a police car drove by, the children would get very excited. I always thought it was incredibly sweet how the officers knew that young children hero-worshipped them and how they would make a point of slowing down and waving. Some even flashed their lights, which absolutely thrilled the children.

The experiences of the past week had me wondering if I would ever get to the bottom of Billy's attitudes. I was reminded of what I had known right from the start – Billy wasn't like other people. I hesitate to say that he wasn't 'normal', because what is normal? But I did know that he wasn't right. I could tell by the blank look at the very back of his eyes. I could tell by his personality, his mannerisms and behaviours, his speech, and even by his aura of uncertainty.

I could tell.

It's like he doesn't know how to be. He surveys; he copies; he overcompensates, becoming too friendly and then too accommodating. All of it is his persona. It is in the way he watches people, and scrutinises them. He watches, and even squints, as if to catch a clue in the silence. His composure is off as well – too premeditated and then too aloof – as if it is habitual behaviour, or sort of rehearsed.

Are those things normal? Maybe I wasn't normal for noticing.

I didn't know for sure. What I did know was that I loved him. Despite and because.

PART II

MASKS AND TRIGGERS

INTRODUCTION
(During)

The human mind is a wonderful device. It can protect us from extreme pain and suffering by blocking out what is too hard to cope with. Without my knowing, Billy's mind was doing just that, blocking out the traumatic events of his childhood in exactly this way. The memories are there, they are just locked away, until something triggers them to surface. Many times this happens in the form of a flashback; when thoughts, actions and emotions that have been repressed are brought to the fore, triggered by either internal or external circumstances, evoking the original trauma.

The memories that are evoked are obviously emotionally loaded and the very fact that they can appear uncontrollably and unpredictably makes them all the more difficult to deal with. They can take up residence without any invitation and so many things can be triggers that it is impossible to keep them in check or to have any control over them.

As the years went by, and as Billy got older, it was becoming harder and harder for him to continue wearing his mask and suppressing his memories. Triggers out of his control were causing him to have flashbacks more and more often. All those years, nobody knew what was actually going on in his head . Not even me. Then in 1997, the floodgates opened and all the horrific memories bubbled to the surface. It was out of his control. His mind had taken the burden for so long, shielding him from the pain, until eventually it was in overload. It then quickly became apparent that, in essence, I had lost my husband. The man in our house looked like Billy but it wasn't him.

4

NEW MOON

If you ever find your way back home
Please send me a sign
You know you're not alone
If you ever feel you're so low
Please send me a sign
Please don't forget me

'Remember Me' by James K

We all have defining moments in our lives, moments that we remember even years later. Moments that change the course of our lives or who we are.

One of those moments for me happened on 20 December 1997. It must have been a Saturday or Sunday because neither of us had gone to work. The morning of that day had started out as one of those ordinary, forgettable days of domestic life where periods of routine chores and household jobs make up the hours as one moseys along in a bubble of normality. It seems nothing noteworthy is remotely capable of happening other than cleaning getting done, laundry getting washed and groceries getting bought.

I was at home while Billy was out Christmas shopping with my sister Sophie. Billy hated shopping at the best of times and avoided it the rest of the year but, with Sophie along for moral support, he braved the Christmas crowds. It wasn't just all the people who made Billy uncomfortable, it was also standing in queues waiting to pay and, worst of all, actually paying for purchases. He almost never bought things and then only when he absolutely had to. He often made me gifts and always made my birthday, Christmas and anniversary cards, which I always thought was incredibly sweet.

By the time Billy had been gone for a few hours, I was well into cleaning the house. I sang along to the CD that played in the living room as I dusted and tidied. I have always been one of those people who actually like housework. It isn't a chore for me. Completely immersed in music and work, I jumped when the ringing of the phone interrupted me. I ran to pick it up… and, in that instant, our lives changed.

'Hello?' I answered, struggling not to sound out of breath.

'Alix?' I recognised Billy's sister's voice, but instantly felt a shiver of fear as I heard her sobbing, 'Oh, Alix, I don't know how to tell you…'

'What? Tell me what? What is it?' I asked in a panicked, jumbled way.

'It's Mam… oh, Alix… she's gone.'

'What? What do you mean? She's not …' I knew what she meant, but, at the same time, my mind was stuck in disbelief.

To be honest, I don't remember the rest of the conversation. But I do remember sitting on the arm of the chair in the living room after hanging up the phone. I couldn't quite get my head round it, especially since we were planning to ring Billy's mum, Hannah, when Billy returned from shopping – ironically, to wish her happy birthday. I watched through the front window to the road and there I sat, for I don't know how long, waiting for Billy. Even Ben appeared morose. He lay perfectly still with his head resting on the floor between his two front paws. His eyes looked heavy and sad as he stared at me – the droopy, chocolate saucers watching my every move. As always, he was completely in tune with my mood and had picked up that something was wrong.

The shrill ring of the phone abruptly shattered the silence again, sounding extra loud and totally intrusive. It had taken on a Judas-like quality, having been the bearer of such awful news, I suppose. It was odd but I actually had a different feeling towards the phone itself, like it had let us down or something. The ring definitely sounded harsher somehow. With a feeling of detachment, I recalled how, as a teenager, the phone seemed to have had its own identity then as well. Back then, when it was silent, it seemed to be moodily withholding what was in its power to give. That afternoon it just seemed cruel.

'Answer the phone, you geek!' Sophie's voice broke through my thoughts. The answer machine had kicked in, which, I have to say, was not uncommon. We are 'screeners' and anyone who knew us well knew that.

'Oh, well, I guess you have the vacuum on or something…'

I didn't pick up; I couldn't face talking to anyone.

'Billy just dropped me off. Mission accomplished – big time,' she joked. He'll be home any minute… no peeking!' she warned before hanging up.

I drew in a big sigh and wondered how the hell I was going to tell Billy. I felt nervous and sick. I wanted so much to protect him and shield him from the pain. I wildly thought that perhaps I could just not tell him but, of course, I knew that was ridiculous. I just simply would have done anything to make it all go away. Like *Bewitched*, I wanted to perform some kind of magic – to go back and erase the shock of the day. But my name wasn't Samantha and I couldn't wiggle my nose.

Not long after, I saw him pull into the driveway, his lovely little head visible through the driver's side window. I got off the chair and stood at the window. I had a powerful, regressive, even instinctual urge to suck my thumb in an effort to comfort myself, just as I used to do all those years ago in childhood. I watched him jump out and open the sliding door, pick up some bags and put them under his coat. He glanced up at the window, saw me and smiled. He looked pleased with himself as he touched his nose with his finger, telling me to stop being so nosy. I thought my heart would break.

I couldn't bear the thought of him having to hear such news. He seemed so happy and I was going to wipe the smile off his face – in an instant, with just a few small words. I dreaded telling him and hated to be the one to have to do it but, at the same time, I wanted to be the one. I didn't want him to have to hear it from someone else.

All too soon, he was there, standing in front of me. He looked at me and our eyes locked. For an instant, time stood still. A feeling of desperation coursed through me, a feeling that made me want to cling on to him for dear life, as if I knew that, as soon as I opened my mouth, all would be different. In no way could I have known that that instant was the last one we would ever have as *that* couple.

But, looking back, it was as close to a premonition as I was going to get. I saw that he recognised in my eyes that something wasn't right. I don't remember the words I used – the horrible words I used to break his heart. I do, however, remember the look in his eyes. It was a cold, hard stare, with a blankness behind it that seemed to mean more than it should have done. A shiver went right through me.

Without any further verbal exchange whatsoever, Billy turned and, rather clumsily, walked away from me and retreated downstairs. I wasn't sure what to do.

After some time, I went downstairs to see if I could do anything for him. I really didn't know what to expect. I could only imagine how I would react to news of my own mother's death, even though it didn't bear thinking about, but I really didn't know how Billy would handle it. When bad things happened, Billy tended to laugh them off. I knew such a reaction was because he was putting on a brave face, not that he didn't care. He always had trouble showing his emotions and I never quite knew if that was just a guy thing or yet another legacy from his childhood. I had always assumed that it was probably a bit of both.

There had only been one other occasion when I had witnessed Billy's reaction to someone dying. I remember it clearly, as it is one of those things that tend to stick in your mind for ever. We were in Cardiff at the time and Billy's mate Callum had tragically and unexpectedly died. He had known him since childhood but had reconnected with him when he bought a flat around the corner from where we lived. I was friendly with Callum's fiancée and the four of us often got together. His death was such a shock and was so appalling, especially since he left behind his lovely fiancée and was so young, with so much left to do.

When Billy found out, he cried openly. He grieved and, in time, life went on pretty much as normal. But Billy's relationship with Callum had been easy, without any conflict, so I couldn't shake the thought that his reaction to his mum's death was going to be very different. I could feel it in my bones.

I began to isolate incidents in my head, between Billy and his mum, going back years. I started replaying in my mind things that had been said, which, in turn, made me realise just how complicated Billy's feelings towards his mum actually were. It gave me the first glimmer of dread that the grieving process was going to prove immensely difficult for him.

When I went downstairs, I found Billy sitting at the desk in the office. He sat completely still, his face filled with emotion. We were surrounded by an almost palpable stillness, somehow intensified by the irritating drone of the dryer. Laundry that I had put in before the phone call had become forgotten and was unnecessarily tumbling round, wasting electricity, and daring to interrupt the thick silence.

I didn't know what to say. I desperately didn't want to say the wrong thing. He clearly hadn't been crying but his ashen face and tensing facial muscles spoke eloquently of his torment. I couldn't take my eyes off his face. His expression communicated something that I couldn't quite put my finger on. In some ways, his countenance was utterly descriptive, yet oddly, and confusingly, I was having significant trouble reading it. I ended up just asking him if I could get him anything. He just shook his head sluggishly from side to side as if it took an enormous effort, as though his head suddenly weighed more.

I felt utterly useless as I clumped slowly back up into the kitchen. I sat in silence in the living room, in the same chair I had sat in before. The house felt quiet, as if Hannah being gone had somehow made a difference – ridiculous, of course, especially since she had never even been there. It was as if just knowing she was alive and well had somehow contributed to the ambient noise. It was quieter, hollow-ish, without her.

About an hour later, I heard Billy come up and get my address book out of a drawer, followed by the dull thud of his leaden footsteps as he slowly descended back down into the basement. I figured he was going to phone Lauren. I went to the top of the stairs and heard the beeps of the phone emanating from the darkness below, as he pressed the numbers. There was an interval of silence before I then heard his muffled voice... then silence... then his quiet voice resumed... then silence again. That pattern repeated itself for a time until a beep signalled the end of the call and the silence took over.

I went down to see if he was all right but he told me to leave him alone. I felt so helpless as I resignedly went back upstairs. Eventually, what seemed like ages later, he came upstairs. He came into the living room and slumped down on to the couch for a moment before he sat forward and put his head in his hands. I had been sitting in the dark with only the Christmas lights on. On my own, I found the lights somehow soothing but, with Billy there, I felt like the festive cheer they represented was both disrespectful and insensitive. I also felt guilty for having lit a fire, sort of selfish – like it was somehow wrong that I didn't want to feel chilly – as if the awfulness of the situation would only be properly validated if we were completely in the dark and cold.

He looked up. A flicker of firelight, dancing against the grey pallor of his face, contorted his features giving him an unnerving look. I realised immediately what the haunting expression – the one that had crossed over his face from the moment that I broke the news to him – reminded me of. He looked like a tormented child.

The room was still imbued with that same absolute silence that often follows in the wake of death, which, coupled with his demeanour, seemed sacrilege to break.

Over the next hour, he relayed snippets of the conversation that he had just had with Lauren. Apparently, Hannah had died in her sleep. Heart trouble they thought, although, as far as we knew, she had no history of it. She wouldn't have known what was happening. It was very quick – peaceful even. She had just gone to sleep. Her bedding wasn't messed up; she hadn't struggled.

Lauren had obviously been told those things to give her a grain of comfort, not that they weren't true, just that giving her the knowledge that Hannah hadn't suffered gave her something to hold on to – it was perfectly natural. I'm sure Lauren had attempted just that when she told Billy the same things, although I'm not sure it made any difference to Billy. I think, for him, she was just gone.

He still hadn't cried and I wondered if the enormity had even registered. It didn't seem to have but, then again, it was impossible to tell what he was thinking. His lack of tears made me nervous and uneasy. I wished he would cry, thinking that it was bound to make him feel better somehow.

We sat in silence for ages… until we ended up having an argument. Well, it would have been an argument, if, in fact, I had said anything back. It had started when Billy had asked me if I would phone work for him, his voice sounding so flat and expressionless as he made his request. I said that of course I would, and then hesitantly asked if he wanted me to book some flights.

'No need,' Billy stated firmly, his muted voice suddenly roused with instantaneous temper.

'What do you mean?' I asked, totally surprised. I hadn't expected that response at all.

'Leave it, Alix. I'm not going… end of!' he barked.

'I'm only trying to help,' I replied, gently by anyone's standards, but the look on Billy's face told me he thought otherwise.

'Just shut it!' he shot back. He made to leave the room and, as he did so, he put his open hands up beside his ears in an exaggerated, frustrated manner, as if he didn't want to hear anything else. He let out an angered sort of grunt as he retreated down the basement staircase. As usual, he was acting as if I had spewed vile recriminations at him – his response, once again, completely out of proportion with the reality of the situation.

★   ★   ★

Crash! A chair was violently knocked over as the largest of them lunged forward.

'Wahoo, blah-oo, bwah-oo, bwah-oo…' is all Billy heard of the argument.

'You bloody well took my money! You do my fucking head in with your thieving ways. I'm gonna do for you, you fucking bastard! I'll teach you!'

'I fuckin' never touched your pissing money!'

'Bwah-oo, bwah-oo, bwah-oo…' On and on and on.

A plate was thrown at the wall and exploded into pieces on contact. Mashed potatoes and gravy slid down the nicotine-stained wall to accumulate on the floor amid a pile of sausages.

'You fucking twat!'

'Bwah-oo, bwah-oo, bwah-oo…'

'Fucking pack it in, you pair… Are you fucking listening to me?'

'Jesus bloody Christ, you're going the right way for a bloody good hiding, boyo!'

Billy pulled his legs up and put his arms round his knees. Hugging himself and gently rocking back and forth, he looked from one to the others, praying they'd stop.

'That's just like you, you selfish fucking prick!'

'And you're some fucking saint, aye, twat features!'

All three faces were twisted in anger. One got hit across the face with a back-hander. Blood splattered across the wall, adding yet another pattern to the already stained woodchip.

As per usual, the rage-fuelled bust-ups and the slanging matches produced a chaotic jumble in Billy's head. Almost every day in Billy's dysfunctional world, no matter where he was, someone was yelling and carrying on over something. It wasn't always directed at Billy, but it was almost worse to have to watch.

During such violent outbursts, Billy's mind was sent spinning into an uncontrollable turmoil. A confusing mix of angry voices started to sound as if he was hearing it all from under water and angry faces became distorted, swirling relentlessly in front of his vision. Sometimes he covered his ears, but that really only muted the already strange sound, making the noise even more distorted.

He was subjected to these terrifying rows on so many occasions, in many different scenarios, until he became extremely deft at knowing when yet another row was imminent. Raised voices, for whatever reason, meant inevitable conflict. And conflict was an inevitable part of Billy's immediate surroundings.

In order to cope, Billy shut down at the first sign of any form of disagreement or confrontation. In his mind, mild annoyance led to emotional outbursts; they, in turn, led to possible bloodshed, and that led to inevitable chaos.

★   ★   ★

The few times that I had asked Billy if he wanted anything, he had snapped at me, so I decided it was best just to leave him be and to let him set the level of my involvement. I just had to hope that he would let me know when I could help and what I could do.

He was understandably fighting with a maelstrom of emotions but the over-riding one seemed to me to be one of anger. That confused me, I have to say. I mean, yes, I know anger is one of the stages of grief, but it didn't seem like that kind of anger at all.

I knew I needed to delve deeper. I let my mind zero in on past concerns relating to Billy's relationship with his mum. Once they were dissected, I realised that I actually had previously acknowledged them on some level. I reminded myself, or perhaps admitted to myself, that there *had* been a sort of undercurrent between Billy and his mother (that only Billy had shown). And, although they were on pretty good terms when we left Cardiff and moved to Canada, I began to realise that that really had only been on the surface. I came to accept that there had always been a conflict of emotions going on in Billy's head to some degree with regard to his mother – an underlying sense of something that, although he had never expressed it openly, I had picked up on.

Revealing that to myself worried me, mainly because it seemed to me that the people who are more likely to experience difficulty when dealing with a loss are the ones whose relationships with the deceased had been troubled. Feelings of anger, guilt, remorse, regret – any number of destructive feelings, really – about all the things that weren't said or done or put right, can become overwhelming when one can't do anything about them. Unfinished business and all that. Obviously, that isn't the case with everyone but it must be harder to come to terms with things, and ultimately harder to grieve, when there are 'issues' to sort out on top of everything else.

I rather suspected as much with regard to Billy's relationship with his mum but really I was just grasping at anything that could help me to understand Billy's obvious torment. I literally had no personal experience of such feelings. Of course, my family unit had its own annoying dynamic, mainly to do with normal sibling rivalry and classic birth-order behaviours, but there were no unresolved issues, at least not of any significance.

Understandably, the lack of conflict in my past, and the obvious surfeit in Billy's, gave me significant cause for concern. It was so obvious to me that, if the tables were turned, I would have been incredibly sad, as well as experiencing a range of other emotions, but anger wouldn't have been one of them. My concern over Billy's sense of entrenched anger fed my worry. I fought against it – because I really didn't want it to be true – but I knew that it was. He didn't appear to be angry at Hannah for dying, or angry that he hadn't had the chance to say goodbye, or angry at the unfairness of her being taken before her time. I sensed profoundly that it was an anger that went deeper than that. I sensed contempt. But somehow I was also reminded of his vulnerable, childlike quality.

★   ★   ★

Billy was lying on his back in a field that ran along the river, down at the bottom of Llanellog Hill. It was familiar territory, as it was his usual route of choice either to or from his mam's house. He didn't know why he had gone there, really. He wasn't running to his mam's house, he didn't want to go there. He was just running away. He didn't have a plan; somehow, he just found himself in the field just down the hill from her house.

Old man Jonesy's farm was just across the river and Billy could hear the farmer's son shouting abuse at his dog. He did not like Jonesy's son, but there was nothing he could do. He couldn't risk being seen, or getting caught.

He tried to put the noises from the farm out of his head. He had other things to think about. He watched the wispy cotton candy overhead turn into thick rain clouds. The sky seemed to have changed so quickly, Billy couldn't help but wonder if he had dozed off. He turned over on to his belly and began pulling out blades of grass as he thought about his trips out with Mr Andrews. Immediately, he felt annoyed with himself. Annoyed that he had been stupid enough to believe that Mr Andrews cared about him. It hurt him to think about how excited he had been the first time he was allowed to go out for the day – even if it had been just to a football match. When he had found out that his brother was going as well, he had been beside himself with excitement.

Absentmindedly pulling out handfuls of grass, Billy chastised himself for being so stupid. He clawed at the earth beneath the grass until his fingers were sore and caked with dirt. He turned over on to his back once again but couldn't shake that feeling of hopelessness. He had had a bit of hope three weeks before, for about three hours, but the clouds overhead seemed to confirm a different story. He felt like they looked – grey. But most of all he felt discarded.

About a month before, he had built up the courage to try to tell his mam about going to the football. At first, he hadn't wanted to say anything about what happened on the drive back to the home, especially because he didn't want to say anything that might put a stop to possibly seeing Jon. But, in the end, he was just desperate to get away from there, so he told her as best he could. He wasn't quite sure how to put it into words but he thought she would understand. And, he thought, she would save him. She was his mother; surely that stood for something.

For the first few weeks, he imagined she was sorting it all out. Every day, he expected to be told he was going home, or at least getting moved. But nothing happened. He hadn't seen Mr Andrews. Well, he'd seen him, obviously, but not alone. So that was a promising development. But he couldn't help thinking that something more should have happened. And sooner.

About two weeks later, while Billy happened to be looking out of an upstairs window, he saw his mam entering the building. Any earlier, or later, he would have missed her. He was excited. She was coming to get him. She had understood what he had tried to say. He went to get his bits together, then he sat and waited.

Two hours later, she still hadn't come up.

Two days went by.

Two weeks went by.

Then Mr Andrews took him out again. They didn't see Jon. Mr Andrews said that their mam wouldn't let Jon go out with them any more. Billy felt as if he had been stabbed right through the heart. As far as he was concerned, there were only two explanations. Either she hadn't believed what he'd told her, or she did, but she didn't care. What was worse, she obviously cared more about Jon because she had stopped him from going to meet them.

With the rain hitting his face, Billy decided that he wouldn't think about his mam any more. He wouldn't let himself. She became consciously dismissed, yet indelibly imprinted on his heart.

★   ★   ★

Later, I went to bed, unsure of what else to do, but tossed and turned all night, aware that Billy wasn't beside me. He never did come to bed that night. He just dozed on the couch as he sat in the dark.

The next morning, he was quiet but nowhere near as withdrawn as the night before. He took the dog for a walk and things were definitely better. I thought I should try to get him to talk about the funeral when he got back in case he had just said that he wasn't going to go because he was still in shock. I thought he might change his mind once the initial shock had worn off. On the other hand, I didn't want to risk him becoming all withdrawn and angry again if I brought the subject up. I knew I had to, though, especially as I felt obligated to tell him that he might regret not going and, in time, wish that he had.

I managed to pluck up the courage later that day but, as anticipated, he absolutely refused to discuss it and shouted, 'You don't know what the fuck you're talking about, Alix… just fucking leave it, will you!' The strange flash of anger returned with a vengeance.

I actually started to sing, *sotto voce*, singing words I didn't even know I remembered. I sang a song under my breath that I had sung when I was six years old at Sunday School. That in itself was odd, not the least because I wasn't particularly religious. Well, I was, but not in the regular churchgoing kind of way.

*　　*　　*

'Jesus loves me, this I know, for the Bible tells me so… Little ones to Him belong, They are weak but He is strong… Yes, Jesus loves me… Yes, Jesus loves me… Yes, Jesus loves me… The Bible tells me so.'

I was singing quietly to myself – the choice of song simply because I liked the tune. We were in the camper van, all packed up, and were driving down Cadboro Bay Road just alongside Oak Bay Junior High School. After singing the first verse, and forgetting the rest of the words, my mind was taken off singing. Almost immediately, I sensed, although perhaps not entirely comprehended, that something wasn't quite as it should have been. It came to me before I even knew why, or what, it meant – a hint that tension was in the air. It wasn't enough to upset me but, in the moments that followed, I paid close attention, as if important information could be garnered just through examination alone, or a concentrated effort at awareness.

Mummy was looking for something and she seemed slightly agitated. She opened her handbag and pulled a few things out. Daddy pulled over to the side of the road. He seemed a bit cross. I was in the back and couldn't really hear what was being said between them but I didn't think much was really that wrong as Kate hadn't even looked up from her Mad comic.

Daddy drove round the block and headed back towards home. He was definitely cross. He pulled into our driveway rather quickly and then Mummy jumped out and quickly ran up the side steps into the kitchen.

'What's wrong, Daddy?' I asked.

'Your mother realised she wasn't wearing her wedding ring and she's worried that she has lost it. She'd better get a move on or we'll miss the ferry!' he replied insensitively, as much with the question as the inconvenience.

In no time at all the door opened and Mummy came out. I watched intently as she locked the door. Then, as she turned towards the van, I detected a slight upturn at the corners of her mouth. She jumped back in the van, amid visible relief, and Daddy reversed out of the driveway in much the same manner that he had driven up it just a few minutes earlier. I knew without being told that Daddy didn't like to be rushed, or late.

'Are we going to miss the ferry?' I asked worriedly, the apple not falling far from the tree.

A few cross words were exchanged between Mummy and Daddy before I got my reassurance. Then, after some further discussion – none of which I could make out over the noise of the engine and the traffic – all was OK again.

There had been a problem. I knew it. I didn't quite understand what it was, or why, but I knew it.

I also knew when it had been resolved.

★   ★   ★

I can't say that I wasn't hurt by Billy's harsh tone, because I was, but I also knew it was just the grief talking. All I could really do was to respect his wishes. I certainly didn't want to keep on at him and for us to end up mad at each other. With Hannah having just died, it was the last thing I could let happen.

However, even if I had wanted to release some of my pent-up feelings through a heated exchange, I wouldn't have known quite how to go about it. I have never been able to argue properly with Billy, probably because I wasn't used to arguments during my childhood. I never saw or heard my parents yell at each other, so I guess I just wasn't programmed that way. Granda shouted and became angry on more than one occasion but, in my head, and in my scrutiny, that was something completely different – something I almost forgot, if 'forgot' is the right word. Daddy may have raised his voice from time to time but it was never over anything worrying. And Mummy never shouted back. At worst, I mostly only sensed discord. Sometimes, it was the words that were used rather than the volume at which they were spoken. Certainly, the tone of voice was a clue, but often it was simply a slight alteration in manner that alerted me to something that otherwise might have gone completely unnoticed.

With a child's unerring antennae I recognised things – which usually caused me to store them, as children do, for future reference, until I could understand them. There was never a time when I witnessed, or heard, a heated exchange, not even on television. And if there was a disagreement, it wasn't hidden or swept under the carpet. My sisters and I were just privileged to act as witnesses to non-aggressive conflict resolution.

'I shall tell Lauren we can't afford the air fares,' Billy said, breaking the silence, interrupting my thoughts.

It seemed that Billy had given it some thought, especially having come up with an excuse, so I figured he must have made up his mind. At first, I worried what everyone in Cardiff would think if we didn't attend the funeral. I was sure they wouldn't believe that we couldn't afford it. For one, I knew they were under the inaccurate impression that because we had moved to Canada we were well off; and, two, they would know that I could borrow the money from my parents if I had to. In the end, though, I concluded that I couldn't worry about what people thought. It was up to Billy and I had to go along with what he thought was right, support him and just hope that he could live with his decision. I wondered if perhaps I should buy the tickets anyway, just in case he did change his mind. It would be awful if he decided to go, only to find that he had left it too late and couldn't get a flight.

But I decided not to. And it was a good thing, too, as Billy didn't change his mind and proceeded to refuse any attempt on my part to talk about his mum's death.

Christmas came and went. We cancelled everyone coming to ours on Christmas Eve and we didn't go to the Christmas dinner at my parents' house. It didn't feel right celebrating the Christmas season;

besides, I knew Billy wouldn't go anyway and I didn't want the hassle of trying to make him.

On 5 January, we both went back to work and, although Billy wasn't himself, he seemed to be coping, at least to a certain extent. However, now the anger had taken up permanent residence. Sometimes, it was inconspicuously hiding in the basement, but I wasn't fooled. I had the niggling feeling in the back of my mind that, instead of dealing with the loss, he was actually only pushing it aside.

I didn't know it at the time, but I couldn't have been more right. What I also didn't know was that there was no room left in his head for anything else to be stored away. Not only that, but the pain of Hannah's passing was chipping away at all those things that he had previously suppressed, and these were all now clamouring to break the surface of his consciousness.

An extremely explosive concoction had been simmering away inside Billy since he was a young boy. A cauldron of emotions made up of a huge portion of betrayal, a dollop of abandonment pain, an overflowing scoop of anger, a pint-sized measure of shame and generous seasonings of fear and sadness all churned away inside him. For as long as he could remember, he had tried to keep it all from erupting. Neither of us knew that on that day, 20 December 1997, the cauldron started to bubble over, and it took a few months for the whole lot to burst out. The chaos of feelings in his mind had been fermenting for so long that, when it did eventually boil over, what was left was a layer of scorched matter at the bottom. Not only were we left with the mess from the overflow, but there was also the burned-out cauldron to deal with. And I had no idea how to clean it up.

5

PATIENCE

I wanna feel the rain falling on my face…

'Baby You Know', by James K

As winter gave way to spring, Billy's mind gave way to a prolific and profound mental unravelling. Bulbs, carefully planted amid much anticipation the autumn before, surreptitiously turned into tulips, and all the while I watched as Billy blindly succumbed to his ever-expanding darkness. The more desperate the situation became, the more I wished it was still winter – if only for the fact that I somehow felt comforted by stormy weather.

I have never been the sort of person who gets depressed on cloudy days. I have certainly never been able to relate to the notion of seasonally affected disorder (SAD). And a good thing, too, given that we lived in the Pacific Northwest, where rain was indeed plentiful. I suppose it's fair to say that I have always liked rainy days. Perhaps not more than sunny days, but certainly as much. In fact, it is probably more accurate to say, simply, that I love weather. Around that time, then, more than ever before, I was especially partial to wet weather days. And, when those days graced me with their presence, Ben was treated to an extra long walk.

During those first months of Billy's decline, I think I enjoyed my walks with Ben more on the darker, wet days simply because I encountered far fewer people. And thus was spared the agony of exchanging false pleasantries with many of the neighbourhood's regular dog walkers. By that stage, I took great pains to avoid as many as possible, although, as the weeks went by, I didn't even notice the few die-hard walkers – my mind becoming far too preoccupied. Eventually, I began to crave being out in the rain, just to experience the feeling of rejuvenation that specifically came from feeling the rain on my skin. It was a tangible feeling of empowerment that I realised was guaranteed to be found while Ben and I walked briskly, alone together, during the heaviest of downpours. I sought it out almost addictively.

After one such therapeutic excursion, Ben and I arrived back looking very much like a pair of drowned rats. As we entered through the kitchen door, there was no Billy waiting with towels at the ready. Instead, I quickly took my wet things off as Ben waited patiently. With my coat off, and minus my soaked trousers, I stood in the kitchen in just a sweatshirt and knickers, feeling oddly uncomfortable – as if the person just down the stairs was a stranger, instead of my husband who had seen me in less clothing thousands of times before.

As I quickly rubbed Ben down, I heard a familiar noise emerge from the darkened basement. A noise I had heard many times over the past few months – the sound of yet another beer being opened. I had taken to listening obsessively from the kitchen, anxious to hear something, anything, that let me know Billy was all right.

Then there was another sound, something that jogged my memory. That also was a familiar sound, but I couldn't quite put my finger on it. The realisation hit me seconds before the smell confirmed my suspicion. It was the flick of a lighter. Damn, Billy was smoking. What a shame, I thought, he hadn't smoked for three or more years and he had been so proud of himself when he quit. It was just another thing that confirmed to me just how low he was.

By the middle of 1998, Billy was in a very poor mental state. Things had gone from bad to worse – much worse. He was totally burned out and didn't seem to have any coping skills at all. It was as if he couldn't think any more. He couldn't even make choices or decisions about the simplest of things, sometimes even refusing to speak.

He was on the sick from work and spent all of his time in the basement. It was mostly a storage area, with only part of it being used as living space. The biggest area, where all our camping equipment and

Christmas decorations were kept, covered most of the basement and was completely unfinished, with exposed stud walls and concrete floors. The washing machine and dryer were also there, which I hated because it was incredibly spooky at night and there were always spiders and cobwebs, no matter how much I swept. The only finished section comprised of an office of sorts, which mainly housed an old desk and bookshelves, containing my old psychology and child-development textbooks from my time at university, and an open area at the bottom of the kitchen stairs that we used as a second TV room. It was dark at the best of times, being below ground level, and the only little window that let in minimal light Billy kept covered. I had always called it the 'Black Hole' and definitely then, more than ever, it seemed a fitting name. We hadn't done any decorating down there since we moved in – something upstairs always seemed to take precedence – so it was like a 1970s explosion down there, with horrendous wood-panelled walls, hideous wall-to-wall orange shagpile carpet and an even worse Partridge Family sofa. There, Billy isolated himself.

I couldn't understand it; we had a perfectly good living room upstairs that was much more comfortable *and* a million times more pleasing to the eye but, day after day, night after night, there he stayed. I could only assume that Billy sought out this dingy and depressing place as it somehow suited his mood. I hated every minute he was down there but I was grateful that we at least had somewhere he could go, as it obviously allowed Billy the space he needed. I also, selfishly, was glad that I didn't have to see it first-hand. I don't know what would have happened if we hadn't had a place where he could detach himself. I really felt that, if I pushed him, he would take off, so at the time it was an acceptable solution for me. It also ensured that I could keep an eye on him, safe in the knowledge that he at least had access to food and a warm, dry place to sleep. It really was that bad.

As each day slid by, he was taken along a path that began in denial, hardened into an ugly resentment, then leaped to a bitter and painful estrangement from everything. He had become morose and filled with a strange kind of melancholia. A decline that I suppose, if I'm honest, was a gradual thing that had just sort of crept up on me until one day he was completely withdrawn.

With the benefit of hindsight, I would have to admit that the decline had not been immediately evident to me. I mean, I think things had been going wrong for quite some time before I consciously allowed myself to notice, but by then he was completely withdrawn and in a bad way. But I *had* known *something* was off – something just hadn't been quite right.

I remember I thought that if I could just think my way through it I would be able to uncover a perfectly logical explanation. I *remember* thinking that, and I even know that it was 1 March 1998 when I first noticed that change, but at the time I guess I just wasn't letting my consciousness identify it. Of course, the memory can be very mysterious. It can file things away that you don't even know you have noticed. Billy's behaviour, in the months leading up to his breakdown, had been evident and I can see that with hindsight. But at the time, I just stored it away. I still find it extraordinary that I was able to recall that I *had* thought about that change in Billy but at the same time I also knew that I didn't address it.

In the months leading up to the moment when I actually conceptualised the problem, he had been subtly changing. One of the only things that could have been pinpointed was that his movements seemed younger. Well, not quite. It was more like he was acting like a teenager, but at the same time I knew he wasn't doing it deliberately, or even consciously. At the time, I didn't compare his behaviour to the movie *Thirteen Going on Thirty* because it wasn't out then but, looking back, that was exactly what it was like. His body language had changed. A nuanced, non-verbal shift in his body movements had occurred that suggested teenager-ness.

It *was* a gradual deterioration over a two-month period, but I had been busy with work and I had also been single-mindedly focusing on my infertility, so it really isn't that much of a surprise that that behaviour had gone unnoticed. And I don't think the end result would have been any different even if I had seen it coming.

Either way, by the end of the summer, he was clearly very ill. He appeared listless, without energy, and would go for days only getting off the couch to go to the toilet. He wore the same clothes day in, day out and was unshaven. This, in itself, was so unlike him; he had always been so finicky about his appearance. He had lost loads of weight, as he barely ate a thing, and had absolutely no interest in anything. His clothes hung on him and he always looked unkempt. Buttons were done up incorrectly, or not done up at all, shirt-tails were un-tucked – everything he wore was perpetually in need of laundering.

He also had a terrible, haunted and hurt expression at the centre of his eyes that I had seen for so long by that point that I'd forgotten when I'd first noticed it. It was at the part of his eyeball that, when you looked at it, really looked at it, it took you straight into his soul – the part that left him naked every single waking moment of every single day. A dark pool that no amount of alcohol, drugs or masks could ever cover. I'm sure, if there had been a way, Billy would have found it. I hated to witness such raw pain, especially in the man I loved, but I was almost obsessive in my scrutiny of it. Maybe I thought that, if I looked at it long enough, and understood it, I could somehow make it go away. All I knew was that it made my heart hurt. An actual, non-specific, unidentifiable pain that I felt within me. I absorbed it, and it hurt. It truly hurt, in a way that is indescribable and unique and actually completely different from the pain one feels from one's own physical ailments.

He had simply become a lost soul.

I was desperate to fold my arms around him and offer comfort, but he had an off-putting aura about him that persuaded me not to. I felt utterly powerless. I tried relentlessly to get him to go to the doctor's, but to no avail.

Eventually, I had to do something, so I went to the doctor myself to try to get him some help. Our GP was very good and, after hearing all I had to say about how Billy had been and how worried I was, he agreed to phone Billy at home. I just hoped that he could convince Billy to accept help.

To give him his due, he did as much as he could. He got Billy to agree for me to take him to his surgery and he was then able to prescribe some medication. I so much wanted everything to be all right again that I naively thought that maybe that was all that was wrong. Maybe he just had some sort of chemical imbalance that could be sorted out with medication. I wanted to believe that.

Unfortunately, it wasn't long before I was back to my original theory. Something had to be causing all the turmoil. Such an all-encompassing decline must stem from some concealed suffering nucleus. There *had* to be something at the root of his behaviour, I just knew it. I may have no idea *why* I know, but surely, if one feels something that strongly, it would be extremely unwise not to pay attention to it. I also knew that Billy was in denial, but denial is only a coping mechanism, no more than that. I just didn't know what he was trying so hard to cope with. Maybe Billy didn't know either. I surmised that it could be subconscious, or buried so deep that he didn't know how to let it out.

I tried many different tactics to get through to him. I became an expert at reading his moods without him even speaking. I knew when he was upset; I knew when he was angry; I knew when he needed me; and, most of all, I knew when he was completely unreceptive, in which case I hardly spoke to him. At those times, there was no point in trying anything as he was oblivious to my presence.

Over time, his increasingly unreadable immobility lowered the level of expectation I had for anything that could remotely be seen as favourable or promising feedback to such a degree that even the merest suggestion could gladden my heart. One afternoon, I went down to the basement and he lifted his head up and looked, not quite at me, just in my vague direction. It evoked a warm surge of gladness in me.

During one of the unresponsive, zombie-like states, as he was lying in the dark with the television on, I walked past him to put on a load of washing. He didn't even seem to notice that I had walked past, so I stubbornly decided to turn the TV off, mainly to see if I could get any sort of a reaction. Still there was no response. He didn't even acknowledge that the television was off. I went back upstairs and, for the rest of the night, there was no movement. The light stayed off, as did the TV.

It was a strange time. I constantly felt like I was existing somewhere between lucidity and utter insanity. I clung to any vestige of strength that I could muster. I adjusted and readjusted my evaluation of the circumstances, clinging desperately to any residual shred of normality, and managed to retain my sanity with the last remaining fragment of my mind. I perpetually worried that if I didn't make a concentrated effort, and my mind went down a particular road, the balance might just be tipped.

Looking back, I wonder how I did it – how I actually got in my car after work each day and drove home, knowing what I was going home to. I know there were times when I wanted just to keep driving. There were also many times when I wanted to crawl under a rock and hide, but somehow I always made it home. If nothing else, Ben was there to help keep me on track. I knew I couldn't rely on Billy to see to Ben's needs, since he couldn't even see to his own, so I had to make sure Ben was fed and taken for a walk every day. Thank God for Ben. I suppose I could have taken him with me and stayed elsewhere, although I thought perhaps, if I couldn't reach Billy, maybe Ben could. I had read somewhere that just being with a dog can lower your heart rate by releasing endorphins into your system. And I had also heard about the positive effect that therapy dogs can have, so I figured having Ben around might actually help Billy.

Obviously the atmosphere was tense but, to be honest, when you are actually living through something, I don't think you are fully aware of what is going on, at least not to the full extent. I am sure if I read an account of what our life was like then I would have thought it sounded awful, but, when you are actually *living* it, somehow you just get through each day. I was, at least, going to work every day.

Undoubtedly, I would have gone bonkers if I had to be at home under such circumstances without a break from it. I just developed a routine that I could live with. I never asked Billy what he wanted to eat because I was aware that he was not capable of making even the simplest of decisions, so I made sure there were always things in that he could just grab to eat if he was hungry. Sometimes, I cooked a casserole or stew, hoping that the smell would entice him to eat. Sometimes it did, sometimes it didn't, but at least it gave me something to do. Something that made me feel as though I was at least doing *something* for him.

On the days that he didn't seem to be as unreachable, I would try to get him to talk. Somewhat worryingly, whether he answered or not, his eyes were constantly shifting from side to side, as if he were looking for a way out – a preternatural door – a way into or out of his own private and desperate abyss. It was incredibly hard because often he would say things that either scared the hell out of me or hurt me, but I had to try my hardest not to seem shocked or upset. I hoped he would say something that would help me to make sense out of it all, but he never did. He just said that he didn't love me; that he wouldn't care if Ben was hit by a car; that he felt like he was in a dark hole; that he would be better off dead… and so on. And, through it all, there was nothing that could explain to me why he felt that way.

As appalling as it was to hear, I knew it was about what his words represented – what they really meant, rather than the words themselves – that was revealing. He didn't feel *anything*. That's what he was trying to say… feeling nothing meant he felt nothing for anything, not nothing for Ben and me, and that made a difference.

I was so determined to get to the bottom of it all and, perhaps, that determination was the thing that eventually caused Billy to leave from time to time. Actually, 'run away' is really a more accurate way of describing Billy's absences, because that was really what he did. He ran away. I think he knew that I could see through the façade to the person underneath, and *that* was dangerous. I don't think it was a conscious thing, to run away, but I do think somewhere in his mind he thought that, to get away from the truth, he had to get away from me. I don't know how I knew that, I somehow just did. It was as if he was running away from something in his head and, if I got too close, or asked too many questions about his past, he would leave in an effort to keep it hidden. As if he wanted to bury his past, forget it, perhaps even pretend that it had never happened. I didn't know which.

I guessed that maybe that was why he was so remote with me at times. Maybe I, or at least my questions, somehow reminded him of the things he wanted to expunge from his memory. I didn't know for sure but I believed he thought that, if he didn't tell anyone whatever it was he was hiding and left, he could make it go away. He didn't realise, you see, that pain and heartache travel well. You don't just leave your troubles behind you when you go to another place.

It was clearly never planned. Once, I even came home to find he had gone and left a plate full of food on the table. He had made it for himself, and then left before he ate it. I didn't hear a thing from him. Then I came home a few days later to find him in the basement sitting in the dark. One minute he was there, then he was gone, then he'd be back again as if nothing unusual had happened. He seemed obsessed with running away – figuratively and literally. It was as if he was a rebellious teenager. Strange behaviour for a grown man.

★   ★   ★

With all his strength, Billy strove to free himself – striking out with fists and feet, and twisting and jerking himself in the hope of slipping out of the vice-like grip. But the restraint proved too strong. Physically and mentally, his defences were down. He could feel himself falling, shrinking, dissolving… and he could hear the jumble in his head – like a kettle on the boil.

The strip of yellowy-orange light under the door mesmerised him. At first, it seemed to be taunting him, teasing him that freedom was so close, yet so far. He wondered for a moment if it would have been better if it hadn't been there at all, but then he realised that that wasn't the case. That glow gave him a focus. It drew him in, and he had been relieved to give in to that pull. It centred him, internally, inside his head.

Some time later, it was hard to tell how long, the interference in his head stopped. The thin strip of light flashed big and brightness flooded his vision. A dark form seemed to move through it somehow and then, with a sweep and a click, the thin, bright strip returned. Somewhere beyond the strip he heard footsteps fading away.

Without thinking, Billy shuffled away from the yellowy-orange line. He wanted to breathe and he craved fresh air, hoping to restore some of what he had just lost. He climbed up, knelt on the sill and put his forehead against the cool, smooth surface. At the same time, he slid the sash upwards and crawled out.

Utterly weak, and miserable beyond words, Billy allowed himself to be guided by the lunar glow. The moonlight could make everything almost as light as day and it cannot be denied that that increase of visibility usually aided Billy's journeys, but in some ways it was more of a hindrance. When you are trying to get away without being seen, it's a case of the darker the better. But, as always, Billy couldn't plan his escapes according to the weather, or the time of day. Often, it would be a spur-of-the-moment decision. When, or if, he went was never anything to do with the weather. And, actually, there were pros and cons whatever the condition. When it was raining, it was better in the sense that there were less people out and about. People also rushed more, which tended to mean that they weren't likely to take much notice of him. It was also worse, though, mainly because it was hard, and inconvenient, to stay dry. And wet clothes, even in the summer, ensured that Billy became uncomfortably cold.

That night, as he stopped by a tree still within the grounds, Billy's courage gave way. A great sob shook him from head to foot. Tears, which he would have been determined not to shed in front of anyone else, rolled down his cheeks. He was only a little lad and that wicked night he had been struck helpless yet again. His nights were not the bedtime-story, flannel-jimjams, warm-milk kind of nights. His days were not about eating boiled egg and soldiers, walking in the park feeding the ducks, or taking trips to the beach and making sandcastles. His mornings certainly did not contain Weetabix, or vitamins, or goodbye kisses. They never had. But Billy still knew that he wanted them to.

When Billy ceased sobbing, he noticed that the light was fading. Clouds had rolled in. Everything at a distance grew indistinct. Only the tops of the trees stood out sharp and clear against the sky. A great stillness had descended. His surroundings, now uninhabited by shadows, closed in around him. Even the grass at his bare feet seemed motionless and asleep.

He was only wearing his pyjamas. He knew he had to go back.

★ ★ ★

I didn't really know where he was during those times away. He would often appear back very dirty and unshaven, suggesting that he had been sleeping rough – the mere thought of which filled me with confusion and horror. On other occasions, he clearly had been in someone's home as he was at least clean. But I never knew for sure where he had been.

Many people were shocked that I didn't question him on the matter. With hindsight, I can see that during that time he was drawn to chaos. He, in a sense, recreated the environment and behaviour patterns he knew best – where his responses to things seemed more acceptable than they did in the nicer side of town, in our stable life. My 'goodness' and my functional childhood was what he couldn't feel comfortable with. He ran away to the seedier side of town. He hung out there and frequented the rougher neighbourhoods. He spent time with those who were dysfunctional themselves.

He surrounded himself with people who drank too much; with people where violence, cheating and deception were commonplace. I think it reassured him. I'm sure he thought that he fitted in better with that lifestyle. The way he acted and thought, his hyper-vigilance and his self-abuse, all made sense. The good life was too good for him. I'm sure he felt like he didn't belong in a 'nice' neighbourhood. His mind was stuck, and it still is in some ways.

I knew I could only really help him if he wanted help and, to do that, he had to be home. Getting him better was the main objective. So, when he was away, I just had to trust that he would come home when he was ready for help. It was because his behaviour was so abnormal that I didn't throw in the towel. If he had just acted like a husband who wanted out of his marriage, I, of course, would have been devastated, but I would have accepted it and moved on.

This new behaviour was something quite different. In order to help Billy, and indeed to cope myself, I had to make sure that when he was home we were only dealing with his mental-health issues. To do that, I had to make sure that other sources of worry or irritation were avoided, which was particularly hard as we were scheduled to have our third IVF attempt during that time.

As the procedure date drew closer, I knew that not only would we not be able to go through with it but we also couldn't even discuss it. I knew that Billy wasn't in any fit state to go through it all. In any case, I'm sure at the time Billy had forgotten all about it. He didn't even seem to know what day it was, let alone anything else. Worst of all, I had to admit to myself that there was no point in even bringing the subject up because, when it boiled down to it, I couldn't, with all good conscience, bring a child into such an environment, regardless of how much I desperately wanted a baby. Having another IVF cycle at that point wouldn't have been fair to Billy. Or our baby.

My quasi-Solomon-esque decision left me feeling like I was shutting the door on my baby girl. It was as if she was in a room, crying, and I wasn't going to her. I'm sure to some people the idea that I knew we were destined to have a baby, and not only that, but that I knew that that baby was a girl, must seem strange. All I can say is that I just instinctively knew it was so. Ever since I can remember, I have thought about my future, especially becoming a mummy, with impatient anticipation. I didn't think in terms of ambitions, although I had a strong sense of my ability to be able to become whatever I wanted. I knew I could be a doctor if I so desired – which I didn't. I knew I could be a lawyer if the fancy took me – which it didn't. That side of things was my choice. Being a mummy? Well, that was simply a given.

*　　*　　*

Mummy and I walked slowly down Cranmore Road, both of us proudly pushing our blue-and-white prams – one a Silvercross, one a generic 'mini' version – as we strolled side by side. Grama was looking after Naomi while she had a nap and Kate was at school. I didn't often get to have Mummy all to myself. Well, Sophie was in the pram but she didn't count because she was just a tiny baby and she slept most of the time anyway, which made the outing even better.

I wore my navy-blue-and-white cotton dress and my favourite red 'Mary Jane' shoes. Mummy had made the dress for Kate, so it was a hand-me-down, but it was finally mine and I was determined to enjoy my time with it as much as possible. I felt grown up wearing it – but, even so, I knew I wouldn't mind when it was Naomi's turn with it because then I would be even more grown up. Closer to becoming a real mummy.

Over my bent arm hung my orange handbag. Inside it was a bottle of milk for my baby, Ricky, a few tissues and a small beaded purse. Before we left, I had undone the zipper on my purse and tipped the coins out on to my bed, as I often did. I got Kate to count them just the night before and she told me I had 22 cents. I purposefully put the coins back in my purse, zipped it closed with a deliberate carefulness, and finally secured it in the handbag. I took my money on our walk but I wasn't going to spend any of it. I was saving it. Kate couldn't understand why I wouldn't even buy just a sucker. But I was determined.

It was a lovely, warm afternoon. Perfect for a walk. Once at Willows Beach, we walked along the esplanade from the Bowker Avenue end. It took a while to get to the halfway point and, once there, Mummy bought me a Fudgsicle from the Kiwanis Pavilion. We sat on a bench seat and looked out at the water. Seagulls flew overhead 'caw-ing' noisily, as usual keeping a close, scavenging eye on all the people below. I squinted to my right and looked across at Jimmy Chicken Island. There were lots of boats skimming along the water in the fresh breeze, sailing both in and out of the marina.

As soon as I finished my treat, I lifted Ricky out of the pram, sat her carefully on my knee and began rocking her. Mummy laughed when I looked at her but I didn't pay too much attention as I was concentrating on my baby.

Before I realised, Mummy discreetly spat on her hankie and wiped round my mouth.

★   ★   ★

Wishful thinking, some may have thought, but it didn't matter. I grew up with such confidence, I didn't need anyone to understand or acknowledge what I knew, which certainly gave me strength, and a dream. Well, enough of a dream to keep me balanced precariously on a knife-edge of hope – but not enough to get the nursery ready, even though I knew the colour scheme I would use, as well as where I would position each and every piece of furniture… especially the cot.

Despite the practical sense of my decision, cancelling the IVF still left me feeling guilty. Guilty for not choosing her, even though I really didn't think it was a 'now or never' choice. I thought I was just putting her conception off until a later date. I was also angry that I had to make the decision on my own, although it didn't occur to me to be angry at Billy. I suppose it would have been a relief to cry, but I couldn't seem to. It was as if the sadness went too deep and was too dark and heavy to be assuaged so easily. The sorrow of it all was weighing me down.

I asked myself so many 'why' questions I sounded like one of my three-year-olds at the nursery. I wasn't prepared for such an obstacle. I knew that God worked in mysterious ways and all that, but I really couldn't make head nor tail out of that one.

Eventually, I did cry – for hours. It happened totally unexpectedly when I came home from work one day. As it happened, it was during one of Billy's disappearances. As I pulled into the driveway, I knew, before I even got out of the van, that Billy wasn't home, as Ben was lying on our bed. I could see his head looking through the window, waiting for my return. If Billy had been home, Ben would have been downstairs with him, protectively lying by his side, as if on guard, steadfastly offering his love and loyalty, ready for battle if he would only have been allowed to help.

I went in, picking up the post as I walked past the mailbox. There was only one envelope. I wasn't paying much attention as I ripped it open. I was distracted by my routine – my routine of checking the house. Ever since Billy had taken to disappearing, I would check around the house whenever I returned. I would scan the living room as I walked down the front hall looking for evidence of his return or departure, whichever the case may be. I would walk into our bedroom, holding my breath as I opened the closet, hoping his clothes would still be there – figuring that, as long as his clothes were there, it meant he was coming back.

Luckily, at that time, I hadn't taken it to the morbid level – the one where he wouldn't be coming back *and* he hadn't taken his clothes because he wouldn't need them. On that occasion, his clothes were still there so next I went into the kitchen, still holding the opened envelope. Everything was exactly how I had left it that morning. I pressed the answer machine – no new messages. I felt so dejected as I slumped on to the kitchen chair.

Before arriving home, there had been the hope that he might actually be there – that something might have happened while I was at work to change everything miraculously and I would have the old Billy back. But he wasn't there. And all the optimism in my poor, hopeful heart dissipated without any effort at all. The house was solemnly quiet and still, the only noise being the hum of the fridge and the clicking of Ben's toenails as he lumbered across the kitchen floor to greet me.

The silence seemed deflating in a way. I suppose it's strange to say that I actually felt the silence and believed that the quietness itself could be descriptive, but I didn't see it as strange. It had happened before. Sometimes the 'quiet' represented a certain calmness, immediately informing me that things were fine. At other times, I immediately sensed unease. That time, I just felt flat and unsure. Perhaps my subconscious was tuned in to certain clues that on the face of it could go unnoticed, but were nonetheless recognisable in the recesses of my mind.

Finally, I turned my concentration to the lone envelope and pulled out what looked like a card. As I opened it, something fell out on to the floor. I leaned over and picked it up. It was a cheque... for $2,000! I couldn't make out the signature. I was confused and then noticed the name and address in the top-left corner of the cheque. It was from Bruce and Marjorie Johnson in Vancouver, with whom we would have stayed if we'd gone through with the treatment.

I immediately understood. I read the card over and over, my sight blurred by my tears. I couldn't hold back any longer. I cried unrestrainedly... for me, for my unborn baby, for Billy, and for my own dishonesty.

I had written to the Johnsons when I knew that we wouldn't be going through with the impending IVF cycle. They had offered for us to stay with them again and I needed to let them know that we wouldn't be coming after all. I didn't tell them the real reason why we weren't going; instead, I said that we couldn't afford it. I guess it wasn't really a lie because, truth be told, we couldn't really afford it, but that wasn't the reason why we weren't doing it. Billy was – only I didn't want to say that because, if I admitted that, then it would be real. And I was afraid I would end up blaming Billy. I felt terrible that, because of what I'd written, they had sent the cheque.

I cried for their incredible thoughtfulness and generosity. I cried for the realisation that the grain of hope I had been holding on to was lost and it hit me that we actually weren't going to go through with it. I cried because I knew then that my time was running out. I cried for my baby girl, lost in the shadows of fate.

Eventually, I calmed down. Ben licked the tears from my face and looked up at me and, as I so often was, I was quite certain he understood my pain. My eyes were puffy and red and the pressure in my head, after crying for so long, was all-consuming. The pounding, a relentless syncopation, showed no sign of abating and put any further thought out of the question. There was nothing for it but to go to bed with a cold flannel on my forehead.

I returned the cheque but, to be honest, I can't remember what I said to them, other than that I was incredibly touched and appreciative. Somehow, I had to put it away – not completely, because I needed to come to terms with it myself – but away enough to ensure I only dealt with it in private, on my own.

As a result of all that, I knew that our marriage definitely couldn't come into the equation. The question of our love and our relationship was not relevant, not for the moment. It could be postponed – and, actually, it needed to be – otherwise we'd have way too much to deal with. The focus had to be Billy. Not me, not us, just Billy.

I also knew that, if we were lucky enough to get to the bottom of whatever was plaguing him, we would be so stretched getting through that that there would be absolutely no room for relationship issues. I also didn't want to create any other problems that we would have to deal with if we were successful in getting Billy back on track.

With that in mind, I never questioned him, made accusations, caused arguments or voiced the things that were in my head. It wasn't easy, by any means, and that's not to say that there weren't times when I became enraged or cried or said something I shouldn't but, on the whole, I kept it away from Billy.

In order to concentrate on Billy and not our relationship, or what it was all doing to me, I first had to put the whole IVF struggle on the back burner and then ask myself some important questions. First, was any of it about our marriage? Second, was he worth the effort? Third, and probably most important, could I deal with whatever he was doing or wherever he was when he wasn't home? Because, if I couldn't, I would have to walk away right there and then.

The first two questions were easy to answer, but I had to think a lot about the third question – and, believe me, I thought of every scenario. In every instance, I knew I would stand by him. I could do that because I was so certain he was mentally ill. He wasn't in control of his mind or his actions. It was almost irrelevant if he was cheating, or doing anything else – that was so far removed from the main issue. It then occurred to me that I didn't need to know. If I was willing to stand by him no matter what, then I didn't need to know.

It was during that time that family and friends were thinking that I was the one who was in denial. I can't say why or how I so adamantly knew I had to hang in there and not give up. What I ended up saying to anyone who voiced those opinions was that I would reassess our relationship and what I wanted out of it when Billy was himself again. Before that, I just simply wasn't prepared to give up on him. Perhaps if Billy had ever been cruel, violent or abusive towards me in any way over the years, or perhaps if I hadn't been with him for so many years prior to his breakdown, as I called it, things would have been different. As it was, I had been with a loving, caring, sensitive man for thirteen years. He was just troubled, and had been all along to some degree, and that certainly didn't justify my turning my back on him.

Don't get me wrong – everyone's concerns about me did make me think. I did nothing but think. However, I never wavered in my determination to stick by Billy. I just couldn't. I did a lot of soul-searching but I also probably overlaid my feelings with too much thinking. I didn't really acknowledge my feelings consciously and, even if I had, I don't know that I could have identified exactly what they were.

In hindsight, I think I used music as a way to try to pinpoint my feelings. Then I used my analysing as a way to make them intelligible to me – to help me see that my reactions to what I could and couldn't choose were what would shape the outcome of my life.

Needless to say, I listened to music a lot. I spent hours just driving the van, with Ben in the back, listening to music and thinking. I know that everything is different in the grip of strong feelings, so I tried not to react too quickly or to make rash decisions when things were most stressful, but to mull things over in my mind before I decided what best to do. That I did in the first few months of Billy's breakdown but, as time went by, I couldn't *do* much, which was what I found to be the most difficult to deal with.

I found that, for the first time, I could actually see that something good had come out of my infertility. Through that struggle, I had no choice but to realise that what was happening was out of my control. The struggle with Billy was out of my control, too, and I had to adopt a similar strategy. I couldn't fix what was happening. I could just choose how I was going to deal with it – which was to hang in there and keep my own personal faith. I accepted that I couldn't control how Billy was, but I was determined that I could still try to get to the bottom of it.

By the autumn of 1998, Billy was no better and I was getting nowhere in my quest for answers. I decided that I needed to take drastic action. After a lot of deliberation about what could have triggered it all, I realised the only thing that happened around the time of Billy's breakdown was the death of his mother a few months earlier. I figured it must be connected, and I began to wonder if he was feeling guilty for not going to the funeral.

I decided I would get two tickets to Britain. I thought it would give Billy a chance to go to Hannah's grave and maybe get some peace. Maybe he just needed to say goodbye and find closure.

I booked the tickets for December as I had two weeks off work. I didn't tell Billy my plan. I wanted to present the tickets as a fait accompli, so he couldn't try to talk me out of it.

He refused to go. After initially being upset, I decided that I would go whether Billy went or not. I told him he didn't need to decide if he'd come with me until the day of the flight. I hoped he would change his mind but, as the day of departure drew closer and he wasn't showing any signs of wanting to come, I started actually to look forward to time away, although my reason for going was still to try to figure out the connection. If Billy still wouldn't go back to Wales, there had to be a reason.

I started to think it was more than guilt about not going to the funeral. It was more likely that whatever stopped him going then was continuing to stop him. I just didn't know what that was. I hoped something would fall into place when I got there.

Of course, an added bonus with going away over Christmas was that it took me away from the situation at home which would have been so much harder to bear during the holidays, especially since Christmas had always been such a special time. It would have been too much of a painful reminder of how bad things were.

I don't think Billy thought I would really go through with it and actually go by myself. I must admit it was hard to go alone but I reminded myself how, during one of Billy's periods away from home,

I had gone camping by myself. Looking back, it sounds so sad but I hadn't been sad all the time. I had Ben with me and I was proud of myself for going. It had been rather scary at night – Ben and I in our tent, alone in the dark, with only the nylon protecting us from the forested spookiness and its nocturnal inhabitants. But I remembered that that weekend had ultimately made me feel strong. Going to Wales alone was a much more daunting challenge, but I felt the same sense of strength and pride in myself as I sat on the plane with the empty seat beside me.

My flight was very late arriving at Heathrow, although we had left on time, so, by the time I got to Cardiff, Billy had rung many times. I was actually surprised that he had even noticed I wasn't there and was obviously worried. For someone who wasn't showing any emotion, I was a bit taken aback that he had the ability to be worried.

He rang every single day I was there, which I have to say somewhat lowered his credibility. I asked Billy's family questions about his childhood but I didn't actually find anything out. I was no closer to understanding Billy but, if nothing else, at least the trip had taken the pressure off me relentlessly trying to figure it all out.

By the time I was on the flight home, I had already regressed back to roaming around in my hugely populated subconscious. Quite by accident, I stumbled across the realisation that being so far away had actually helped me to see that it wouldn't just all go away, even if I did figure out 'the why'. And I realised that Billy wasn't going to get better until he decided himself that he didn't want to live like he had been doing. Whatever the problem was, he couldn't get help until he wanted to – and asked for it.

Although I considered things to be awful, I don't really think, at that time, Billy was in a bad enough place to want to do anything about it. At that point in time, even if I had found out something that explained it all, it wouldn't have made any difference. Billy hadn't yet reached the point where *he* needed to get better. It occurred to me that I was helping him to cope, or at least making it less hard. That's not to say that Billy wasn't in turmoil and he certainly wasn't enjoying what he was going through, but he wasn't in hell and, truthfully, that was because I was making sure he wasn't.

Having said that, though, I don't think I should have just left him to it either. I felt that, whatever I did or didn't do, I couldn't walk away. Yes, maybe that would have shocked him into reality and forced him to get it together, but because it seemed to stem from Hannah's death, and I knew he had been in children's homes, it wasn't too much of a stretch to think that he suffered from abandonment issues. I really believed, if I just left him to it, it would do more damage than good.

In any case, my decision to go to Wales was the best thing I could have done. Getting away from it all was so good for me; it was so nice to laugh again. My sister-in-law Lauren and my niece and nephew had always been able to make me laugh and then was no different. There were times when we were absolutely hysterical. My mind was taken off Billy for the first time in almost a year, which was a bit strange, actually, given that I was with *his* family.

Before I went, I had thought that I would be reminded of him all the time; in fact, for the most part, the opposite was true. I knew then that it was up to Billy. I needed to let him fall – all the way until he hit rock bottom.

I dreaded going home.

94

6

ICING OVER A
SECRET PAIN

And it makes me cry
To see this life passing you by
To see the wonder missing from your eyes
And feel that chasm in your soul
And hear compassion turning sour

'It Wouldn't Take a Miracle' by Dirk McCray

The months of turmoil and upset were taking their toll. Billy was so unpredictable. I was wearing myself out trying to figure out his next move. It was a ridiculous tactic, of course, as there was no pattern at all to his behaviour. He was just existing day by day. His only thought was how he would take his next breath and, more importantly, how he would get his next drink. His abuse of alcohol had taken on new heights in his attempt to self-medicate. He was engaging in what a lot of people do in the quest to escape – he drank… and he drank… until he didn't do much else. Of course, that was only making things worse, compounding his feeling of anxiety and depression and not giving his medication a chance to work.

His drinking also became a hurdle in my pursuit for help from our GP. He seemed reluctant to believe that Billy's problem went deeper than alcoholism. I remember he said to me that he thought Billy might be an alcoholic and perhaps I was having trouble accepting that. I was so mad at myself because my initial response to that comment was to cry – which I hated because I felt like it lowered my credibility. I managed to croak between sobs that I wished he *was* just an alcoholic because then I would know what the problem was and he could get some help. I certainly don't mean to diminish the seriousness of alcoholism in any way by that comment because I know it is a dreadfully hard disease to overcome. I just would have been relieved to have had a diagnosis, *any* diagnosis, to tell you the truth. I just knew that alcohol wasn't Billy's particular demon.

I managed to compose myself and added that Billy wasn't messed up because of his drinking; he was drinking because he was messed up. I was embarrassed I had become so emotional but I achieved something that day – I got our GP finally to understand what I meant.

Although I had realised, while I was in Wales, that Billy needed to hit rock bottom, I was still determined that I would be there to catch him when he fell. Intellectually, I knew Billy needed to hit his own rock bottom before he could really get better and I acknowledged the fact that I was cushioning that fall, but knowing that fact and actually doing something about it are two different things – especially as I just didn't think he was mentally capable of actually surviving the fall.

Perhaps I was protecting him too much but, while there was an element of real danger to his wellbeing, it was incredibly hard to sit back and watch the fall-out without intervening. I knew I wasn't ready for that. I was so worried he would end up dead if I didn't keep an eye on him. I know that psychiatrists say that, if someone really wants to commit suicide, they will, no matter what anybody else does, but, my God, it was so hard not to be constantly in 'protect' mode.

He was so messed up. It got to the point where I just wanted him to be happy again – even if it meant that he wasn't with me. And it was all taking its toll on me. The majority of the time, I felt like any attempt that I made to help was futile. In fact, 90 per cent of the time I felt as though I was talking to a brick wall. However, as I had grown up with a mother who always tried to make the best of a bad situation, I did my best to as well – even though the bad situations weren't remotely in the same league.

I can still hear my mum saying, 'It doesn't matter that it's chilly. Now, we don't have to take our cardigans off.' My sisters and I always laugh at that comment in particular, especially when Sophie imitates her. So I'm sure at least some of the reason why I handled the stress in the way I did was due in part to a certain amount of learned behaviour from my own childhood. And I found, more than ever before, that I went about my days in a careful, considered, rational way, playing out the subliminal notion that I had assimilated years before – perhaps the residue of a 'functional' upbringing. A perfectionism or an ideal which, I suppose you could say, was in some ways as much detrimental to me as it was beneficial.

More than anything, I found physical toil the best form of therapy for my mental distress. I decorated the dreary basement in an effort to make the surroundings brighter and less depressing – not that it helped Billy any but it looked much better nonetheless. I then tackled the spare room and the bathroom, then moved outside when the weather got warmer in the spring. In the early summer of 1999, I single-handedly dug up all the grass at the back of the house, going down into the ground a good six inches, before laying down fabric and crushed rock, and developing rockeries and beds for planting a variety of plants and shrubs. As with most projects I undertook, I was rather compulsive in my approach and would often be at it for hours on end – even into the early hours of the morning in some cases. It got to the point where my neighbour, with whom I was quite friendly, would joke about it, saying that I could never hide the fact that I was stressed. The bright lights or the sound of digging drifting through her bedroom window in the middle of the night were a dead giveaway. I definitely earned the nickname 'OCD girl' but at least it was a harmless stress release and I got jobs done into the bargain. I suppose I wasn't prepared to throw in the towel, so I threw myself into the garden instead.

Throughout that time, I became aware that my brain was one of the only things that was keeping me sane. I know it sounds odd, but my subconscious inner workings often lifted my spirits. I say 'subconscious' because I didn't purposefully manufacture them. Countless times, I found myself very low emotionally, and then something would change in my head and I would find renewed optimism. I became very grateful for that ability. I don't know if other people experience that, but I suspect they do. Perhaps some people just aren't in tune enough to recognise it.

It is very hard to explain how I could become optimistic when the situation hadn't changed. I could be by myself, upset at the hopelessness of the situation, and then I would feel stronger. Of course, sometimes a song lifted my mood and gave me strength – surely everyone experiences that. And, actually, to be fair, that did happen a lot. But that was a mood change that came about through something that I did – I listened to music.

At other times, my resolve would lift after thinking of Hannah or Callum but, again, those were things I was actively doing to feel better. The most incredible mood changes were the ones that just happened, simply as a result of the magnificent abilities of the human brain – without any external help. I found it so miraculous that I even began to feel a bit sorry for people who have never experienced truly hard times because they won't get to experience such an organic ability. I mean, I think we find our greatest strength when we most need it, so it stands to reason that, if we never need to be strong, we won't get a chance to see what we are capable of.

As well as that miraculous and spontaneous lift of my mood, I also gained strength and knowledge from a very different source. For as long as I can remember, I have been in touch with something or someone – perhaps even more than one – that manifest themselves from 'beyond', in times of need. Strange as it sounds, they visit me. Not visually, like angelic apparitions dressed in white, floating around my front room, or like John Travolta, with the long hair and the wings, trolley dodging at the grocery store… but, come to think of it, if the mental images I conjure up of these ethereal visitors are anything to go by, they're not completely unlike that either.

Words of encouragement and solution literally just arrive in my head, although not heard or seen in print. It is more like they are words that I can feel – at least, that is the only way in which I can attempt to describe it. And, along with feeling the words, I feel a presence. I don't even need to be aware that I am actually in need of anything, or in any particular state of mind, for these visits to occur. In fact, the portal to these dalliances seems to be almost exclusively of their bidding, not mine, which I suppose increases my belief in the authenticity of their existence.

But, then, I have always had a stronger belief in the spirit world than many, so that isn't particularly strange to me. I have dabbled with Ouija boards, hovered near ceilings in séances, and experienced enough premonitions to recognise these phenomena. Non-believers snub and rebuff such things, but spiritual connections happen all the time; siblings separated at birth, who both name their first child Elliot; a wife rushing home, for no reason, to find her husband unconscious on the kitchen floor; people changing their minds about leaving town on a doomed flight. It's the sort of communication that one has no particular reason to believe under normal, rational circumstances – things that can be dismissed as coincidence – unless, that is, they have truly touched your life… then you believe.

The existence of both of those abilities secured, deep within me, a focused determination and the faith that, no matter what happened with regards to Billy, I would be OK.

I remember I was out walking the dog and I had a sort of epiphany – a real 'ah-ha' moment. I remember exactly where I was standing at the time and it is over six years ago now. Out of the blue, I felt totally comforted. I had been stressed out and very upset but, in an instant, it all evaporated. It just came to me that, whatever happened, I would still be me. Even if the worst happened, whatever that was, next week, next month, next year… I would still be me. And I would be OK. It was a huge relief. I felt a little less worried, a little more optimistic, perhaps even hopeful to a degree. That's not to say that I wasn't stressed out again as soon as I got home, or that I didn't have times when I wanted to explode through the frustration of getting nowhere, but it did give me staying power.

Of course, as well as the involuntary help from my brain, and the otherworldly episodes, there were still the more conventional problem-solving sessions which also achieved similar results. I regularly experienced periods of excessive thinking – just my way of keeping myself in check, I suppose. I had a steady, internal, even rhythmic, compass of detecting cause and effect. A spectrum that swung from an analysed diagnosis to its various outcomes. Practically with every action I took, I ran through the implications in my head in the seconds before I made a decision or actually engaged in it. This was another scale on which Billy and I were at opposite ends – where his behaviour could again be described as like that of a teenager.

I sometimes wondered if I was making excuses for Billy, but I would reassure myself that I wasn't. I played devil's advocate a lot but I always came back to the same place. I knew it, but I couldn't always feel it – even from beyond.

It was during one of my thinking sessions that I realised I had been right to trust myself and stick to my belief that I wasn't making excuses for Billy – even though I heard from many people that that was precisely what I was doing. That day, I happened to be driving along Beach Drive. Ben was lying along the middle bench in the back of the van. Through the rear-view mirror I could see the fur on his head blowing in the sea breeze – especially the long bit sprouting out of the end of his earflap that I couldn't quite bring myself to cut off.

I was driving on autopilot – my head completely elsewhere. Pretty soon, I was drifting back through the shadowy tunnel of time and I found myself looking back to a day long ago – 25 years to be exact. I was nine years old. The memory came back to me completely unbidden and unexpected, taking me by surprise.

Echoing back to me along that dusty corridor of the past came a mingling of familiar voices, smells and sounds, dredging up long-forgotten fragments until the full memory eventually emerged and crystallised. I subconsciously parked at Cattle Point, which was undoubtedly a good thing, as my mind wasn't paying close enough attention to driving safely. Exhumed and exposed, the memory lived again.

★   ★   ★

We are at my grandparents' house in Mosborough, South Yorkshire. Mummy is there, as well as Naomi and Sophie. I can smell a mixture of coal and lavender. The consistent ticking of the clock on the mantelpiece seems to be exaggerated, as does the sound of a horse trotting past the window – the clumpity-clump of its hooves in time with the clock.

It is the last day of our holiday. Granda is raising his voice at Mummy. I feel my muscles tighten, along with my lower tummy, not so much that I think I might break down, but enough so that I begin to scrutinise everything – and I mean everything, all at once. His words are harsh, angry and accusatory. He's blaming Daddy for us living in Canada.

I can see through the window to the chip shop over the road. I wonder if the people milling about outside can hear the shouting. I look over at my sisters. Sophie is sucking her middle fingers – her pointer finger stroking her cheek at the same time, and Naomi is twisting her hair round her fingers. Granda is turning away angrily, leaving the front room, his handsome face miserable. There is a helplessness about him. My sisters are both crying. Mummy is quietly angry – I can tell by the look on her face and the way she is standing.

Granda is just about to pass me and walk through into the kitchen when he stops, turns me round and propels me through the kitchen with his hand firmly on my back. My back feels strangely cold, yet somehow warm as well, right on the bit of my back where I feel his touch. Grama has put the kettle on – I can feel the warmth from the cooker as I am pushed past it. I recognise the smell of gas and Fairy Liquid mingling together in the air around me. I can hear Grama tidying up, dishes and cups clanking against the stone sink.

Granda shoves me through the back door into the garden. 'Ger out!' he yells. The door slams shut behind me. I go up the garden path and stand at the bottom of the garden.

Sucking my thumb, as I often do when I want comfort, I look over the hedge to the field beyond and replay in my mind's eye Mummy's stiff quietness, Grama's nervous activity, Naomi's hair-twisting and Sophie's sucking. But, mostly, I replay how Granda looked, and the cloudy mist that I saw around him. Granda is a big man but I am picturing him smaller for some reason. I feel warmly comforted, yet my skin feels cold and prickly. I'm not sure whether sucking my thumb has caused this feeling or not, but I like it. I also feel a bit confused but I don't rightly mind that.

I watch the cows grazing for a while – listening to the sounds of the neighbouring farm. It strikes me, with a rush of clarity, and something akin to a revelation, that he is just sad. He pushed me and shouted at me and looked so angry and yet I knew I hadn't done anything wrong. I was just standing there – so it mustn't have been about me at all. It must be about him. He just doesn't want us to go back to Canada. He doesn't mean to be nasty. I am sure that when we have gone, and the little cottage is quiet once again, he will be feeling worse about his outburst than we are.

This is so startling a thought that it takes me a moment to adjust to it. Still sucking my thumb, I am thinking, poor Granda. I feel so sorry for him.

★   ★   ★

I don't know why I remembered that all of a sudden. I hadn't thought about that probably since the day it happened. The strange thing was, I felt like I was actually there. Before that day, whenever I had been thinking of the past, I had been 'looking' back to it – the memory appeared in the past tense. For example, 'I remember we went to California...' and so on. That day, though, I was reliving the experience. I smelled the smells; I felt the feelings.

Now, knowing what I know, I can see that it was a proper flashback, which certainly gives me a greater understanding and sense of empathy for Billy. Back then, I realised that unexpected memory, or whatever it was, so long concealed, had confirmed to me that I have had the ability to properly empathise from around the age of about nine. Well, earlier actually, because I was eight on the Tijuana trip. It also confirmed what I knew, or thought I knew. No, I *really* knew. I hadn't been making excuses then and I still wasn't. Granda really was devastated over our impending departure. Of course he acted inappropriately but, to my mind, he was terribly sad and that was what came through to me.

I think, even as a very young child, my way of looking at things had already been established. I am just that way. And I don't mean that past experiences made me that way, I mean that that way of thinking was just in me. I never held Granda's behaviour against him and I wasn't going to hold Billy's behaviour against him either. Also, I have to say that both of them were good, loving men; they were just tormented by their emotions.

If Granda had ever been truly nasty to me, I wouldn't have been forgiving. It was the same with Billy. I knew he loved me and he had never done anything to deliberately hurt me in all the years we had been together. In fact, quite the contrary. He did things that he thought protected me, or, at the very least, shielded me. He sometimes tried to come across as bolshie and streetwise, but there had always been a sensitivity and overall vulnerability to his bearing that gave me no reason to suspect him capable of intentionally causing me pain. Anyway, my memory of Granda confirmed to me that I wasn't making excuses.

Unfortunately, others did not hold the same views. I felt like my marriage was under a microscope. Family and friends were all putting in their unsolicited two cents' worth. *Unsolicited.* That is probably what pissed me off the most since I never once asked for their opinion or asked them what I should do.

Samantha and her sister Tracey were the only ones who trusted my faith in my marriage. I knew they didn't think I should 'kick him to the kerb' like others had said – some quite literally, I might add. Samantha also told me about someone she knew who had had a breakdown and how it had taken him a couple of years to get through it, and also that he was still on medication and probably always would be.

Her sharing that helped me in two ways. First, I wasn't expecting Billy to recover overnight, although admittedly I prayed and fantasised that he would. So, when he didn't, and it went on for months and months, I didn't lose all hope.

Second, I knew of the person she was referring to and he was someone to be respected and thought highly of, which reminded me that mental illness can strike anyone and that it is nothing to be ashamed of.

Unfortunately, although I appreciated Samantha's words immensely, she still lived in the United States, so we didn't get a chance to talk very often. I was very frustrated. I wouldn't be getting such a response if Billy had had some physical ailment. No one would tell me to dump him if he had cancer. In fact, if I had, I would have been the one at fault in that scenario. Yet, there I was, standing by my mentally ill husband, and I was the weird one!

It is so sad that, as a society, we seem to be focusing so much on keeping ourselves happy that we aren't paying sufficient attention to other people. Modern women joke about how wives treated their husbands in the 1950s, and, while I admit that the idea of greeting your husband at the door with a ribbon in your hair and a smile on your face, in a 'June Cleaver' kind of way, *is* pretty funny, it seems now to be too far the other way.

There was an occasion when I was with a bunch of girls having a hen night; a few of the married girls were talking about their husbands and what married life was like. One woman said that her husband was a real '90s man, and that she wouldn't have it any other way. 'I'm not being any man's mother!' she had said emphatically.

'Doing things for the person you love isn't a bad thing,' I stated.

'What, like cooking and cleaning for him?' she laughed. 'I bet you even make your husband's packed lunch every day.'

'As a matter of fact, I do,' I said. 'I love making his lunch. We love to do things for each other.'

'Whatever. You are just repressed and you don't even know it,' she accused.

Someone else, probably thinking there might be tension, changed the subject. She needn't have bothered. The comment hadn't annoyed me in the slightest because I knew it wasn't true. If something makes you angry and you're honest with yourself, you will most likely find a grain of truth hidden somewhere and, if there isn't, or if you don't take issue with it, you won't get angry. I simply knew that I wasn't repressed. I genuinely loved doing things for Billy, but he had always appreciated whatever I did and had never taken me for granted. If he ever expected me to do something, it would have been a completely different story altogether. Also, I'm confident in sticking up for what I don't like. I don't do windows and I pretty much never iron anything for Billy. 'Not in my contract,' I would jokingly reply if the subject ever came up. I think it comes down to the fact that, if you are authentically happy with however your marital dance plays out, then it doesn't matter what you, or your husband, does or doesn't do.

It turned out that the woman with the '90s man was divorced a year later.

She had made those comments years before Billy's breakdown. I can only imagine what she would have said about me 'hanging in there' when I was getting nothing out of the relationship. After the breakdown, Billy wasn't capable of giving me any support, be it emotional or financial. Did that mean I should have bailed out?

Whatever happened to the vow 'in sickness and in health… for richer, for poorer'? Of course, I am really only talking about long-term relationships and/or marriages that are entered into on the right basis. I am not talking about casual relationships, or marriages that should never have happened in the first place. I am assuming that love was there to begin with and that there is something worth preserving.

I think it's ironic that, not that long ago, I would have been *expected* to stand by my man. Yet, there I was, some thirty years later, completely surrounded by self-help books and 'ego-massage for the self-absorbed', with *no* books on putting your spouse first. Even on television there are very few programmes that address a wife or husband sticking by their spouse through a rocky period. There aren't many role models for staying together. People are taught that relationships are disposable. They aren't taught that, as long as your welfare and safety is ensured, putting your spouse before yourself isn't the wrong thing to do. Ending a relationship may well be the easiest thing to do, but that doesn't mean that it is right. Sometimes staying together takes strength; sometimes splitting up takes strength.

I felt like it wasn't anyone else's business whether we stayed together or not. I know plenty of people who have left their partners because others made them feel they were being weak if they stuck it out. I wasn't going to let that happen to us. I guess it depends on how you look at it, but sometimes it's a problem within oneself that is at the root – a reflection of how people feel about themselves, not how they feel about their partners. It isn't because their partners aren't pretty enough, or smart enough, or 'whatever' enough. It isn't necessarily anything to do with lack of love. Maybe if more people realised this, they might not take it so personally and might be willing to work through things. I know it can get complicated and it is easier said than done but, ultimately, I think a relationship should only break up if, at the bottom of it all, there is no love left. If love is gone, I have no problem with divorce. But can you be so sure it's gone? I couldn't.

I realise a lot of the time husbands or wives walk out on their partners and the choice is taken out of the remaining spouse's hands, but that wasn't the case with me. I would have either had to tell Billy to leave or to leave myself. And there was no way I was going to do that.

I certainly thought that the reason why people were saying that I shouldn't stand by Billy was only because they couldn't understand what he was going through. I didn't really understand much myself, but I knew enough to know that it wasn't Billy's fault. Before long, I resorted to telling people either to pretend Billy had some sort of cancer of the mind, or that he was my brother. One isn't expected to turn their back on their children, their friends or their siblings if they are going through a bad time, so why should spouses be any different?

Thankfully, my suggestions did seem to make a difference, at least to the extent that the majority of people gave up on trying to convince me to 'think of myself', and just let me get on with it.

Time passed, and with it came the sense of a sort of begrudged acceptance – although 'acceptance' isn't quite the right word. I certainly began to forget what life had been like before Billy's breakdown. It felt like we'd been surrounded by stress for so, so long. It felt like for ever and a day – but it had been more like two years. Throughout this time, my projects ensured that our surroundings changed, although the atmosphere and Billy's mood didn't.

During one of Billy's rare lucid moments, he said that all he wanted to do was sleep. Yet I knew sleep eluded him, his mind churning with what I assumed to be endless distressing and painful thoughts. At least that was what the look in his blank eyes portrayed. He again said that he wanted to end his life, but 99 per cent of the time his apathy appeared to overrule that thought. He simply couldn't muster the strength to do anything about it. It was such absolute apathy that it seemed to take on a life of its own – a big, breathing, black hole. He was teetering on the edge of it and I was terrified that at any moment it would swallow him up.

As the weeks passed, Billy's behaviour had really begun to worry me. On one occasion, I had gone into the kitchen and I'd seen Billy standing by the sink. I am certain he didn't know I was standing there and, for some reason, I didn't make my presence known. I watched as he turned on the tap. He clenched his fist under the running water until it got too hot… and he held it there. I was shocked because it seemed he was actually trying to hurt himself. I was confused and scared by that thought. I replayed it over in my mind, hoping that I was making too much out of it, and somehow came to a worrying possibility – self-harm. I surprised myself reaching that conclusion, and am not really sure how I did. Maybe I had read something about it years before, during my time at university, and had then stored it away in my subconscious. I don't know how I even knew to call it 'self-harm'.

I looked it up in one of my old psychology textbooks and, from what I read, it seemed that there are different reasons why some people with mental-health issues can resort to such a terrible attempt at relief. I read that sometimes self-harm can be a way of dealing with extreme feelings that have built up over time and have become quite unbearable. Apparently, when the level of emotional tension inside becomes too high, causing oneself pain acts as a sort of safety valve, a way of relieving the pressure. Feeling that pain ensures they feel *something* at least, instead of just feeling numb or dead inside. I can sort of see how people who don't cope well could use self-harm in a kind of misguided attempt at gaining some sort of control over their feelings.

I didn't want to believe that Billy had experienced that, yet I had to admit to myself that it was a distinct possibility. I knew he hadn't been engaging in self-harm in the years I had been with him before his breakdown, but nor did I think that the burns and cuts of late were the first time he had self-harmed.

I wasn't to know how right that thought was… or that he dreamed of feeling safe; or that he doubted he ever would. As a child, his experiences had taught him many things in his short life, but nothing more than what he had learned as a very young lad – that the world was not a safe place, and nobody could be trusted. It's a difficult truth to cope with when you're an adult, but especially sad when you're not quite eight years old.

★　　★　　★

For as long as he could remember, Billy wished he was anyone but himself. He wished more than anything that he was loved and happy. But he wasn't, and he feared on both counts that he never would be.

Sometimes, when he felt particularly overwhelmed by the torrent of his emotions or the pressure in his head, or if things were especially bad, Billy went on the run. Running away achieved only two things, though – temporary safety and temporary reprieve – and thus a break from the fear of the known. But it obviously posed safety issues of its own – lack of shelter, lack of food or exposure to situations that were utterly unsafe for one so young. Indeed, these were all of the reasons why children should never be left to their own devices and why, under normal circumstances, most parents take the responsibility of supervising their children so seriously.

However, even taking all that into account, Billy was still, more often than not, better off running away. But it was hard living rough and, of course, sometimes he simply couldn't get away, even if he may have desperately wanted to. There was also the fact that the volcano in Billy's head wasn't diminished or changed by running away. His soul had been wounded too much for that.

In a desperate measure to help himself, all Billy could think of doing was to run away, which he couldn't imagine ever stopping. However, one day, quite by chance, Billy discovered another method of relieving some of the pressure and, in some ways, it was preferable. He had thought about running away that day mainly because a group of boys, including Billy, were going to be taken to the swimming baths. Billy particularly hated going there. Well, the swimming part was all right, and the bag of crisps before they left was quite nice – it was the after bit that he hated. Just hearing about going swimming gave Billy the instinctual urge to escape.

Unfortunately that day, before they went, Billy had no chance to get away. Just before they were due to leave, Billy was told by Mr Henry to go into the classroom to get his car keys. Billy particularly hated going in Mr Henry's car. None of the others went, but he could never figure out why not. As Billy went off in the other direction to get the keys, he heard Mr Henry being asked to help the headmaster with something before they left.

'Chapel, when you've fetched the keys go and wait in my car,' Mr Henry shouted down the passage.

Billy obeyed. He walked to the car feeling an overwhelming sense of dread, but at the same time he felt a glimmer of satisfaction. Mr Henry mustn't have realised that his Woodbines were with his keys. Billy could feel them pressing against his belly underneath his underpants. Two minutes later, Mr Henry jumped in the car. Billy felt sick – partly, but not only, from the fear that Mr Henry might notice the cigarettes – and had to swallow bile back many times on the way.

When they got there, Mr Henry followed Billy into the changing area and stood while Billy and all the other boys got undressed. Billy was shaking as he took off his clothes, but his mind was conveniently focused on praying that no one would see what he had hidden. It's funny how one's mind can switch to less important matters when nothing else can be done. Somehow, he managed to conceal his secret stash and rolled his clothes up in a ball. The cold water felt nice and Billy was glad to get in, but the time went by too quickly.

He dressed without drying himself, anxious to get his clothes on. He felt sick again so he didn't bother to eat the crisps. He carefully put the cigarettes in his coat pocket so that Mr Henry wouldn't notice them.

On the way back, Mr Henry ran out of petrol. He was so angry. But Billy secretly thought it was funny – not to mention lucky, as he knew the bus didn't go past Mr Henry's 'parking spot'. They got the bus back, but got off two stops early, just so that they had to walk through a concealed wooded area.

That night, with the volcano in his head getting bigger, Billy lit one of the cigarettes. He had intended to smoke it, just glad to get one over on Mr Henry, but he realised as soon as he took the first drag, that obviously stealing his cigarettes wasn't going to make things even.

That realisation sent him plummeting into despair again. He had been stupid to think that stealing his poxy cigarettes was going to change anything. For a moment, he sat and watched the red glow. Then, without even thinking about it, he stubbed out the cigarette on his arm. For the first time ever, the pressure in Billy's mind released a bit, while all his senses were drawn to the pain searing through his arm.

He quite liked it.

* * *

Once again, I felt sure that something major in his childhood was at the root of it all. It surely wasn't something that one first discovers in middle age. I rather thought that, when Billy became an expert at repressing all of his pain, he hadn't needed to engage in self-harm. But then, as an adult, after his breakdown, when that unresolved trauma – whatever it was – came back to torture him, and with his increasingly irrational thought patterns, he had simply regressed and resorted to some of the methods of coping that he had used back then.

Perhaps I was negligent in not realising what a danger he had become to himself. I had no clue that a cut to an arm or a burn on a hand could actually have been self-inflicted. It wasn't until he spoke about the details of how he had actually planned to end his life that I began to take it much more seriously.

It was horrible, not only because the thought of losing Billy was appalling, but also because he said that at least if he was gone I wouldn't be getting hurt any more. The logic of that escaped me, but then that was how his mind worked.

I went to see our doctor to tell him about Billy's harmful and worrying behaviour, what he had said about ending his life and to ask for advice. He told me to watch him closely, not to hesitate in ringing for an ambulance if the need arose, and that he would do what he could to have him admitted to the local psychiatric hospital for treatment.

I also read all I could on the subject. One book said that usually when people are talking about suicide it isn't as much of an immediate threat, although one must always take suicidal tendencies seriously. Apparently, the biggest threat is when they have stopped talking about it. Often, when people make up their minds to kill themselves, they feel so relieved to have found a way out of their misery that they become happier once the decision has been made. That really made sense to me, so I concentrated on looking out for any elevation in his mood. I didn't know whether I was coming or going, as I was then dreading what I had been hoping for.

Of course, his vocalisation of wanting to end his life seriously concerned me, but I didn't feel the need to act any more 'hands on' than I already had been – until a day in the late summer of 1999. That day, I knew I had to take action immediately. It is strange how you can worry that you won't know when to intervene but, when the time actually came, I just knew. There wasn't any uncertainty. No indecision.

As soon as I saw Billy that Monday, I knew instantly that something was different. While up until then he had been withdrawn, that day he had become practically catatonic. He was basically motionless, although he was periodically rocking back and forth, which was certainly scary enough, but interspersed with his silence were spurts of what I can only describe as delusional outbursts. I recall asking myself during one of the quiet rocking states, what happens when a mind splits? What happens when so much shit happens that it cracks into a hundred pieces? Is there a glue that can piece it all together?

I phoned my sister, Naomi, and she came straight round. I have to admit, part of me did wonder if he was exaggerating a bit, which was one of the reasons I rang Naomi; I knew that, if his behaviour didn't change in front of her, then he truly was in a bad way. The other reason I rang Naomi was that I needed some added emotional support.

I recognised the seriousness of the situation, and knew an ambulance needed to be called, but couldn't seem to pick up the phone. I think because I knew that the police would accompany them – it was a mental-health issue, and police always attended such call-outs – it worried me significantly enough to prevent me from following through. It was strange because I *knew* the call needed to be made, and I wanted them to be there – but at the same time I didn't. There had simply been so many occasions – like the incident in California – where Billy's reactions to, and opinion of, the police had been over the top. Fair enough, I didn't completely understand what was behind those negative attitudes, but it was natural of me to be concerned – especially as he didn't react well to the police under normal circumstances. And, clearly, the situation we found ourselves in was far from normal. Thank God, Naomi was there. I was completely out of my depth, and felt, for the first time, that I needed support. Crucial support. And thank God she stepped up to the plate, took charge and made the call herself because I honestly don't know what would have happened next otherwise.

If my memory serves me correctly, the paramedics stayed in the kitchen. I followed the policemen and Naomi downstairs… because I really did think that everything would be OK. That confidence lasted as long as it took for my gaze to fall on Billy. If I hadn't witnessed it, I wouldn't have believed it; Billy changed. If it hadn't happened so quickly, maybe someone, other than just me, would have seen the transformation. But it was instantaneous. My Billy was lovely. The Billy before they arrived was very ill. But this Billy was nasty. And he exuded unpredictability.

I know one of the policemen spoke to him. Not for long – probably just a few sentences, although I have no memory of what was said, until one of them suggested they all go upstairs to have a word with the paramedics. I sensed that they thought they were making progress, but my tummy told me otherwise. I didn't trust Billy's compliance. I don't know why, I just didn't. I could tell the police had relaxed a bit. Inside I was screaming for them not to. It only took a few moments for us all to proceed upstairs, with Billy obediently following behind one of the policemen before the rest of us took up the rear. I could tell they were definitely under the impression that they were gaining Billy's co-operation. I still wasn't so sure. Then all hell broke loose.

Basically, it rapidly became apparent that the only reason Billy agreed to go upstairs was because down in the basement he was trapped. In the kitchen there were three potential escape routes. I came to this realisation literally two seconds before he made a dash for freedom. Maybe the policemen weren't as relaxed as I had thought. Maybe *they* had been acting as well. In any case, they reacted swiftly and grabbed Billy, but their touch sent him ballistic and the situation erupted into a violent struggle. Billy became increasingly uncooperative and it ended with him being dragged out of the house and down the front steps by his arms.

I don't actually know what was happening around me at that point. I don't know what Naomi was doing, or the paramedics come to that. I had tunnel vision and all I saw were two policeman wrangling with a madman. But it wasn't a madman… it was my Billy.

They threw him in the back of the police car and sped off. One of the paramedics said that they would be taking him to the ER and that I should let our GP know. Then they too drove off in their empty ambulance.

My vision returning to normal, I walked down the front passage. The mêlée had caused significant damage. Pictures had been knocked off the walls and black scuff marks had been left up and down both walls. Outside, plant pots that had been placed lovingly up the front steps lay broken and scattered at the bottom – bits of terracotta, dirt and plants were strewn up the path. I felt like I was watching a bad episode of *The Bill*.

Don't get me wrong – I knew the police officers weren't to blame.

I absolutely appreciated that the paramedics' safety was a number-one priority, especially when dealing with the unpredictability of a patient with a mental-health issue. It was just such a shame that they couldn't have stayed in the background and let the paramedics deal with Billy. Although I guess I can come to that conclusion with the benefit of hindsight.

Obviously I drove straight to the hospital, though I definitely shouldn't have been behind the wheel of a car. Once there, a lovely nurse told me he was in a locked room waiting to be seen by a psychiatrist. I remember feeling utter relief. Unfortunately, I was so naive. I really thought that, in light of Billy's difficult behaviour, which lead to what transpired with the police, together with my and our GP's request to have him sectioned, would have been all that was needed for the psychiatrist to come to the same conclusion. I really thought that would have been enough to ensure he would finally get the help he so desperately needed.

But that wasn't to be.

I was absolutely flabbergasted to find that the ER psychiatrist just let him go. I couldn't fathom why on earth they hadn't even spoken to me. Surely there must have been some questions that I could have answered better than Billy could. I was the one that was seeing it all first-hand after all! Granted it was happening to Billy, but he wasn't seeing it. I was shocked but there was nothing I could do. I felt utterly alone.

When Billy emerged he walked straight past me and out the front door. He completely ignored me. I happened to turn and look down the hallway that Billy had just come from and saw a female doctor watching me. And then I understood.

I had assumed that the psychiatrist was a man. I wanted it to be a man, I suppose, although I hadn't conceptualised that until I saw he was, in fact, a she. I felt such frustration because I just knew that Billy had conned her; something that I seriously doubted he would have achieved with another male.

My theory was proven right as soon as I got to the parking lot. Billy approached me, came right up to my face – within a very few inches – and laughingly, yet horribly, said that I would have to try much harder than that. He then chuckled, in such a repulsive way, before

113

turning and simply walking away. He arrived home about three hours later as if nothing had happened and retreated immediately downstairs.

I was beginning to completely lose confidence in the medical system and wished we were living in the UK so much that I was reduced to tears more and more frequently. I also began to feel with each passing week that, as more time was being wasted, my growing frustration was soon going to start having a serious impact on my faith.

By the time that next episode occurred, in early September, I wasn't trying to have him committed. It would certainly have been a bonus if he had been, but I wasn't holding my breath. I had come to the point where I just wanted to shake him up a bit and I suppose I had reached the stage when I was ready to let him hit rock bottom – so much so that I was willing to set up the fall and then even go as far as to trip him up. It wasn't something I had planned to do, but on the night in question the opportunity arose and I took it.

Billy had gone off in the van that weekend and, by the Sunday night, he hadn't returned. I was angry because, unlike other times, that specifically impacted on me as I hadn't had the use of the van all weekend and it looked as though I would have to figure out some other way of getting to work in the morning. Of course, any time Billy wasn't home it upset me and I worried about him, which obviously affected me, but I hadn't felt that he was doing anything that specifically put me out. That did, though, and it annoyed me. I was fast approaching the end of my tether and he was skating on thin ice.

I was getting ready to take the dog out for a walk and I noticed that the van had pulled into the driveway and Billy was sitting in the driver's seat. He didn't get out, he just sat there and, although it was dark, I could see, from the light of the street lamp, that he was drinking. I am sure he wasn't thinking at all about what I was thinking but I felt like he was waiting for me to go out and tell him to come in and that pissed me off. I knew I had made things easy for him but that was pushing it. His behaviour was making me feel sick. Drowning his sorrows in the darkened basement was one thing but drinking and driving repulsed me.

I held off on taking Ben out but, after a while, I decided that I couldn't make Ben suffer just because I didn't want Billy to think that

I was trying to accommodate him. As I walked past the van, Billy looked up at me and smirked. It wasn't a smile and it made me see red. I opened the door and, with a look of disgust on my face, I asked, 'What the hell are you doing?'

'Don't worry about it,' he replied with a nasty attitude.

'For Christ's sake, Billy, sort yourself out!' I snapped. 'This is getting ridiculous!'

'Just fuck off!' he growled.

I looked away and kept my head down, but I could see him out of the corner of my eye. I had to close my eyes then, and take several gulps of air, which I exhaled in a long breath out, to stop exasperation spilling over within me. But I couldn't stop my anger that time. 'Don't you dare speak to me like that! I have never done anything other than try to help you!' I cried.

He started the engine and, in that split-second, a conversation that I had had months before with my friend, Tracey, came miraculously back to me. Perhaps I held on to that conversation because she is a person for whom I have a very high regard and hold very close to my heart but, whatever the reason, I remembered what she had said at exactly the right moment.

For some reason, we had been talking about drinking and driving. I can't remember what had initiated the discussion, but the long and short of it was that she had said how AA says that, if someone who has been drinking insists on driving, you aren't supposed to try to stop them, you are supposed to phone the police and report them. I remember thinking there would be no way that I could do that, but there I was in that exact situation. 'If you drive, Billy, I *will* phone the police. It's one thing to be in self-destruct mode, but I am not going to stand back and let you kill some innocent person.'

'Over-dramatise as usual, why don't you?' He just looked blankly at me. His eyes were so cold and hard.

Inside my head, my mind was screaming, 'Who is this madman?'

He called my bluff and drove off. I knew I had to follow through with my threat. I had never issued idle ones before and I wasn't going to start then. I knew, if I didn't phone the police, in effect, I was condoning such behaviour. Billy could then continue on this path and I refused to be part of it. I also saw it as an opportunity to make something bad happen. Hopefully, something that would shock some sense into him.

I had made the decision to phone and report him, however hard it was actually to make the call. Not because I wasn't sure that it was the right thing to do, because I was positive it was, but because I had to overcome my lifelong hang-up that only 'trailer trash' called out the police under such circumstances, especially when reporting a spouse or family member. Phoning for an ambulance, even though the police came, was different somehow, probably because it was truly for a medical issue, so it wasn't so degrading. This was unlawful and, to be truthful, his behaviour embarrassed me. I didn't want the police to judge me. I didn't want to be associated with a person who would drive under the influence.

So I knew I didn't have a choice. I had to phone no matter how uncomfortable it made me feel. I fleetingly thought about what the neighbours would think, but then I realised I really didn't care any more.

As I walked back into the house, it felt like I was moving in slow motion, although I wanted to rush to make the phone call. A patrol car arrived very soon afterwards. It turned out that one of the officers had accompanied the paramedics on the previous call-out. They drove around a bit and then returned and said they had seen no sign of him. I felt so let down. Not by them so much, more fate really. I wondered if anything would ever actually go my way. The officers were still sitting in the patrol car at the front of the house when I happened to notice our van coming slowly down the road approaching from behind the police car. I was praying that they would notice him but they were both looking down, filling out some sort of paperwork, I presumed. Billy, obviously spotting them, turned into a side street which, thank God, was a cul-de-sac. I knew he was trapped. I was sure he would have been shocked to see that I had actually phoned them.

I saw my chance to put the final nail in the coffin and I seized it. I went out to the police car and told them that I had seen him and pointed to where I knew he would be. Another car arrived at this point, which was a blessing really, because in it was a female officer, who made the initial approach towards Billy. That simple fact made all the difference. She professionally and empathetically treated Billy in a manner that I think only a female officer could have done. Not that male officers wouldn't have handled the situation well – it was more that Billy would have responded differently to a male officer. In any case, she defused the situation and gained Billy's trust and co-operation which, ultimately, ensured an uneventful outcome. It was the hardest thing I have ever had to do. Even the police officers seemed surprised that I had gone to such lengths.

After the female officer had taken Billy to the station, the male officer from the last time asked me what I was doing with someone 'like that'. I was shocked at his remark and simply said, for what felt like the hundredth time, that it wasn't about us. I suppose he got the backlash from all the other people who had said the same thing to me. I was fed up and he was the one I snapped at. I told him that he wouldn't have said that if Billy was my brother and that our relationship had nothing to do with it. I could tell by his reaction that he just thought I was another doormat of a wife putting up with shit and making excuses. He told me that I didn't have to stay with him, which only served to bug me more, so I just turned and went inside.

To be fair, he had probably seen countless dysfunctional domestic situations and I understood that, because of that, he may have had a jaded and cynical view. I just wished he could have seen our situation for what it was. Not for my sake really, more for his, to show him that, sometimes, good people get into trouble.

I knew he was also basing his opinion on what happened the last time. I had heard from my sister Sophie, who, it turned out, knew the other officer through her work, that Billy had actually broken his fingers during the scuffle that ensued when they were trying to get him out of the house. I was sure the officer was basing his opinion on what had happened to his partner rather than anything I had said. Whether it was because the other officer was being compassionate, I don't know, but thankfully he didn't press charges over the broken-fingers incident, which he could have done.

Once in the house, I watched the police car drive off. I was so frustrated that even the police officer thought I was a doormat but I realised that I actually wasn't embarrassed by the whole interaction with him, most likely because I knew I was right.

It turned out that, at the time, the incident didn't get the result I had hoped for, especially since Billy was back home within a matter of hours. The only thing to come out of it all was that Billy had his licence suspended for a year, but he didn't seem to care. He was also advised to go to a detox centre. I was all for that. I thought that in such a place they would be bound to address the reason behind Billy's self-medicating. Billy refused to go, though, and continued on his path of self-destruction.

I knew I needed to remain strong but I was running on empty. When I finally went to bed that night, I lay awake, unable to sleep, agonising over what to do next. Over the course of the next week, I reminded myself, for the millionth time, that my infertility had made me strong in a way that I wouldn't have been if I hadn't gone through it all. I had lived with the ache of childlessness for ten years at that point and was well versed in coping with that heartache – a sorrow that was, and still is, unendurable. And yet, despite my pain, which lay close to the surface, I had managed somehow to survive and, through it all, finally to come to understand what it meant truly to have faith. I simply had to draw on that strength again.

I was tired, though, so very tired of swimming upstream. I knew it was going to get worse before it got better; that is just how it usually is. I simply couldn't imagine where I'd get the strength from to deal with any more. I remember thinking that God must think I am indestructible. I was sure he had made a mistake. I'm not. I'm really, really not. I wasn't then and I'm still not. I didn't know what my breaking point was, but I felt that I was really very close to it then.

I suppose when you don't know how long a struggle is going to be, it is easier somehow. You just plod on, one day at a time. When faced with the knowledge that it would be going on for years, it was exhausting and potentially soul-destroying in a way I had never known.

Calling the police obviously hadn't worked, and that really had been a hard thing for me to do. Breaking a police officer's fingers and going berserk hadn't got Billy placed anywhere. Even trying to get him admitted to the psychiatric hospital with our GP's help hadn't got us anywhere. What else should I have done when Billy was released from the emergency room by a psychiatrist who didn't think talking to the patient's wife was important – a psychiatrist who believed the 'story' of a delusional patient? Should I have stood in the emergency room and screamed at the top of my lungs until someone took notice? I really didn't know what else I could have done.

People tell you to ask for help but who the hell do you ask when no one is listening? If taking such drastic measures and going to such lengths wasn't enough, what else was there to do? I understood that, in order to get help, Billy needed to *want* help. I had to come to terms with the fact that that is just how it is. But the main problem was that the system required that the patient asked for help themselves, which Billy wasn't doing. Of course, that really frustrated me – mainly because it seemed to me that all the seriously mentally ill people out there, whose lives were genuinely threatened, who needed help the most, were precisely the ones who weren't capable of asking for it. When a person can't even function, how the fuck are they supposed to get help?

I was very frustrated that we were living in Canada. I felt that, in Britain, I could at least have got him sectioned, but we weren't and I had to think of something else. It took me a while to get there, but I realised that I really, really would have to make him hit rock bottom. And there was only one way to do that. It was risky but I realised there was no other alternative.

I had to leave.

7
FIGHTING TO BREATHE

If I could find a way
To turn it all around
I would feel whole
It's all falling down
You're not around
I'm over the edge
I don't want to be
Waiting all my life…

'I Would Feel Whole', by James K

I found myself standing in the kitchen after work the next night. Billy had passed out downstairs after drinking himself, yet again, into a stupor. I had no idea where he got the alcohol. I had long since refused to buy any but there are always ways and means, I suppose.

I had made the decision that I needed to leave but I was cannily aware that that was the easy part. Stopping all the questions in my head, second guessing myself, and *following through* – they were the difficult bits.

The stillness in our little house was so acute it was a tangible thing. I sat down at the kitchen table, listening to that stillness, like I always seemed to do, and I began to feel less agitated. My skin felt all prickly and cold; that familiar feeling which, as always, was oddly comforting. I thought of Hannah and I immediately felt a sense of peace come over me. Experience told me to trust that prickly skin feeling. How could I not let the idiosyncratic, eldritch-like atmosphere in the kitchen engulf me and my consciousness? And how could I then deny its message or its power? It gave me an overwhelming feeling of empathy for Billy and it told me that I had made the right decision. I felt like I had Hannah's approval or something and that reinforced my confidence. I still had a dogged determination to help Billy through it all, but I realised that that wouldn't change if I were elsewhere. I wouldn't let it.

There was only one problem. I knew, before I could leave, I would have to take some drastic safety precautions. As a result of Billy being suicidal, our GP had already instructed me to guard Billy closely and not to leave things around that Billy could get his hands on when I was at work. So I had conscientiously hidden money, medication, car keys, knives, garage keys, rope… anything I could think of, really. I even hid the phone. Admittedly, that was ridiculous, completely counter-productive, and was actually worse for me in the long run because it meant that I couldn't ring him from work to check on him.

Knowing I was going to be away overnight felt different somehow and had me ransacking the whole house. I guess I felt more of a responsibility because *I* was leaving *him*. I suppose, actually, it was guilt-driven.

I went through the whole house and removed anything at all that I thought might be dangerous or life-threatening – knives, forks, scissors, razorblades, bleach, cleaning products… the trouble is, when you start thinking that way, you begin to see everything in a different light. And where do you stop? Christmas decorations? Tent spikes? I see now how frantic I must have been. Didn't I think that he could just break some glass with his fist and slit his wrists with a shard of it? What would I have done then? Moved out with the windows strapped to the roof-rack?

*　　*　　*

'Is the moon home to anyone?' Billy asked himself philosophically, while lying awake one night, feeling frighteningly alone and particularly pensive. He could see its full circular form high in the night sky through his curtain-less window. The light shone into the stark dormitory – bare except for the other nine beds, inhabited by nine other boys, probably all awake, and probably all feeling just

as alone. The rays from the full moon lit up the room and, although Billy liked the ethereal glow, it also, somehow, increased his loneliness. If he had been outside, he would have relished it, and subsequently not felt lonely at all, but there, in a room full of boys, he felt desolate. Billy couldn't decide whether it looked magical or mysterious.

As always, Billy was anxious, but he tried religiously to take his mind off his present situation and to focus it elsewhere. He wondered again, if anyone, or perhaps anything, considered the moon to be home. Maybe just plants grew there. And if that were the case, then Billy wished he was a daffodil. Maybe the moon was covered in daffodils and that was why it was yellow. That thought led to something else, which led to the question of what 'home' actually meant to him.

The word was often said but Billy was increasingly confused as to its true meaning. He could remember, shortly after he had first been taken into care, that he had cried, and Miss Davies had shouted, 'Stop it, or you'll never get to go home ever again!' He could also recall one of the other lads crying, 'I want to go home...' But then this nightmare was called a 'children's home', which seemed to Billy to be the ultimate contradiction, for surely no one would want to go there.

Home. Home? He didn't possess any conceptual idea of what it really was but, based on what he had heard and seen, he associated the word 'home', at least at first, with warmth, safety and comfort. He couldn't really imagine where he had got that idea from, for that had never been his personal experience. Certainly with his mam, brothers and sisters, it had been none of those things. In fact, before his dad had walked out on them, 'home' had been an awful place that he had done his best to avoid. That realisation made him feel sad. It seemed that, over time, the word 'home' had become synonymous with sadness – incorporating hurt, as well as anger, and finally emptiness along with it. He thought he might have considered the house where he had lived, before being taken away, as home; he couldn't quite remember, but he certainly didn't over time. Mostly, it was just Llanellog Hill Crescent, or 'The Crescent'.

Eventually, he stopped associating The Crescent with home, most likely out of self-preservation, and with it came the feeling that it wasn't 'his' any more. He actually began to think that he had nothing, and no one, to connect himself with. No physical tie. No emotional grounding. He was free-falling. Nothing mattered. No one cared.

It was too easy to climb out of bed and walk to the window, drawn to the moon. It was too easy to punch the window. And it was lovely to feel the warmth trickle down his arm. Was this what comfort felt like? Maybe this thick, sticky, ruby redness was home. The release was warm, safe and comfortable.

*   *   *

I see now that our GP meant for me not to leave things like my painkillers, Billy's meds or long kitchen knives lying around. The 'lying around' bit was the operative word. Billy's suicidal tendencies at that point weren't premeditated or calculated. He was so apathetic and worryingly enervated that he didn't possess anywhere near the mental capability to *plan* his suicide. He was worse than that in a way. He wouldn't have been capable of *looking* for rope, or pills… or anything. But he would have used them if they were sitting out on the kitchen table. But, of course, I am, at the very least, marginally obsessive-compulsive. Naturally, I went overboard and took away anything I could think of. I also did it, simply, because I loved him.

I don't think Billy even noticed.

Eventually, with the house 'safety' blitzed, I left, taking Ben with me. I felt so awful taking him away from Billy but the cold, hard truth was that I couldn't trust him to look after Ben properly. Looking back, I see that separating them really was the first thing that got Billy to start to fall. His mate had deserted him.

*   *   *

'Please, miss. Can I go out to it?'

'No, Billy! You'll have to wait!'

'Please, miss! It's hurting its neck!'

'Will you shut up! If there's any more carry on, you'll not get it at all. Just pack it in!'

Billy stood looking out of the window, kicking the wall absentmindedly. His foot hurt, as much from kicking the hard stone wall as from having to wear shoes that were two sizes too small. He knew better than to complain about his pain – any kind of pain. No one would have listened anyway, so he figured he might as well keep it shut. Besides, he was more concerned about the dog. It looked lonely and scared out in the yard by itself. He began thinking about how great it was that he was actually going to take it home with him. He couldn't believe it when he had been given permission, out of the blue, to go home, but he was even more shocked to learn that he was being given a puppy. He had no idea why, but he didn't want to question it. He couldn't remember the last time he was given any kind of a present. He couldn't wait to stroke it.

'Miss?'

'Chapel! Will you piss off and stop mithering me, you irritating little shite. I've got enough to sort out without you making all that racket.'

Billy stopped kicking the wall and concentrated on the boisterous brown and black mongrel. It was tied up with a bit of rope and Billy could see it straining against his neck as he struggled to get free. He related to its plight and recognised their common bond immediately.

Behind him, a knock on the door pre-empted Mr Plant slithering into the room. Billy knew who it was without seeing him or hearing him speak. Among other things, the smell of his bad breath entered a room before he did; the stench of mothballs permeated his clothes, and his whole body held a definite pong of the same stinky stuff his dad used to put in his hair – all of which turned Billy's stomach and made his skin crawl. Billy's hatred for Mr Plant, and what he used to do, was somehow all wrapped up in his head with the reminders of such smells. But they weren't the only things that Billy recognised. There was the squeak of his shoes, a semi-cough sort of noise he used to make when he was nervous or when other adults were around, and the telltale jangle of coins in his trouser pocket. He often had his hand in his pocket, turning the loose change over and over. Billy didn't know what the coins were in aid of but, whatever the reason, he always did it. Billy didn't mind the noises, though, because they warned of the man's approach. That was both good, because he could perhaps hide, and bad, because he knew what to anticipate. All of the signals involuntarily caused Billy to stiffen in dread.

Standing there at the window, Billy wanted to disappear into the wall. He imagined his body becoming smoke and seeping through the cracks in the brickwork. He stopped wheedling about the dog. He stopped kicking the wall. He stood as still as a statue. He needed a wee but would rather have pissed himself than walk past Mr Plant. He wished he was a puddle of wee that Mr Plant hadn't noticed, and then stepped in. Billy liked the idea of splattering his noisy, fancy shoes – that would sort out the squeak. Better still, he imagined he was a pile of dog shit that had got stuck in the sole of his shoe and was tracked all over his house making it stinky and dirty. Billy suppressed a grin *while picturing the mess on his precious carpet, in his posh house. The grin didn't stop him from feeling petrified, though.*

Billy heard Mr Wee Shoes ask Miss Jones why Billy was getting a dog.

'Some bloody stupid idea from some tosspot in Social Services,' was the reply.

'Why's that then?'

'I don't fuckin' know? What you askin' me for? I'm just doin' as I'm told, that's all.'

'I'm going to ask Bernie.'

'All right, aye. He'll know.'

As soon as Billy heard the cough, the squeak and the jangle fading away down the passage, he relaxed his shoulder muscles — well, all his muscles really. Billy didn't know if he had muscles in his fingers and toes but, if he did, then they'd have been tense, too. With a jolt, he realised that he'd been so wound up by Mr Plant that he had forgotten about the dog. He quickly stood on his toes to strain a bit further just as the dog had managed to strain against his rope. Billy felt guilty for taking his mind off him.

'Can I go to the toilet, miss. Please, miss, I'm bustin'.'

'Hurry up! I don't wanna be stuck here any longer than absolutely necessary.'

Billy raced off with Miss Jones's loud voice shouting after him, 'Don't run, Chapel!'

Billy ran anyway. He didn't want to bump into Mr Plant making his return. By the time Billy got back, he heard their voices again. He stayed out of view, listening as best he could.

'They're giving dogs to the boys when they go home so that the dog can help them to come together better or something. It's just some prat's idea to unite the families — fat lot of good it'll do.'

By the time Billy was allowed to go to meet the dog, he was beside himself with excitement. He didn't show it, though. He didn't want anyone to know how much he wanted the dog. He thought that they'd take it away from him if they knew how much he already loved it.

Once back at his mam's house, he was thrust yet again into emotional turmoil. Time hadn't stood still while he'd been away. He was shocked to see how much his baby sister had grown. He felt like an excluded outsider and very, very left out. He thought he should just leave and go on the run again but he knew that the dog, which he named Wendy, deserved more than that. He wanted her to have a proper home.

Billy soon became disillusioned over the 'proper family' idea. His mam didn't seem to like her at all, and his brother kicked her only moments after they had arrived when she got in his way. Of course, Billy kicked his brother in return and then got a clout from his mam 'for causing trouble'. Apparently, or so Billy was told, there hadn't been any problems when he wasn't there – which he doubted because Jon was always up to no good. Billy knew there was no point in sticking up for himself; he always got the blame for everything anyway, and he knew she wouldn't have taken any notice. He felt upset and misunderstood. Then Wendy came over and licked him… and he felt so, so comforted. In all of his seven years, he never once felt like that before.

For two nights, Billy slept on the kitchen floor beside her. She wasn't allowed in the house at night but Billy sneaked her in once everyone was in bed. He daren't risk taking her to his room so, instead, he lay on the cold, hard floor with just a coat under him.

In the morning, after the second night, Billy awoke to no Wendy. He frantically ran around the house calling for her. Then out the back. Then up and down the street. No sign whatsoever. He didn't notice that her lead was gone, too. 'She must have run away,' his mam said unfeelingly, hiding her deceit.

Billy ran crying from the house and out on to the street. He ran and ran, across the field adjacent to his mam's house, all the way down the hill, and veered left, through the next estate. He ran until he couldn't run any further. Once at the river, he rested for a moment to catch his breath and then ran back along it, heading east. Upon reaching the bit where the river narrowed, he skilfully, albeit recklessly, scrambled across using some conveniently positioned slippery rocks as precarious stepping stones. Safely across the other side, he ran straight into the woods, and climbed up into the highest tree. He sat sobbing, 'She wouldn't have left me. She wouldn't…' He cried until he felt sick. 'I thought she loved me… what did I do wrong?' he said to a bird, up in the sky. But the bird didn't stop. 'Why did she leave me?'

Back at the house, Billy's mam had just returned from the shops having spent the money on milk, bread and potatoes. Billy, though, stayed in the woods all night. He knew his brother would have taken the piss out of him for crying, so he stayed well away.

Billy wasn't at the house the next morning when the social worker came to *check up on him. When he did go back, his mam just said, without looking at him, 'You've done it now! You're going back. Mr Plant is coming to pick you up this afternoon.'*

*   *   *

I told Billy that I would come over literally just to drop off food and medication. I thought that that was probably pandering to him too much but it was impossible to know what he thought of the idea. He was so inert that I got absolutely no response from him. Sometimes, it felt like I was talking to someone in a coma. And right from when I first started going over, he seemed completely vacant and devoid of emotion.

It was hard to judge whether I was doing the right thing or not. I couldn't tell one way or the other as nothing changed and everything was just as horrendous as before. How does one gauge an inanimate object? It was breathing, but that's about it.

During my darkest moments, I was driven to making whispered bargains with God. I also resorted silently to reciting the Serenity Prayer: 'God, grant me the serenity to accept the things I cannot change, the courage to change the things I can, and the wisdom to know the difference.' People with addiction issues don't have the monopoly on that prayer. It *is* a litany generally associated with AA, but it was a valuable mantra for me as well. I first heard it in the film *When a Man Loves a Woman* with Andy Garcia and Meg Ryan. At the time, I must have stored it for future reference.

I knew I had done the right thing by both mentally and physically distancing myself from Billy, but I found the whole sorry mess excruciatingly hard and I experienced tremendous guilt. I very much had to struggle to keep it together, especially at work. I couldn't let the children see my pain, which, of course, put me under a great deal of stress as I fought to keep it all separate. The pressure was building but, for the most part, I managed somehow to control it.

One day, though, I flipped at my mum and Sophie. 'Have you ever asked yourselves why *I* have had all the crap? My chronic pain, all the surgeries, my infertility, all this shit with Billy… It's because God only gives you what you can handle! Billy needs a wife that won't leave him. I was meant to be Billy's wife because I know it's not about us! I know not to take it personally! I'm proud it's happened to me – it means God knows I can handle it, so just let me decide what's best to do!' I ranted.

They just stood there with their mouths open and I went upstairs crying. I don't remember what exactly triggered it, but I do remember how frustrated I felt a lot of the time. Nobody could see it from my perspective, or so it seemed. We didn't bring it up again. In a weird way, I *was* proud.

Staying back in my childhood home gave me an unexpected advantage. Just being there allowed me the distance I needed to be able to recognise just how much my world had altered. In fact, my life had changed so radically and so harshly I hardly recognised it as my own. I also hadn't anticipated just how much instigating my physical removal from our marital home would be of benefit to me emotionally. Achieving the physical distance obviously gave me some perspective and a chance to step back and see things more clearly.

It was evident that, over the previous two years or so, all that I believed and everything that was familiar had become so unfamiliar. Everything was oddly skew-whiff. What I thought, what I had always believed, was obscenely off kilter and the only thing that I could think of that might possibly stabilise my compass was to go back to a time when I felt connected and real, in its most innocent and purest form.

It didn't take much for me to realise that my 'past' self was who I needed to reintroduce myself to. I thought that the easiest way to accomplish that was to spend time going through all the things that signified who *that* 'me' really was. At the first opportunity, I went down into the crawlspace of my parents' house, retrieved my old trunk filled with memorabilia from my childhood and lugged it up to my old bedroom. I spent the next few hours lying on my bed, unpacking all my keepsakes and, with them, pulling recollections out of the dim subconscious recess of my mind. I was kind of compelled to linger over the items before me – fingering them, imagining them to be clues to an enigmatic me, which, of course, they were.

I familiarised myself with everything and I quickly became entrenched in reminiscence. I listened to all my old records while looking through my old scrapbooks, all in a concerted effort to finally reunite myself with that other me, the young me – who wasn't really so far away.

It seemed funny to be comforted by those things again; everything was so *familiar* and that familiarity was my magnetic north. Strangely, ever so quickly, all those things reconnected me with that time in my life when everything was stable and full of promise. All of it had been such a part of my lovely childhood, things I had subconsciously left behind. I had almost forgotten them, but just being in my old room, surrounded by signs of the time, filled me with nostalgia that was, perhaps, tinged with a certain pang of sadness, if I could call it that. I was back to a time when I was exquisitely unprepared for the path that was to become mine – unprepared in the sense of my naivety. Blissful naivety. It was wonderful to remember and feel that simplicity.

The music helped to transport me back to those days – the old songs becoming markers of key moments in time. Looking at photos, reading all the comments from my friends in my annuals and reading old letters, I became trancelike in my wistful remembrance. Remembering who I was – me, before Billy. Up until then, I hadn't fully realised just how much the collective treasure of my childhood experiences had been safeguarded in my mind. It took seeing my old 'stuff' properly to reacquaint myself. The way I had kept all the details of my 'high-school' self in my brain space put me in mind of keeping special things in a hope chest or an old shoe box that had been decorated with glitter and pink felt-tips, covered with words like 'private' and 'keep out' – in much the same way that Tatum O'Neal's character, Addie, in *Paper Moon* kept her treasures in a 'Cremo' tobacco box. She and I carried our treasures everywhere. Ensconced in my old bedroom, I had put my focus on them.

I took out my past and held it up to the light. An aggregate slide of childhood that, for the first time in years, I took the time to scrutinise. Just seeing the overall, singular assemblage brought me to a parallel place, a realm separate and unconnected to my present. I felt a strange need to protect it, or to protect my ownership of it. It was mine… and I didn't want to share it. Alone in my old bedroom seemed to me to be the perfect place to have dissected it.

Reflecting on my past had been the right thing to do. I had sought refuge, and I had found it there among my innermost thoughts. It had been there all along, I just needed to uncover it. The whole process had helped such a lot and certainly gave me the mental distance that I both craved and needed. But, most of all, it made me confident that some day, somehow, it would all be OK again.

Billy didn't take the separation well, which gradually became evident as the state of his appearance, as well as the house, declined even further. Actually, I am not sure if Billy was actually getting worse or if it was just becoming more obvious how much I had kept on top of things and, as a result, masked things. It was torture not cleaning up when I dropped the food off, but I vowed not to.

Everything seemed to deteriorate so fast. I had been so consumed with guilt over leaving and concern for Billy that I hadn't given a moment's thought to the everyday little things. It just happened that one day I got there and I was confronted with chaos. Pots of dead parched plants littered the front steps. Decaying hanging baskets, light from the lack of any moisture in their dirt, swung in the lacklustre wind. Groupings of once colourful and healthy perennials, strategically placed in clusters around the garden, sat withered and neglected. And that was just outside. Feeling responsible for their premature death and the shabbiness of our property, I was preoccupied as I let myself in. My mind was filled with a myriad of thoughts floating around, filling up my brain space. It was like I was half-asleep. Quite similar, in fact, to the feeling one has when woken from a deep sleep by the harsh ring of an alarm clock. When erratic thoughts of 'What time is it?'... 'What day is it?' crowd into a semi-conscious jumble.

I pushed the door open, conscious that it took more effort, and realised why as I stepped over a mountain of coats and shoes littering the mat. As I brushed past the doorframe, my jacket caught on a rogue nail that was jutting out of it. The material ripped as I tripped over a hammer, lying out of place, just inside the doorway. I half-noticed some nails scattered on the hall floor, but I was too distracted to dwell on them. I put the food in the fridge and left quickly. Too quickly perhaps, but my discomfort made me so overwhelmed I couldn't wait to escape.

I felt better once I was in the van driving too fast with all the windows wound down. I may have felt renewed optimism when I was safe in my childhood bedroom but the harsh reality at our house pendulum-swung me firmly in the other direction again.

The next time I drove over, I mentally built myself up, mile by mile, sick-makingly nervous of what I could potentially, realistically, be confronted with. Realistically, I knew it was going to be at least as bad as the time before. I didn't get a chance to garner much strength, though, as I only had about a three-mile drive, so, when I found myself approaching the corner where our street turned off Cedar Hill Road, I accelerated and drove straight past it. I continued driving up past Doncaster Elementary, along the back of K-Mart and then circled, automatically, back along Shelbourne Street. Obviously, I needed to give myself more time, although I didn't conceptualise that at the time. I guess I simply knew that I couldn't possibly not go, even if I was desperate to avoid it.

As it happened, that time, for some reason, I elected to walk round the back and go in through the kitchen door. Maybe, subconsciously, I was attempting to avoid the horticultural signs of neglect that were more evident from the front approach. The back steps were in poor repair and somewhat rickety but I suppose I didn't feel depressed by the sight of them as they had always been that way.

As I clumped heavy-footed up the steps, I realised I actually quite liked their dilapidated appearance. That was probably only because I couldn't fix them personally, so I didn't feel responsible for them. Right, something to work on there then – my self-inflicted pressure, not the stairs. I put the key in and turned it, but the door wouldn't open. I could see the latch disengage, so I knew it wasn't locked from the inside, but I couldn't waste time trying to figure out why. I was too anxious to get in the house, so I ended up going round to the front.

The view was pretty much as before. Seeing it still made me feel guilty. When I went into the house, I didn't even bother to pick up the post. Those few weeks were probably the first time ever that envelopes weren't opened and the contents dealt with on the day of receipt – bills paid, paperwork filed, envelopes, minus the plastic window, straight to the recycling box, along with any junk mail. Suddenly, our house was becoming one of those other kinds of homes. The ones where bills were left unopened for weeks, and various leaflets and fliers littered the kitchen work surfaces.

As I walked through the front hall, I don't recall seeing the hammer, although the nails were still scattered on the hall carpet. I could hear the telly on downstairs, and was aware of a tiny bit of movement – evident by the telltale squeak of the couch springs. I shoved the food into the fridge, absentmindedly pushing things out of the way to make room; anxious to make an escape before Billy realised I was there. I quickly suppressed a cough – a precursor to my inhaler being fished out of my handbag, as the airless, stale and smoky atmosphere caused my airways to tighten almost immediately. My wheezing seemed extra loud as I shuffled down the hall and out into the night, gulping at the freshness with hunger.

After a few more visits and a few more door disorders, I got there to be faced with the necessity of entering through the basement door. We never used that door and had bins against it on the outer side. All I had to do was pull the bins out of the way, but that wasn't the point. *Why* couldn't I use the front door? Or the kitchen door for that matter? But, surprisingly, I wasn't asking myself that question. I was caught up with having to go in through the basement door because I knew what that would mean. I would have to pass Billy in order to get upstairs.

I very quietly opened the door. I couldn't hear the television but I could see the telltale flashes of bluish light flickering in the cavernous darkness. As I approached the couch, I was struck by the silence. Obviously, the volume on the telly was right down. I got a lump in my throat as I suddenly remembered how I always used to tease Billy over never using the 'mute' button. I was scared shitless at the prospect of looking at him. I was acutely aware that there was no movement. As I got closer, I started shaking. I couldn't tell if he was alive.

After a bit of a mental delay, I found myself bending towards Billy's prone lifeless body. My movement had almost been involuntary, as if my mind hadn't connected how my body had got in that position. I was horrified to realise that my brain was intending to get my body closer to check if he was breathing. Oddly, my conscious mind and my body were somehow disconnected and something in my brain was playing the part of the puppet master. He controlled both – getting my body to move before my mind knew why. I don't know why I thought of the puppet master as masculine.

When I saw the faint rise of his chest, it felt like an hour had passed. I chastised myself for having acted in such a dramatic fashion as I quietly went up into the kitchen, which actually didn't look much worse than the day before.

Looking back, even though it sort of feels like it happened to someone else, I do remember that I *had* felt silly for being so over-dramatic. And I know that I hadn't acknowledged the door situation at all. I didn't even check why I couldn't open the doors. How could I not have *seen* the seriousness of that situation? I guess that is denial at its finest.

I'm not sure if it was the next time, or later on, when I finally noticed the state of both the front and kitchen doors. I know I had gained entry through the basement, and had left the same way on numerous occasions, but I really can't recall at what point I realised that both the upstairs doors had been barricaded from the inside. They were actually nailed shut with bits of wood criss-crossing the length and width of the door. There was so much wood you could barely see the true colour of the door. I truly can't remember what I thought about it. I obviously wasn't totally *compos mentis* myself. I didn't do anything about it, I know that. But I don't know why I didn't. I guess because of the 'D' word again.

Then I got there one day to find he wasn't in. The house was eerily dark and still. Blankets had been tossed up over the curtain rail in the living room and the front bedroom, blocking out all light. My window dressing in the bedroom had been pulled down and slung in a corner – the other hung twisted and stretched as it dangled off the end of the pole. Strangely, I noticed there were no illuminated digits on the video or the clock radio. Everything had been unplugged.

When I walked into the kitchen, I immediately noticed the absence of the fridge's hum, which, of course, added to the unsettling ambience and understandably intensified my concern. I looked around in shock. It was a doss house. In a matter of a relatively short space of time, our lovely place had been transformed into a completely different dwelling. It was no longer a home. My stomach dropped as I noticed his keys on the kitchen table. I thought that meant he wasn't intending to come back.

Something overflowed in my head. I backed up with my hands over my mouth until I met with the wall and literally slid down it into a crumpled heap on the sticky, dirty floor. Why the hell I even *noticed* the state of the floor is beyond me. It was as if, seeing the keys, which I felt had been deliberately placed in full view on the table, had sent me over the edge.

Since the breakdown, I often felt that Billy left me clues or signs or something. Due to my obsessive penchant towards order, it was always noticeable to me when something had been moved or put in a different place. Billy had always thought it hilarious and would often tease me about it. The keys 'lived' on a hook in the kitchen. Billy always put them there, too, automatically. For years and years, he had never put them anywhere else. I don't for one minute think that his reason for always putting things in their place was the same as mine. I think his stemmed from a need to please. It was as if, when we first started living together, he had watched my every move to find out the 'right' way of doing things, and had then adopted them too. I just knew that by putting the keys on the table he knew I would notice them, and I felt he was telling me he wasn't intending to come back. I know that sounds bizarre, but he had been doing things like that for years. He had always moved little things as a joke, just to make me smile.

*   *   *

I awoke with the usual grogginess that always followed a spell under anaesthetic. There was no other feeling like it. I was used to it. So used to it, in fact, that I recognised every step. First, I became aware of the noises that were indicative of only one thing – hospital. Machines beeped. Trolleys, gurneys or wheelchairs rattled past. Phones rang. Then, the smell hit my nostrils, around about the same time as my eyes opened. That unmistakable smell. Then the feeling of each individual thing. The tube up my nose. The tube down my throat. Dry mouth. Sore throat. The drainage tube out of my belly. Pressure in the abdomen. Catheter. Pain across my pelvis but, at the same time, the lovely relief from the other, horrendous pain. I knew I had about two hours before I started throwing up.

I'd had emergency surgery at 2.00am so Billy wasn't there. I didn't mind. Actually, I was glad. I hated having to worry about how he was when I felt like shit. It was just easier if he wasn't there. I was oddly independent when in pain. I tried not to be. I knew Billy and my mum wished I were different. They wanted to look after me, but I couldn't let them. I didn't know why.

I turned my head unintentionally and felt the tubes pull restrictively. My bedside travel clock read 5.55am. I said 'Thank you' in my thought voice – acknowledging my cosmic greeting. And then I saw it.

The bunny ornament.

I smiled weakly, barely able to respond, and I knew Billy had been there. Putting it there was the best thing he could have done. He knew just what to do. He knew I would have hated hand-holding, or brow-stroking. He knew that the bunny would make me laugh. He knew that I would take it to mean that he had been thinking about me and that he loved me.

The ornament turning up in strange places, without any warning, had been an in-joke of ours. It had started around Easter time, a few years previously, probably around 1992, when I had made a comment about it being moved from its 'place' on the mantelpiece. Billy had teased me relentlessly about my ability to notice when things were even a millimetre out of place. It had taken him a long time to realise that it really was just a quirk of mine. From then on, Billy began moving the ornament on purpose. When I put it away at the end of that Easter, Billy somehow got it out again. It appeared a few months later, out of the blue, sitting at the kitchen table. I was hysterical when I saw it.

Ever since then, every once in a while, it would turn up. Once, he put it in the driver's seat of the car, with the seatbelt across it, so that I would see it when I went out in the morning. Then it wouldn't appear for months… then it would turn up in the bath, or sitting on the couch with Billy's earphones on, or in the tent on one of our road trips. The hospital one was the best to date.

★   ★   ★

When I saw the keys, I basically lost the plot. It was so obviously something that he knew I would notice, but then again he didn't appear very capable of thinking about anything… but that kind of made it stranger in a way. I can't *explain* why, really. I just *knew* that the keys meant something.

★   ★   ★

As soon as her mam went to bed, little Lauren Chapel sneaked into the scary darkness and quietly hurried down the passage. She bravely and determinedly descended the stairs and slipped into the back room. She stood on the chair by the window, lifted the latch and pushed it open just a fraction of an inch before she quickly returned to her bed. She hoped the morning would bring a sign from her brother, Billy – or 'BB', as she liked to call him. Lauren loved him very much. The way she looked up to her big brother made Billy feel very brave and strong. Strangely, he felt weak and timid at the same time.

Months before, during a rare home visit, Lauren told Billy that she would leave the living-room window open for him so he could get in whenever he wanted to. She didn't understand why he wasn't allowed to live with them and, in her innocence, thought that if she left the window open he would come back.

At first, Billy laughed at the suggestion, but he thought about it later and realised it would actually be a good idea. The very next time he ran away from the children's home, after a particularly bad incident, he managed to make his way back to Llanellog Hill Crescent and, sure enough, the window was open. Sometimes, he just went in for the night, and left in the morning before anyone woke, and sometimes, in the morning, he crept up to the loft to hide out during the day. It depended on the weather and how tired he was.

Lauren tried so hard not to miss a night, even though a lot of the time she fell asleep before she could fulfil her task. She always felt incredibly guilty if she awoke in the morning to the realisation that she hadn't opened the window.

Whenever Billy came, he always let Lauren know that he had been there. Sometimes, he left a pebble on the windowsill, or a leaf on the stairs, or some other sign. Obviously, he didn't always manage to get there. In fact, in all the months she left the window open, he only managed to get there two dozen times or so. But, when he had been there, she always knew. This, in itself, was incredible because they had never verbally discussed it. Every stone, every leaf, every stick was a message. They told her he was OK. They said, 'Thank you.'

She hated the times when weeks would go by without a sign. But then, out of the blue, something would be left. Once, she awoke to a feather on her pillow.

She shouldn't have had to feel that guilt, or that worry. She was just a little girl.

*   ★   ★

I cried until I was an exhausted snotty mess. I don't know how long I remained like that but, at some point, my usual coping mechanism took over and I decided to clean the house. First, I pulled my hair off my face and secured it up with a scrunchie, blew my nose with what must have been a whole box of tissues, and then washed my face with cold water. That done, I efficiently, swiftly and mechanically checked all the food in the fridge. Obviously, it hadn't been unplugged for long as everything was still cold. I plugged it back in and then pushed the extension lead as far as I could behind the fridge, in an effort to make unplugging it again more difficult. Then I got stuck into cleaning.

Afterwards, I had a long hot bath. My tense neck muscles were absolutely desperate for relaxation and, strangely, I found myself actually enjoying the solitude that staying at my parents' house had not allowed. By the time I got out of the tub, it was late and I figured I might as well stay overnight. I went to bed and lay in the dark, trying not to think about things. I knew I would be awake all night if I did. I was soothed to a certain extent after the hot bath and soon drifted into a deep, yet troubled, dream-filled sleep.

Some time later, I found myself being dragged up from the bottom of the ocean. With effort, I broke the surface of sleep, woken by the sound of a commotion in the back garden. I crept out of bed, slipped down the hall and into the darkened kitchen, where I went straight to the back window and carefully pulled the curtain back, ever such a tiny bit, and peered out. I squinted into the darkness, taking a moment to become accustomed to the poor visibility.

Amid the vague shadows, my fuddled brain registered the sighting of a nebulous silhouette, lurking just below the porch window. My breath caught in my throat and my heart began pounding but, amazingly, I wasn't scared. Well, not exactly. The dark form then perched on an upturned bin and reached up to the window. The branches of a tree just inside our property line swayed back and forth creating illusory images that materialised, then vanished, in the inconsistent glimmer of moonlight. A street lamp, on the road behind our house, was too far away to offer any help, so I couldn't make a positive identification. However, the absence of fear led me to conclude that it was indeed Billy.

I couldn't begin to fathom what he was up to. I ducked into the spare room off the kitchen and hid in the shadows, as Billy stumbled in and went downstairs. Drunk again.

Soon everything was quiet, with Billy presumably asleep. I walked to the porch and stood staring at the window. I told myself that Billy had just forgotten to take his keys with him when he went out, but part of me logically knew that that wasn't the case. Certain things had to have been premeditated. For one thing, the sliding porch window had no proper lock on it, so beforehand he would have had to remove the piece of wood that we had positioned along the bottom of one side, in order to be able to slide the window open from the outside. But there had also been a kitchen chair placed in the porch, under the window. There was no possible reason for the chair to be put there unless it had been to aid the process of getting in. It had to have been planned.

It was like I was two people. Person one was explaining everything away and totally forgetting the previous meltdown and person two was seeing all the horrendously obvious clues. The bits of wood still remained nailed every which way across the back door, right beside the window. I didn't give them a moment's thought as the first person told the second person just to go back to bed. Which I did.

I lay there, trying to stay calm, telling myself that I was over-reacting and that he wasn't really that bad, telling myself that he really had just forgotten his keys. Then, illogically, I told myself that I didn't need to worry about him being suicidal because at least his apathy was saving him on that score. That, of course, didn't make sense, as planning to get in via the window certainly wasn't the behaviour of an apathetic person. But, at the same time, he was absolutely apathetic. So how had he gone out in the first place? And why? One thought contradicted the next, but I didn't see it.

I convinced myself again, as I drifted off to sleep, that he really wasn't alert enough to kill himself. And a strange doublespeak, that always transformed all negatives to positives, played over in my mind as I made it all OK in my head. I had learned early on in our relationship that, if you let them, it is easy for the good things to overshadow the bad. Actually, for me, I think the good sort of dismissed the bad.

A few hours later, I sat bolt upright in bed, startled back into consciousness, woken by a terrifying picture running over and over in my mind's eye of me putting food in the fridge and having to make room for it, suddenly realising that the fridge shouldn't have been full. I desperately tried to recall how many times that had happened. My train of thought then switched to recalling how I had noticed that the kitchen didn't appear any messier and things generally weren't becoming more untidy. I remember that I had taken that to be a good sign.

Sitting up in bed in the quiet darkness, hot and sweaty from anxiety, I had a moment of clarity. Billy wasn't getting better. He was getting worse. I raced into the kitchen and flung open the fridge. Holy Fucking Christ, he hadn't eaten anything for days! Earlier, I had plugged the fridge back in and checked that the food hadn't spoiled. Why hadn't I noticed *then* that nothing had been either eaten or opened?

Obviously, the kitchen hadn't been more untidy because he hadn't been using any plates or cutlery. I stumbled into the living room and slumped on to the couch. I pulled my knees up and hugged my legs, rocking back and forth. I suddenly thought that maybe that was Billy's weapon. Maybe his method of choice, to take his own life, was *apathy*. What if he was giving up and his mind was killing himself that way? As if the demon in him wanted to end it all so much that, when his mind wouldn't co-operate and get his body to find some rope, or to find some pills, he had thought, Right, I'll get you, ya bastard. I'll make sure you don't do *anything*.

I began to realise that something was wrong. Very wrong. I couldn't save him from that. There was nothing left for me to do. I couldn't remove his brain or hide his mind. I couldn't save him from himself. No amount of love could do that.

Then, I finally let myself acknowledge the barricaded doors business and the climbing in through the window business. And I began to permit myself to begin to unravel what the fuck it was all about. I couldn't figure out why he had behaved so strangely and erratically. For the first time, I admitted to myself that it might be some sort of a paranoid, delusional break from reality. It was all so weird and I was mortally petrified. Billy was sick. Maybe even crazy. Something terrible was happening. It was so obvious.

I felt sick and ran to the bathroom. I sat on the floor, leaning against the cold porcelain, dry heaving into the toilet bowl. There was nothing to come up, as I hadn't eaten since breakfast. I got up and went to get some water and stood in the pitch-dark kitchen and drank three big glasses in as many minutes. I again returned to the couch, feeling completely different. It was as if the water had numbed me from the inside out as it travelled down my oesophagus and into my stomach. I had acknowledged the truth to a certain extent, but here is where the 'D' word made its appearance yet again. I went to bed.

I awoke the next morning amid a distinct aura of detachment. The feeling was completely unexpected, especially since I remembered the stress of the night before and I knew I had experienced some mental clarification. I remembered, too, the numbness. It was a feeling that had been utterly discernible the night before, and it remained. It wasn't altogether pleasant; in fact, it was rather disconcerting, but, honestly, it was welcome. The sense of appeasement could not go unnoticed, nor could its uniqueness. If only for the fact that it was unwilled. I left early to go to work.

Maybe I should have stepped in that morning and demanded psychiatric help from somewhere… but I didn't. And I don't really know why, except for the fact that I had no idea who to turn to. I had already tried the obvious and had resorted to things that I never thought I would do in a million years. There was no doubting he needed help. He was so spiritually crushed and so mentally withdrawn. It was as if he was completely consumed by the belief that he didn't deserve other people or something. I don't remember that day at work.

I returned to the house after work. The drive over wasn't anxious, I do know that, but I couldn't tell you what I was feeling. I didn't know what I was supposed to feel. I had absolutely no compass.

It wasn't until I got there that I realised that I hadn't even stopped at Thrifty's for milk or anything. I again entered through the basement. I didn't even think to try to go through the other doors. I just walked right in. I didn't think about waking Billy up or checking to see if he was breathing. I guess self-preservation had kicked in big style. As I walked past the couch, I didn't even look at Billy. But it wasn't as if I didn't look on purpose. I didn't think about it. I jumped when he spoke, absolutely not expecting it. I couldn't make out what he had said, though. His voice was so weak it could almost be described as a pathetic whisper. Then he spoke again, his voice gruff and faint, from weeks of disuse. I still couldn't make out what he had said. His face looked so vulnerable.

Then I said quietly, 'Do you want something to eat?' in a voice that sounded as if I was coaxing a sick child.

As soon as the words were spoken, Billy's whole demeanour changed. The vulnerable look gone in an instant.

'You need to eat something, babes,' I said in that voice again.

'Do I?' he said.

If my eyes had been closed, I would have thought someone else had come in the room and was talking. His voice was completely different. It reminded me of *The Exorcist* when Linda Blair's mouth moved and the demon's voice came out. I'm not saying he was possessed, I just noted it, that's all.

'Of course you need to eat, Billy,' I added, trying to placate.

'I don't want to!' he growled.

I backed away from him involuntarily.

'Fuck off!' It was practically a grunt.

'Do you want to die? Is that it?' I shouted, horrified at my own short fuse. Then, desperate to salvage something, I said soothingly, 'You need to eat so you can have a tablet. You know how you can't take them on an empty tummy.' I desperately wanted to get an Ativan into him.

'Why don't you just give me the bottle. I'll take one later.' His voice sounded weirdly normal, and it made me feel even more uneasy than the exorcist voice did for some reason.

'You know I can't do that,' I said softly.

'Why? Do you think I'd take them all?' he replied even more softly. Sickeningly nice. I didn't even answer. Then he said, 'I don't deserve to die that way.'

'No, babes, of course you don't. You deserve to get well.' I was so glad he seemed to be coming round. We were having a conversation. He was actually talking!

He looked at me, adopting the strangest expression, and with the most repulsive grin on his face. Then he said, almost laughingly, with the other voice returning, 'No, sweetheart, you got it wrong. You think you're always so fucking right all the time. Well, I'll tell you something, shall I? You're not. You. Got. It. Wrong. I'm not going to top myself with pills or hang myself from the support beam in the garage.' I gasped and I think he heard me because he continued, 'Yeah, that's right, sweetheart. I checked to see if they were strong enough… they are, by the way. Did that surprise you? You fat barren bitch!' Then he just sarcastically laughed for a minute or two – which felt like for ever – and then finished by saying, 'That would be too quick.'

I just stood there, emotionless. I was sort of wondering why I wasn't crying. What I had just heard cut like a knife. He *doesn't* love me, I thought. He must hate me to say those things. But, actually, that's what did it for me. Hearing him speak that way to me generated a huge glow of strength from deep within. In an instant, the feeling I had towards him was severed. Cut dead.

8

STRANDED UP IN
THE STARS

As I drown in Holy water
Is there a place that I belong
All your dreams turn into nothing
Came crashing down like a house of cards

Memories are like scars
Dreams that we had burn in broken hearts
It was a bridge too far
Now you're stranded up in the stars

You got up early this morning
To write three dirty letters
Your hands now cold to the touch
Will an angel kiss it better?
Your tear hung down from the star that
I wished upon to save you.

'House of Cards' by Lahayna

I didn't understand… and then I did, just like that.
It was such a relief. My anger disappeared and, more importantly,
my fear dissipated. I was rooted to the spot, three or four feet from the
couch where Billy still had a vile look on his face. I think I actually
even had a smile on mine. And I definitely had the cold prickly feeling
that left me feeling warm inside. The irony of it all was so peculiar. I

mean, he had spouted such nastiness – and it *was* nasty – but it was precisely those things that made me see sense. He *doesn't* hate me, I thought. Don't you see? It was the poison in him. His lifelike mental illness had slipped up, in my eyes, by making him say two things – 'barren' and 'sweetheart'.

My Billy would *never* have said those words. 'Barren' was way too hurtful and cruel. And 'sweetheart'? Billy *never* called me 'sweetheart'. He called me 'sparrow'.

So I knew. He was just trying to push me away. It wasn't really Billy talking. It was his mind, his mental illness, or whatever. I didn't know what, or why, or how, but I realised in that instant that my poor, poor husband was in there somewhere. And he needed me to get him out. I had to find him and somehow, some way, I knew then that I would. He was acting like an animal, at his worst, and yet I felt my best. Well, the best that I had felt in months at least. He was vile, but at least he was talking. He was being horrendous, but at least that was better than being comatose.

Then, incredibly, as all those thoughts realigned in my head, it all changed again. Right before my eyes, Billy visibly shut down. I felt and saw him depart. I was too stunned to react. What the hell just happened?

It was weird. I kind of felt like I had felt that way before, a long time ago, but I couldn't quite place it. Billy retreating again, and so swiftly, sent me sliding back to the pre-numb state of hope and disappointment, optimism or sadness, worry versus relief – and all that those emotions entail. Those conflicts of emotion had inhabited my head for so long by that stage that they had become habitual. My head was comfortable enough with their presence – accommodated them to a certain extent. It was my heart that wanted to get away from them. I was so completely, emotionally wrung out.

I got in the van and drove away. I felt like it was the only thing I knew how to do. Days went by and, all the while, Billy remained withdrawn. In fact, I began to wonder if I had imagined the unsettling outburst of a few days earlier. But the more I thought of it, the more I began to dwell on what he had said about taking pills, checking beams and not deserving to die. I ruminated many a nocturnal hour, playing over in my head, 'I don't deserve to die… I don't deserve to die…' over and over. Until, no… no. That wasn't what he had said. He had said, 'I don't deserve to die that way.' *That way.* What way? I played it over and over. In the van. In the bath. In my bed. Changing diapers. Picking up dog poo. Over and over and over. Then I remembered the last bit. 'That would be too quick.' What would be too quick? What did he mean, *too* quick?

And then I got it. He thought, by taking pills, death would be quick. Hanging from the beams in the garage – quick. I felt as if my brain wasn't working fast enough. What was I missing?

★   ★   ★

'Chapel! Didn't I tell you to clean that up?'

'Yes, sir.' Billy was kneeling down on all fours scrubbing a section of the toilet floor.

'Well, get on with it!'

'I am, sir.' He couldn't scrub any faster than he was already.

'Don't you get gobby with me, lad!'

As he walked past Billy, Mr Bowen harshly kicked him on the backside, causing him to fall forward. Both Billy's hands slid outward on the wet surface and he went chin-first down on to the floor. It hurt like hell but his mind was taken off the pain when he noticed drops of his own, bright-red blood on the floor. He quickly wiped it up, praying that Mr Bowen didn't see it. He could get nasty without very much provocation at all – and the mess would have done it.

Surprisingly, or perhaps sadly, Billy really didn't see Mr Bowen as cruel. Indeed, comparing him with the other adults Billy had encountered since living 'in care', he was, apart from a few who never even acknowledged Billy, the best of the lot. But that really wasn't saying much, once the others were taken into account. Those others had all dished out far greater punishments, for far less, so Billy was acutely aware that Mr Bowen could have been much worse. At best, he was one of the few adults in Billy's life who wasn't altogether unkind. At worst, he had a harsh and vindictive tongue and a heavy hand. Often, if Billy got in his way or if he did not obey the one quickly enough, he felt the weight of the other. Unfortunately, the level of what was considered acceptable was being distorted so much that, in some circumstances, he might even have been considered something approaching all right.

Incidents like the arse-kicking scenario happened so often that Billy started believing that, whatever the reason, he deserved whatever punishment was inflicted upon him. Over time, if he did something wrong, or didn't respond quickly enough, and got physically reprimanded, Billy never thought that the adult was behaving in any way inappropriately. The constant occurrence of punishments that never fitted the crime ensured Billy pretty much felt like everything he did was wrong and, when punished, he always felt like he should have got more.

One day, he was kicked for spilling a bit of water. Another time, he was thumped between the shoulder blades for dripping something. So, when he only got clipped round the ear when he dropped a cup and his drink splashed everywhere, he absolutely believed he deserved a harsher punishment. His gauge for the level of cruelty was very warped. And what he considered fair or acceptable was so incredibly off kilter that it bred in him a terrible lack of self-worth, so that he was left feeling completely insignificant. It also had a lot to do with his adoption of a thoroughly entrenched pessimistic attitude.

The thing is, when it boils down to it, children are generally naturally optimistic creatures. It takes such a lot to convince them that things are actually bad. And, when they are, they think that the next day will be better. So, for any child to become pessimistic, things had to have been very bad. For Billy, things had been, and were, that bad.

Billy believed that things would never get better. And he believed that he deserved to be treated badly, just because he was alive. Just because.

*   *   *

Oh my God! I got it, just like that. Billy thought he didn't *deserve* to die quickly… but what does that mean? That he thinks he *does* deserve to die – just not quickly. What then? Slowly? I was getting tenser by the second. I could feel my neck starting to ache, then really hurt. I could literally feel the progression as my muscles wound tighter and tighter. He was torturing himself – literally. What, to death? Was it a kind of… what? Anorexia? Was death by starvation his method of choice?

Then a funny thing happened. I ran to the toilet to be sick. I drank water. And then I felt numb again. I recognised it straight away. Champion. Numb wasn't so bad. Numb I could do.

I also got a migraine. I had no choice but to go to bed. I was lucky it was a Saturday. I slept all Saturday afternoon, and all night, then I stayed in bed all day on Sunday. Mum said she would have the kids for me on the Monday, which was a relief. The migraine had gone but the numbness was still there. It was as though the pressure of protecting him from intentional starvation was too much. And really! What was I to do other than shut it out. Of course it was too much. At night, I had terrible recurring nightmares of Billy looking emaciated, like a concentration camp victim, then him dying and the mental illness moving into my head. Numbness was understandable. And it was something that I literally had no control over. I began to like it in a way that frightened me. I didn't *really* want to withdraw to the point where I didn't care about Billy any more. I fantasised about it, sure I did. But, if I stopped caring, what would that mean for Billy? I still loved him but I found I could no longer worry about whether he'd be out when I stopped by, or if he'd be in but looking terrible. Or if he would be dead. I could no longer hope for anything either. I simply couldn't bear the roller-coaster any more. The up and down of it all was just so exhausting. In some ways, it was just easier continually to be devoid of any feeling at all. I was losing my grip.

For the first time ever, I arrived at the house that Monday morning feeling absolutely nothing. And that was the very day that I found Billy crying. At first, when I got to the house, I had thought he was out. But then I heard his sobs. It took me a while to realise the noise was coming from the bathroom. Eventually I found him, crouching in the empty bath, fully clothed. I didn't know what had changed, but he had some emotion back, and that was good enough for me. For some inexplicable reason, that particular day, he surfaced, after scraping the bottom of the barrel, and decided that he wanted help. He actually *wanted* help.

Initially, I was completely taken aback. Momentarily. But then I jumped back on the roller-coaster and relief soared through me. I found the timing unbelievable, it has to be said. And the irony certainly didn't escape me. Could it have been that something in Billy sensed that something in me had changed? It just couldn't be a coincidence that my *loss* of attentiveness came just before his *gain* of resolve. There was something in that theory, I was sure. I just couldn't be bothered to figure it all out. Analysing that would have meant too much effort in the brain department, even for a head-dweller like me. But one thing was for sure – I wasn't losing my grip. That was just a blip on the screen.

For once, witnessing another person's tears didn't result in me crying as well. 'You'll have to stop drinking,' I told him harshly, strangely proud of my hardened mindset.

'I know,' he croaked, his voice raspy again, from lack of use.

'You'll have to go to the detox centre first,' I dared to add.

'I know,' he repeated.

Relief doesn't even begin to describe how I felt. I phoned our GP immediately, before Billy could change his mind, and arranged it through him. Luckily, there was a bed available straight away. I hoped he would finally be able to get to the bottom of his torment and make some sense out of it all.

The day he was to go, I agreed to drive him. On the way, he was incredibly anxious and wanted to back out. He begged me to take him home. I ended up getting really angry – albeit passively. I know I *felt* really angry, but I'm not so sure that my outward appearance would have shown that.

I continued to drive Billy there anyway. As I was driving, Billy demanded that I give him some Ativan. He knew that I had a bottle of them in my handbag, as he had been prescribed them, but he also knew that our GP had insisted that, for reasons of safety, I was to keep them away from him and to administer his dose myself. Of course, when Billy demanded them, I was adamant that I wouldn't give him the whole bottle. At that point, he started to become worryingly aggressive and very truculent. He was swearing and shouting as I was trying desperately to focus on driving. I knew I shouldn't be driving under such circumstances but I daren't pull over. I knew Billy would try to escape.

All of a sudden, he became strangely calm and tried to say that he just wanted one or two to settle his nerves before going into the centre. I agreed, but I figured he was manipulating me and I didn't trust him, so I got the bottle out myself and somehow managed, God only knows how, to get the child lock unscrewed with one hand while steering with the other. In the confusion, I managed to tip about half of the bottle down the side of my seat beside the door without Billy noticing, so, when he grabbed the bottle and swallowed what he could, he didn't actually get very many, although definitely more than two.

Eventually, I got to the centre and drove right up to the front door. Billy was so mad at me because as soon as we pulled up a man came out to greet us, ensuring he couldn't get away. I told the man that Billy had taken a load of pills, and that he had been very aggressive and apprehensive.

When my eyes met Billy's, there was hatred in them. And rage. But not love, no recognition even. Billy spoke then, in a tone of such aversion, such contempt, that I recoiled. 'She's exaggerating as usual.'

The man looked at me in a way that somehow made me feel better. His expression told me that he knew I wasn't exaggerating and that I had done the right thing. I felt better, but I was angry, too. Simply because Billy had hurt me, because he had fought me, and because he had blatantly lied. But even then I knew it wasn't really Billy.

And then I had to get back in the van and reverse away with Billy more mad at me than he had ever been before. He had such a horrible, nasty and volatile expression on his face it broke my heart to look at him. The further I got, the more the look of pure hatred rose in his eyes, until, finally, I had to turn away. I was devastated. I guess that's what they call 'tough love'.

To be fair, Billy did go in and initially did well. However, he ran away after two weeks. And, as with the incident with the psychiatrist at the ER, his reaction to the police in our home and the whole barricaded door/coming in through the window thing, that, too, was something I had no way of understanding.

Once he was back home, I tried not to show my obvious disappointment that he hadn't stuck with the programme, although the fact that he had been abstaining from alcohol did have a positive effect. He was able to talk more, although certainly not in any great detail. It became evident that Billy's past wasn't really addressed at the detox centre. They did their counselling in a group session in which Billy wouldn't participate.

I was at least grateful that he wasn't drinking as much. Over the next few weeks, I noticed he seemed to be coping better. We started talking a bit when I came round to the house and he definitely seemed more stable.

Christmas was approaching and I was dreading it. I couldn't believe it was a whole year since I had gone to Wales. Billy asked if I would come back home for Christmas. I wasn't sure, although I kept it to myself. I didn't want to bruise his fragile spirit. His aura was so weak and faint I couldn't bear to say no. And I wanted go home.

After all, he had been making headway. Maybe only baby steps, but you've got to start somewhere, right? I decided to redo my contract with myself. I would stay as long as he was willing to receive help and was making progress – even if it was only a tiny shuffle. After all, he was speaking! That had to count for something.

I planned to move back in when I finished work for the holidays but only on the condition that he didn't drink at all. I didn't want to issue an ultimatum as such. I never had, as a rule, and I'd experienced enough to know that, if he was forced to choose between me and alcohol, alcohol would win every time. I wouldn't have taken that personally for I knew there was no contest but, even so, I wanted instead to make it his choice. I just explained that I didn't want alcohol in my life and that if he chose to drink he would have to do it somewhere else. I think, because he was more rational and therefore more capable of understanding what I was getting at without flying off the handle, or retreating, I felt more able to say that. In any case, it was said and things started to settle down.

By the time Christmas was over, Billy was still not drinking. His medication was taking effect and he was much more reasonable, and a bit more healthy. I got back on top of all the things that I had let slide over the previous months and the usual routine resumed. The post returned to being dealt with as soon as it came in and the upkeep of the household generally went back to normal.

All the same, I was unsettled. After all, it was really only the surface stuff that got back to normal. His things were everywhere, yet Billy was still nowhere. I also realised that even though I hadn't been focusing on 'us' – as it really was more about Billy's mental health – I needed to think about it to some degree, otherwise I ran the risk of it all just slipping away without my even realising it. I felt I could do that because he was at least able to hold a conversation, but I was under no illusion that he was really all that much better.

Everything I had read about trying to save a marriage in trouble talked about both partners wanting to make it work. Well, that was where my trouble had been. What if one of you didn't even want to live another day, let alone work at a marriage? Our marriage had been the last thing on Billy's mind, if it had even been there at all. And even then, when he seemed to be on more of an even keel, he still wasn't ready to think about something as mundane as our marriage. I know that sounds harsh but, when your life is at stake, relationships with other people are way down on the list. Billy certainly didn't have a clue what I needed and, even if he did, he wouldn't have been capable of supplying it. Irrespective of any elevation in mood – indeed, ever since Billy's breakdown – more often than not, the only indication I got from his demeanour or his actions that in any way distinguished his relationship to me as closer than just a random acquaintance was the odd verbal exchange or a fleeting look in his eye. It was a look that seemed to hold some level of acknowledgement, or reminiscence, of what we had once shared.

Most of the time, I could have been anybody – just a person off the street who happened to be sharing his living space. I was acutely aware that that wouldn't change just because he was a bit more stable. It was going to take much more than that. Right from the beginning, it had been obvious to me that I would have to be the one to initiate contact, otherwise what fragile connection we may have had would be in serious danger of dissolving for good – which I had done – but as time went by it got to the point where I became desperate to keep any kind of link with him, however small it may have been.

To achieve that, I found that I had to come up with different ways of preserving and maintaining that link. Then, as he got worse, and those attempts at communication failed, and when a hug or any other physical displays of love and support were simply not tolerated or reciprocated, I had to get creative.

One morning, quite by chance, I stumbled across the perfect solution. I had been intending to kiss him on the cheek before I left for work but, as I bent down to him, I saw him stiffen and recoil. It was a very slight movement but it was enough for me to notice. I remember, just after it happened, I had been upset that even kissing his cheek had become too much. I had felt a stab of hurt and, for a moment, my feelings were bruised, but then I told myself, for the zillionth time, that he wasn't himself and it wasn't about me.

As soon as I noticed that apprehension, I knew that he didn't want me to kiss him. But I was right there in front of him, just about to lean forward, so I just sort of stuck my hand out instead. I think it was more out of embarrassment than anything else. I can't remember what I was thinking. Maybe I was just going to touch his face or something but, as it happened, my pointer finger had been sticking out and, before I knew it, Billy copied me and our pointer fingers touched. It was such a simple gesture but I guess because Billy participated it actually meant more than a one-sided kiss. It was small enough for him to accept, yet big enough to secure a connection – even if it was just a tiny thread of a connection.

Perhaps it was more of a spiritual connection than a physical one but, regardless, it was integral and, from then on, it stuck. It became the one thing that he always managed to respond to, except for the intense, unresponsive phases when nothing worked. All I had to do was proffer my finger, gently instigating contact, and he would respond by tentatively reaching out until we touched. More often than not, it would only be a moment before he withdrew again but, even so, as minuscule as it was, I felt like it was keeping him from completely succumbing to the baneful quagmire of his mind.

In any case, more stable or not, he still was nowhere near the point where our relationship would benefit. Billy still pretty much never instigated contact and, on the rare occasion when he was able to handle a bit more intimacy, he was still only capable of putting up with the odd hug, which he literally just managed now and again. But, even so, they were empty cuddles. If anything, they made me feel worse than if he hadn't touched me at all because those limp hugs, the ones where I was doing the squeezing for two, made me feel lonely. More lonely than I had ever felt before. I knew I would have felt less alone by myself.

Throughout my life, I have never really experienced much loneliness at all but, if I ever do, it is in the company of others, usually with the exception of Billy. Even that changed. After his breakdown, having Billy 'there' at the same time as 'not there' gave me a window into the immensity of ordinary human loneliness, and painfully sharpened my own sense of isolation.

People think being around other people stops you from feeling lonely. But, you see, that is what I have always found ironic. For me, feeling lonely isn't about the level of company I keep with other people. I know for a lot of people – most, in fact – being lonely is about being alone. Technically, of course, that is what 'lonely' is by definition. Actually, my dictionary says lonely means '*without companions; solitary*'. So, with that in mind, I guess it depends on whether a person views 'solitary' as having a positive or negative connotation. I have always viewed solitude to be the welcome absence of others. And, strangely, I viewed the time I spent with Billy as *being* solitary – as if the two of us were one person. Maybe that was because we worked so well together.

Before Billy's breakdown, the periods of silence that inhabited a lot of our time were, for the most part, companionable and appreciated. Unfortunately, that wasn't the case after the breakdown. Then, more than ever, being *completely* solitary was my preferred state. Surely there are people out there who know what I mean when I say being *with* people can be lonelier.

What I know for sure is that can I boost my resolve and get strength from myself. Don't get me wrong, I love all the people in my life very much who are important to me. I value them, of course I do. I always have. I spend time with them. Fine. I enjoy it even. Perhaps if I didn't have those opportunities, I suppose I wouldn't enjoy my time alone as much and, perhaps, if I really *was* living a completely solitary existence, with no family or friends at all, I would actually come to crave company. I don't know. But, as it was, I basically just wanted to be left alone.

Without a doubt, during the bad times, I saw less of people but, even before Billy's breakdown, I've always been the type of person who has very few people around. After the breakdown, more than ever, I really just relied on myself. At the risk of sounding incredibly cruel and callous, I didn't get much from my relationships with other people during that time. At least not in the helping-to-feel-better kind of way. I may have bounced ideas or thoughts off the people in my life, and I may have asked their opinion on things but, essentially, when I was sad, mad, scared, worried, happy, excited and so on, it was to myself that I initially turned. If that is what being introverted means, then I guess I am introverted. Put simply, I just got my biggest support from within.

I feel lucky because of that. It's kind of like that buzz you get with another person when you are totally on the same wavelength – and, to be fair, I do get that with other people and it's great. It is simply a bigger buzz when it is your mind and your soul that are in sync and on the same wavelength. I don't really know if it is weird that my best friend is myself. I guess it makes me sort of selfish and I suspect I'm not that great a friend to have. I mean, I get to feel satisfied and pleased if, or when, I help my friends but I'm not allowing them to experience how good that feels. There's a word for that, isn't there?

Despite Billy, and perhaps because of me, the structure of our marriage was crumbling. It had been for a long time but, while all the damage was being insidiously done to the foundation, I could choose not to notice. Then, ironically, with the arrival of a bit of an improvement, it was visible to me. It was falling down. The cracks were becoming more noticeable and it was only a matter of time before it would be damaged beyond repair. I felt like Billy was picking away at it with a chisel and I was the support brace that was starting to weaken – which, as I say, was strange since mentally he was more stable. I suppose, in the back of my mind, I needed him to be so much better than just stable. In truth, I needed a participant. However, in order truly to believe that even if things did fall down they could be rebuilt, and they could be rebuilt stronger, I must have still had something in reserve, otherwise I would have given up, when instead I knew I had to come up with a plan. A plan that involved listening to my intuition and trusting myself to do the right thing. And at that point, that meant giving him some more time and sticking together.

For the months after his breakdown, I alone had to keep us on track, or at least to keep us from going down. I just had to keep on keeping on. But I didn't know for how long, and that was the hard part. I couldn't risk Billy regressing and I was stressed because I didn't know if it would all go bad again. Nothing really had happened to change other than Billy not abusing alcohol. It couldn't all go away just like that. Whatever caused it in the first place was still there so what was stopping it from happening again? I was constantly on edge.

It was obvious to me, mostly by his constant look of confusion, surprise and being out of his depth – that sense of being 'lost' had surrounded his being right from the beginning – that nothing in his childhood had prepared him for the notion of love, happiness or stability. The early damage, whatever it was, had become such a part of him it had persuaded him that he would remain empty and 'not worthy', for all of his life, and to expect nothing more.

I had no clue how to change that. Where would I even begin? The task seemed insurmountable and I knew then, for the first time, that our marriage was in real trouble. And I was scared.

PART III

STARS AND CRACKS

INTRODUCTION
(After)

By the late 1990s I knew for sure my husband was broken – scarred by something. Something he wouldn't, or perhaps couldn't, talk about. At first I told myself that if he had a secret I would have known. We had been together for so long – surely I would have known. But then I realised what an inherent contradiction that was – for if I had known it wouldn't have been a secret. As he spiralled out of control, I had to cling to my beliefs; my belief in Billy; my belief in myself; my belief in us. I needed to find out why Billy noticed the cracks in the pavement while all the while I had been struggling to get him to see the stars.

To say that everything happens for a reason is the sort of thing that is said to try to convince ourselves that things will be all right – to somehow make us feel better. As if the belief that there is some sort of divine path justifies the bad things that happen. Maybe we do it to make sense out of the unfairness of life but whether you believe it or not it seems that this saying certainly enables acceptance and hope where otherwise there might just be perplexity. You may not recognise the reason or be able to figure out why something has happened straight away but eventually it will become clear. At least it will if you are open to such things.

I had become increasingly aware of the synchronicity of our lives. Seeing things that had happened over the span of both of our lives and gaining an insight into why they may have occurred and not only that but marvelling at the outcome and the timing of specific events. Things would have been different if either of us had followed a different path; if we hadn't moved to Canada; if we hadn't had to endure years of endless and futile fertility treatment; if, indeed, either IVF attempt had been successful; if Hannah hadn't died when she did. Even other people's actions, choices and decisions affected *our* lives. So many things out of our control happened to somehow propel us to that place. I could feel it – I just didn't understand it. There was a strange kind of omen that I couldn't put my finger on.

9

IF GOD HAS A
MASTER PLAN

In the dark of the night
In the light of the day
I feel them walk my way
Tell me what have you seen
Tell me where have you been

'Coming Home' by Kevin Young

I arrived at work one Monday, in April of 2000, to find a message that Billy's sister had rung the day before. The note said that she would ring back that afternoon. I felt sick with apprehension. 'What now?' I said out loud.

I was worried something bad had happened again, especially since I couldn't help but be reminded of the phone call that seemed to have been the catalyst of all the heartache of the past few years. I wondered why she had rung me at work. I had been home all weekend so I knew she had not rung there. I was anxious to find out what was wrong, especially since I knew that she wouldn't just be ringing to say hello.

I really didn't think Billy could handle more upset. I tortured myself with morbid thoughts and convinced myself that Billy's sister had contacted me at work because she couldn't face Billy answering and then having to break the bad news. What the bad news was, I couldn't guess, but I was sure it was something terrible.

I dreaded the phone call and contemplated pulling a sickie and going home, or maybe taking the phone off the hook – anything to delay the inevitable. How in God's name was I going to tell Billy?

Things had quietened down since Christmas but we were far from OK. Things had been damaged and I began to have trouble remembering how things were supposed to be. I found myself nervous and jumpy – scared of doing or saying something, anything, that might rock the boat. Billy was better, in as much as he was a bit more mentally stable and his behaviour wasn't so erratic, but he was still very depressed. The medication had been given the chance to work somewhat, as he wasn't drinking at all, but getting the concoction of medications right and then figuring out the right dose is something that in itself takes a long time, *and* the side-effects were such that he was never clear-headed. So, actually, Billy really wasn't all that much better.

And I didn't know how much more I could give.

Billy didn't really remember all that had gone on over the past few years, as if he had been in some sort of fugue state. He certainly didn't realise just how bad it had been at times or indeed for how long it had been going on. I remember once he made reference to something that had happened months before as being just a few weeks before.

The effect of this was that he wasn't capable of recognising what I'd gone through. I knew it wasn't his fault that he wasn't able to recall it all, which I have to admit was probably a good thing, but, at the same time, to be honest, I was desperate to be validated. I so wanted to hear him acknowledge what I had gone through and to know that, even though practically everyone had advised me to dump him, I had hung in there and stayed true to him.

In actuality, though, what I had gone through was nothing compared to what was, and had been, going on in Billy's head, so he really wasn't in a position to give me any compassion. The potentially fatal blow to our marriage, however, was the fact that I wasn't aware of the true cause of his turmoil.

All through that spring morning, I tried to keep my mind off Billy's sister and the impending phone call. I took the children to the beach in an effort to put aside my concerns. I didn't tell Billy that his sister rang for I knew that, if nothing else, for whatever reason, she didn't want him to know. I fed the children and put them all down for their afternoon nap. And then I waited.

When the phone call came, it can only adequately be described as another defining moment in my life. I think, probably, the enormous relief of discovering that no one else had died, coupled with what I found out was the real reason for the phone call, ensured that I will never forget it. Billy's sister certainly had no idea that what she was telling me was having such an impact. She only had to say one sentence and I immediately felt an overwhelming sense of relief, dismay and vindication all rolled into one.

'You know what you asked me when you were over that Christmas?' she said.

'Yes,' I replied, knowing full well that she was referring to my question about whether she had any knowledge of Billy experiencing any sexual abuse while he'd been in care.

'It's about that,' she said, obviously not able to bring herself even to voice the words 'sexual abuse'.

In the time it took for her to explain that a detective investigating historical childhood abuse had contacted her in an effort to locate Billy, whose name had appeared on the list of children who had attended the home in question, I experienced the full gamut of emotions. I was struggling all the while to concentrate on everything that she was saying. I think I probably missed half of it – my mind was so caught up in the enormity of it all.

When I got off the phone, all I could recall was that one of the detectives was going to phone the following day. I just stood by the phone, immobile from every kind of emotional agony. I felt light-headed and so very unburdened. I was relieved but I was also excited, scared, worried, angry, sad, and so, *so* glad.

I couldn't quite believe what had just happened. For two long years, I had fought and prayed to get to the bottom of what had been at the centre of Billy's breakdown and then, completely unexpectedly and totally out of the blue, it was unveiled. It didn't even matter that I didn't actually know what they were investigating. It was enough because I knew what it was about. I knew, without hearing any of the details. I was shaky with excitement and enveloped in an immediate shroud of validation. I was so relieved I felt like screaming from the rooftops the biggest 'I TOLD YOU SO' to everyone who had doubted me. It was so hard to believe that, in the space of ten minutes, I'd gone from being totally stressed out, anticipating the phone call, to such relief.

My mum was the first person I told. 'You'll never guess what!' I excitedly gasped. 'I knew it… something bad *did* happen to Billy… it made him the way he is!' I explained what little I knew and told her I would just have to wait until the detective phoned me the next day. I was on such a high I didn't think about what the discovery would actually mean. I hadn't thought that far yet.

The rest of the afternoon followed in a blur of diaper-changing, snack time and pick-up. It wasn't until the last child had left that it suddenly hit me that it was terrible of me to be so excited. It wouldn't be welcome news to Billy. After all, he knew. He had known all along. It *wouldn't* be a great discovery for him. He probably had been trying to keep it hidden his whole life. I quickly realised my salvation was really a Pandora's box.

On the drive home from work, I couldn't stop my mind from tripping round and round in circles. I wondered – and all those thoughts of mine crowded together in the span of a few moments at the intersection of Fort and Foul Bay, waiting at a red light – I wondered if it would all be too much, if Billy would benefit from exposing his torment, if he would agree to talk to the police, if he would be able to vocalise the details and if I was strong enough to help him through it all. The thoughts came rushing at me, depriving me of air, and were all cause for concern and anxiety. I consciously shifted my gaze to what was positive and clutched at optimism. I decided I wouldn't mention it to Billy, at least not until I had talked to the detective. I don't know how I got through that night without Billy noticing my obvious preoccupation.

The following day, I again received several unrelated phone calls – which of course, only served to heighten my anxiety – before I actually got the one I had been waiting for.

'Hello, Mrs Chapel… DC Liam Harris here, from South Wales Police. Thank you for agreeing to speak with me.'

His soft, melodious accent conjured up an image of my Celtic saviour. The man who belonged to that voice was going to save our marriage. As wildly dramatic as that sounds, it was a certainty to me because he was going to be the catalyst who would unravel the information that I needed to hear.

'Oh... um... yes... hello,' I stammered.

'I suppose your sister-in-law told you who I am.'

'Um, yes... she did,' I answered pathetically. Oh, Christ, I must have sounded a complete idiot. I tried desperately to pull myself together. I had experienced so many emotions in such a short time I seemed to have lost my ability to form proper sentences.

'Do you know why I'm calling?' he asked.

'Um, well... yes... I think so,' I answered, still stammering hopelessly.

'Why don't you tell me what your sister-in-law told you and what you think this is all about.'

After finally finding my voice, I told him what I remembered of the conversation that I had had with Billy's sister the previous day. My heart was pounding so hard I was sure he must be able to hear it. I then said, 'Your records show that Billy was in care and I think you are ringing to see if Billy was abused while in the homes.'

'Do you think your husband holds any information that could be of interest to this inquiry?'

'Yes, definitely,' I replied after only the tiniest hiccup of hesitation.

'Right... has he told you about anything specific?'

'No, but he recently had a mental breakdown of sorts and I have always been sure that something from his past triggered it.'

'Right then... do you think he would be all right with us asking him to tell us what he knows?' he asked.

'I think so,' I answered cautiously.

He hesitated slightly, then said, 'Do you think he would be hostile at all?'

'Oh, um...' I paused, taken aback by his question and not really understanding. 'Er... no... I don't think so. I mean, he doesn't like the police... but that's only because of his past.' I quickly added the last bit, trying to explain and wanting to stick up for Billy. I didn't want him to get the wrong impression. 'Why? Are some people actually hostile towards you?' I naively asked, as an afterthought.

'You'd be surprised,' he replied knowingly.

'Oh, right…' I murmured. Not my world.

'OK, Mrs Chapel. Perhaps you could tell Billy that I rang. The operation is called Operation Goldfinch and we would be grateful to speak with him. Please ask him if he has any information that may be of interest to us and if he would be willing to talk with me. I'll ring you again tomorrow to see how you got on.'

'Yes, OK,' I replied, before he hung up.

At the end of my work day, I drove home, just as I had done the day before. Preoccupied. There was a circus in my head that prevented me from thinking clearly or focusing on the traffic, as I should have been. The proverbial elephant was charging about, already disturbed from his safe place in the room. And the clown? I knew he would be agitated because I was going to take his mask off.

I drove on auto-pilot and, once home, I couldn't remember getting there. As soon as I went in the house, I sat Billy down in the front room. There was nothing for it – I had to broach the subject straight away. 'I have something to ask you, Billy. It is really hard and I don't know where to start. So I'm just going to ask you… when you were a little boy… um… when you were in care… were you abused?'

*   *   *

'Chapel! Get out here this minute! I told you. No talking after lights out!'

'It weren't me, sir. I never talked. Honest I didn't.'

'Now!'

Billy swung his legs out of bed and stepped on to the freezing floor. He was shaken from the shock of the outburst. He'd almost been asleep and it took a moment for the harsh command to register, which seemed to anger the dark figure silhouetted in the doorway. Billy knew who it was.

Upon reaching the doorway, Billy noticed he was wearing striped pyjamas and a dressing gown. Billy was confused, unsure why he had been taken from his bed when everybody else appeared to be asleep and especially since no one had been talking. He was then pushed down the passage – the strong grip of the man's hand pinching between his neck and his left shoulder. He thought it odd that no more words were spoken to him.

He found himself approaching an open door at the end of the corridor. He *was shocked to see that it was a small bedroom, and then realised that the man must actually stop overnight, too. In the short time he had been in the home, he had never thought about who was there at night. It simply hadn't ever occurred to him. He had been too busy pining for his mam and siblings. He hadn't really even clued in when he had seen him wearing pyjamas.*

Billy was pushed into the room and then on to the single bed that had been positioned up against the opposite wall. The room was stark and it gave no clues as to whether it was the man's own room or not. There were no personal touches. Nothing was on the bedside table. No clothes were hanging anywhere. It was just cold and uninviting.

Billy didn't register any potential threat. He had no sense of unease, and wasn't experiencing any concern. Even the manner in which it all came about hadn't alerted him. The man sat down beside Billy and put his arm around his shoulder then leaned down and kissed him on the cheek. It wasn't a prolonged kiss. Billy didn't expect anything bad from such seemingly caring, yet uncharacteristic, behaviour. Shouting and violence were the only warning signals he had learned.

Billy was then pushed back so that he lay on the bed facing the ceiling. It really wasn't until the tall figure stood up, turned to face him and began undoing the belt of his dressing gown and fiddling with the front of his pyjama bottoms that Billy began to sense instinctively that something wasn't right.

He pulled down Billy's pyjamas and then sat down on the bed right beside his bare legs, but Billy had closed his eyes by then so he wasn't sure exactly what he was doing. He heard moaning but it seemed to be farther away than just right beside him and it seemed to go on for a long time. He wasn't sure why exactly, but he felt sick and petrified. He hadn't hurt him; he had touched him, but he hadn't really hurt him. His feelings confused him. More than anything, Billy just wished he hadn't gone with him out of the dormitory without creating a fuss.

Once back in his own bed, Billy didn't sleep at all. He simply just lay there, staring at the ceiling.

The next night it was a long time before Billy finally closed his eyes in sleep. What had happened the night before troubled him a great deal. There had been no chance to tell anyone at all that day, not that he would have been able to as he was more than a bit embarrassed and quite scared. So bedtime found him still the only keeper of the terrible secret.

THE THROWAWAY BOY

It was at that point that Billy's bad childhood turned into a horrific one. The reality of it hit him at breakfast two mornings later. There was little wonder that, after he had a mouthful of toast – more out of fear of refusing to eat than because he had any appetite for it – he was sick. And then during the days that followed, his head full of a strange dark fear and an anxiety that he didn't understand, the sickness welled up again.

It was the beginning of the stuff that permanent scars are made of.

* * *

I silently waited – waited until Billy felt able to answer such a painful and, what I could only imagine to be, embarrassing and potentially shame-provoking question. There was a sort of persistent grimness about him as an aura of something sinister invaded the air around us. Little by little, his vision darkened as he began the slide into the terrible place of his childhood memory. He blinked and his mouth worked a little, then he swallowed, but he seemed to have no notion of how to reply. He didn't move, although I could tell his mind was working overtime, as the burden of the past sat heavy on his shoulders. Finally, just as I was becoming resigned to the fact that he might not even answer me, he murmured very faintly, in a voice that sounded almost childlike, 'Will you still love me?'

The look on my face of initial shock and horror, etched by my anticipation of what was to come, quickly turned to one of compassion mingled with love. 'Of course I will!' I cried.

He stood up then and began quickly pacing back and forth in an extremely agitated manner. It looked a particularly odd action as he only moved a few feet either way. Then the frantic movement of rubbing the back of his left hand, and halfway up his left arm, with the palm of his right, heightened the already tense atmosphere. Every movement, mannerism and action exemplified the intensity of his anxiety.

'Yes, I was,' he finally replied, barely audible. 'A lot.'

I closed my eyes in an effort to stop the tears that had gathered in my eyes and were in danger of spilling over on to my cheeks. I didn't want Billy to misinterpret my tears. He never seemed to judge my emotions with any accuracy at all, tending always to get the wrong end of the stick. When I opened my eyes, the room seemed darker, like the dimmer on the light switch had somehow been turned down, sort of as a reminder of just how sordid this world can be. Deep down, I had known it was true. I had for a long time, but actually to hear Billy admit it out loud was shocking and incredibly sad.

His obvious heartache was a palpable thing, his face etched with dismay. With each tear that dripped down his face and off his chin, I could sense their cathartic power. A power born from years of pent-up, unshed tears that were finally being released.

I hugged him, wanting to nurture and protect the frightened little boy I knew he still was, but I could feel him stiff and resistant within my embrace. After a time, I explained about the phone calls from his sister and the detective. I could see by the gaping look of bewilderment on his face that he, too, was struggling to comprehend it all. His past had risen up and overwhelmed his present in the space of a few startled minutes, and it showed. A look of raw incredulity flickered on his face. It was obviously a bolt out of the blue for him as well.

I knew he needed some space, some time alone to let it sink in. I did as well, so I decided to have a bath. We couldn't talk about it yet. It was too big. I kissed Billy and told him to come into the bathroom if he wanted to talk or, if not, just to sit beside the bath surrounded by the soothing tranquillity of my candles.

I lay in the bath letting the hot lavender-scented water wash over me. The collection of candles, multiplied by the reflection of the tiles, flickered and danced in the darkness, their glow conducive of the desired effect. I could feel myself relaxing but I was aware of a slight feeling of foreboding. I had been certain there was something there, hidden in Billy's past, and I now wondered if it was going to come back – come back, get him and take him. I was so relieved to have finally been given the answer but I was strangely apprehensive at the same time.

Uncovering the truth would undoubtedly give Billy the possibility of salvation, yet it held a potential threat, too. What if confronting it, and in such an exposed fashion, were to drag him back down to the depths of despair? It would certainly cause a great deal of pain, there could be no doubting that. I thought for a moment, just a split-second really, that maybe it would be better to leave it all hidden. Maybe if it all came out it wouldn't actually help, but make it worse. However, deep down, I knew it was best to exorcise it and annihilate it once and for all. Yet again, there I was, faced with the knowledge that we were nowhere near the light at the end of the tunnel. Thankfully, though, my faith still enabled me to believe that there was indeed a light.

I tried to recall when I had first had suspicions that sexual abuse may have occurred. I knew it was before I went to Cardiff in 1998 because it was one of the things I had asked Billy's family about. I think I had had niggling suspicions for ages before, but I hadn't acknowledged them. It was as if they had been bouncing around inside my head, but, with nowhere to file them, nothing to log them under, I had left them unidentified and unexplained. There had been a lot of coverage in the news in British Columbia about the historical sexual abuse of North American Indians in residential schools and also many stories about Catholic priests abusing children as well. All of that certainly made me question, in the light of Billy's breakdown, the likelihood of Billy being a victim as well. There were also little things that had come up over the years that individually weren't particularly significant but, nevertheless, when all the little things were put together, coupled with all the coverage in the media, certainly led me to question.

Then in 1999 I watched a made-for-TV movie about a professional hockey player, Sheldon Kennedy, who had been sexually abused as a young boy by his coach. The film was, without question, moving, and would have been heart-rending and inspirational to anyone who watched it, but personally it really touched me. So many times I was reminded of Billy throughout the movie. It wasn't one specific thing, it was a culmination of lots of things: his behaviour; the way he treated his wife; the way he was sabotaging his happiness and his love of the game; the way he tried to push his wife away; his displays of self-loathing, shame and fear that so reminded me of Billy. All of those things were like a bunch of light switches that one by one had been turned on in my head. However, perhaps the biggest indication came when Billy came in as I was watching the movie. He sat down and started to watch it but, within a very short space of time, his mood completely altered. 'What are you watching this shite for?' he snapped.

I was shocked at his outburst and gaped incredulously at him. Before I could say anything, he announced he was going to bed. At the time, I just thought he was a moody freak and continued watching the movie. I'm not sure when I put it all together and actually came up with my conclusion. It was both a conscious and subconscious thing, I think. There I was, my brain and my thoughts, sort of simultaneously chugging along, when suddenly all my thoughts jolted and rearranged and, in an instant, I had my theory. I did not physically falter from the jerk of my revelation, but I felt as if I had.

I clearly remember that, at the end of the film, Sheldon Kennedy came on and talked in person about his struggle and his fight for justice. How incredibly brave he must have been to go public and report his abuser. I recall thinking that, if Billy had been abused, he would never come forward, so I must have related it to him then, at least to some extent. I just couldn't picture any scenario where that would happen.

Not in my wildest dreams did I expect that the chance for Billy to get justice would actually present itself to him, instead of the other way round. I couldn't believe it.

It would seem that my amateurish attempts at something akin to necromancy had actually paid off. The portent from beyond validated months after its bidding. Hannah must have played a part, or maybe Granda somehow acknowledging my perception. The detective actually contacting us, bringing it all out into the open, and at just the right time, was so fortuitous. Coincidence? Happenstance? I didn't think so. I may have been too long in a hot bath but I believed divine forces must be at play. I thought of it as a serendipitous event that, although kick-starting a journey that would undoubtedly be Billy's hardest struggle, I was convinced it would also, essentially, be a lifeline. It was a benign, yet glorious outcome which resulted from the timely intertwining of a few obliging strings of fate. A result that I didn't even know I had been waiting for.

I was just about to get out of the bath, my prune-like skin becoming chilly in the cooling water, when Billy came in and sat down on the floor beside the bath.

'I don't think I can do it,' he said.

'You *can* do it… you managed to survive under traumatic, even soul-destroying conditions, where others would not have done. I can only imagine the horror you were put through but you have come through it all a sensitive, caring and funny person. All that awfulness didn't make you a nasty man, without a sense of humour, did it?'

'I dunno… I'm just me.'

'Well, you must have been courageous!' After a time, I added, 'That a man could take advantage of a child in that way is vile, so horrendous, it is inconceivable to me. How you ever coped with it I will never know, but you must have been a very brave little boy… and you still are. You were incredibly strong to go through what you have. So you *can* do it. The question is – do you want to?'

'Why should I help the police? They never helped me.'

'It's not about helping them… it is about helping yourself! Don't you see that!'

'They don't care about me… they just want to look good themselves. The big coppers solving all the crimes,' he sneered.

'Billy, who cares about them? Whether they care about you or not, care about yourself! People suffer such terrible things but human beings are tremendously resilient, you know. You of all people are proof of that. Actually, you'd probably be surprised at what you can live through, because I don't think you've ever acknowledged to yourself how strong and brave you've been. You've spent so long trying to push it aside that you never noticed. Living with all those feelings all bottled up will have been incredibly hard, too. Imagine how you might feel a few years from now, when it is all over, and you aren't hiding any more. That has got to be worth it!'

'That's easy for you to say!'

'Oh, I know. It's going to be so, so hard. I'm just trying to show you that you can do it… just think about it, Billy.'

'Aye.' Billy got up and made to walk out of the bathroom. He stopped in the doorway and said quietly, 'I just want live-over days.'

'What?' I asked.

'Live-over days – days so perfect you want to live them over, instead of just wanting to forget them. Maybe the only way is to get it all out once and for all.'

I *knew* we, as a couple, had actually had some damn good days. Days that I certainly considered to be 'live-over days'. Days where everything was perfect. The fact that Billy couldn't appreciate them was a testament to how all-encompassing his torment was. The black cloud cast a shadow over everything.

I hoped he would decide to talk to the detective. It sounded as though he was leaning that way. I knew he would have to come to the decision himself and I would support whatever decision he made. I reminded myself that, if I could survive never knowing the child that was meant to be ours, and if I could survive the last two years not even knowing what I was dealing with, then I could get through that struggle and help Billy to survive it, too. Whatever his decision, he was going to need a lot of support.

Billy thought about it all through that night. He knew that he had been keeping the dark secrets of his childhood hidden away and he realised that he had kidded himself all those years ago when he thought he could just make them go away by moving. He could see that moving had been the right choice in that, if he had stayed in the UK, he most likely would have led a very different life, one probably of crime and self-destruction. It had given him the chance at a better life, which, to a certain extent, he had achieved, but he began to realise that it all had been futile as everything was starting to catch up with him anyway.

When the chance to move to Canada had come up, he had grabbed it, deciding to get away – well away. He had thought that moving would be the perfect solution, surmising that it would be so much easier to forget his past if he was in a completely different country. He hadn't realised, you see, that just moving away, and going on living, wasn't going to take him away from his past. He thought it would. He thought it had to – that distance and time would just sort of cover it over after a while, but it hadn't.

Moving away may have allowed him to compartmentalise all of his bad memories into the place where it all happened, and then to distance himself from that place, but Hannah's death and all his flashbacks were ensuring he was reminded, even in Canada. He had taken himself somewhere else physically but, ultimately, he couldn't achieve what he wanted because he couldn't stop himself from being mentally taken back to the place of childhood. And that place, that childhood place, was the one place he didn't want to be, because he didn't want to be surrounded by all the horribly tangible memories – of all the things that he had tried to run away from, and of all the things he didn't want to remember.

He was terrified of talking to the police and opening up the whole can of worms but he knew that, if he didn't, it really wasn't ever truly going to go away. He knew he needed finally to purge himself – go to the very core of his being, the centre of his psyche, and there he found once again the hidden resources, the strength that pulled him through all those years ago.

It was that strength of character and a determination finally to put the past to rest and start anew – to make some sort of life for us – that propelled him forward and brought him to the decision to talk to the detectives and tell them what he remembered.

10
STILL STANDING

Secrets are deep
Secrets are cruel
Secrets make you everybody's fool
You beat them back down
You beat them back down

'Secrets' by Paul Barns

Billy's decision to talk to South Wales Police was not an easy one. He came to it after a lot of deliberation and, even after countless conversations with DC Liam Harris and the whole thing had been set in motion, there were many times when he questioned the wisdom of his decision.

To think that it was going to be a hard journey was such an understatement. We both had to cling to the belief that Billy was doing the right thing, even though, at times, we couldn't help but wonder.

Also, even though Billy had made the decision to talk to the police, it wasn't as simple as that. The habits of a bad childhood are very difficult to abandon. He had become so accustomed, first as a young boy then throughout his adulthood, at pushing things away that it was not as easy as just agreeing to talk about it for the words to come out. He had to extract and then articulate his memories as slowly, laboriously, painfully and dangerously as if he were surgically removing a tooth without any knowledge of dentistry.

Over the years, he had inadvertently pushed even the smallest memories far, far away from himself. He never wanted to face the memories of his childhood – better to forget them – better still to pretend that they did not exist. But they did. His childhood was built on the foundation of those memories – layered one on top of the other. They were so shocking and painful to bear that he had done the only thing possible. He had obliterated them. This worked well at the time, allowing Billy to cope, in a fashion, but the images he had thrust aside were indelibly imprinted on his brain, so much so that they existed inside him – in his soul. Just deciding that he was ready to expel them didn't mean they would come willingly.

The difficulty of extracting it all meant that DC Harris had his work cut out. First, he had to build up a trust and rapport with Billy that slowly allowed him to open up. He didn't pressurise or rush him. The whole procedure was particularly hard for Billy and DC Harris as it was done over the phone, and also because Billy had adopted a sort of selective mutism on the subject of his past and his feelings, so it was like a double whammy. Not only did they have to access the memory, but Billy also had to figure out how to vocalise it all.

And so, time passed. Throughout the whole summer of 2000, we existed between the phone calls in a sort of limbo. Obviously, there was a lot to get through so it took a long time and meant that many calls were necessary. We never knew when DC Harris would phone back – sometimes a few weeks would go by. Billy dreaded the phone calls but, at the same time, if there was too long between them he would then get a false sense of reprieve – kidding himself that maybe they would never actually phone again. Then, when the next conversation eventually took place, it was with yet another jolt back to reality.

During the phone calls between DC Harris and Billy, I made myself scarce. Partly to give Billy privacy, but also because I didn't want to hear any details. There was just no room in my brain for such atrocities. I could only cope with the knowledge that he was actually abused that way by treating it as though it had happened to somebody else, or was something that I had seen in a movie. I just couldn't go there.

Understandably, there were some very bad days, during which time his cynicism and bitterness completely took over. Days when he would be argumentative, extremely moody or very reclusive. Totally understandable, of course. In fact, I would have been worried if he hadn't been like that. Mostly, though, he was just so, so tired all the time. He looked so obviously weary as well, shrouded in extreme emotion – the exhaustive weight of it.

But it wasn't as hard to witness as it had been in the beginning, because just having the knowledge of what was causing it made all the difference. It enabled me to have a feeling of empathy and a certain level of understanding without worrying about what the problem was. Even so, I couldn't stop myself from worrying that he would be wounded forever by the injustice of his childhood and the dreadful ordeal of reliving it all, his soul being damaged beyond repair. I really didn't know if he would be or not, but I was optimistic that, if he worked very hard at getting it all out and if I supported him as best I could, the gaping, bloody wounds would have a chance to heal and then, one day, he might only have the scars left as a reminder instead of the torment that had been so destructive.

I wished I could just snap my fingers and that, miraculously, time would pass, allowing Billy the benefit of it all coming out without the pain of getting to that point. I was aware that not a day went by when he wasn't haunted by the echoes of his past. There was no respite from the horrible, destructive memories. Day or night, asleep or awake, they were etched on his soul.

Slowly, over time, Billy divulged snippets bit by bit, but never in any detail. He seemed to find it easier to tell me things about his childhood in a way he hadn't before. Actually, he talked a lot about things, considering he still spent most of his time in seclusion in the basement. Mostly, his talks consisted of pieces of information that he would reveal out of the blue. Little snapshots that a little bit at a time gave me a window into his past.

The best thing about his newfound openness was that we could talk so much more about sensitive subjects. I could ask him questions about things that he previously had refused to talk about, like his emotions – how things made him feel, why certain things caused him to become so upset, or why sometimes he became so angry. Obviously, he didn't always *know* why and, most of the time, he had trouble making the connections, and I certainly couldn't always ask him at the time, but usually I could at least bring stuff up and Billy would be receptive.

So many things became clear as a result of those conversations. I learned that the reason he was often in a mood after he'd had a bath was because bath time had been one of the times when abuse took place. Again, Billy didn't elaborate but it still explained a lot to me. He also disclosed how, during the abuse, he learned to fly away.

*　　*　　*

Billy couldn't really say that he was in pain – which was odd, because he was, and he knew that he was, but part of him didn't feel it. He felt like it was as though he was remembering the pain from the first horrific experiences, not what he was currently going through.

His ability to remove himself from it was something that happened over time. The ability had started as a kind of staring – fixating on something until everything around him kind of zoned out. It wasn't a conscious effort that had been learned or developed on purpose. Once, he just found himself floating above it all, on an even better level. If that feeling could have been put to music, or described by music, it would have been the song from The Snowman. *Billy actually liked the experience and wished, in some ways, that he could experience it more often. It was the only time he felt light and free. It was poignant, yet so very ironic, that his best experiences only happened during the absolute worst.*

*　　*　　*

I knew he meant that he mentally flew to escape, as is common with many traumatised children. I had read about that coping strategy – how the mind has a marvellous capacity to escape when the body can't – the subconscious mind providing creative solutions to the horror of daily life. It is viewed as a survival mechanism that psychologists call 'dissociation'. Billy had managed to escape simply by retreating into himself and dreaming. He would escape the awfulness and go to another place, any place he wished. It made his young life more tolerable. He dreamed of having his very own puppy and frolicking with him in lush green fields. He dreamed of being a bird and flying around in the dark night sky, looking down at the world below. He dreamed of cars and motorbikes. He dreamed of simple things – but, to him, those dreams were a lifeline.

I found out why he had an affinity with birds. Well, all animals really, but especially birds. He said that, as a young boy, he always felt like he was like them, that they didn't belong to anyone, and neither did he. He said he used to watch them flying around by themselves and he always wondered if they were lonely, too. He also said that he felt like he could relate to them. I found that particularly odd and, when I asked Billy what he meant, he really couldn't explain it, except to say that he understood the feeling of looking down at the world below.

Now I think I understand it – I think because he experienced so much trauma when he was so young, and he spent such a lot of time mentally taking himself away from the horror, his mind still remembers the feeling of being outside of himself and, to a certain extent, feels comfortable that way.

I also heard about his antics while on the run, how, during the winter months, he would hang around in car parks and lie on the bonnets of cars that had just been parked in an effort to get even the slightest bit of warmth from the engine, and how he liked the night-time best as he could wander about scavenging for food without worrying about being spotted. I found the stories of his nocturnal habits especially touching and it was then that I started calling him 'badger'.

He had bursts where he was so much more talkative. Perhaps it was because, through talking things over with Liam, as he now called him, he had become more in touch with himself and his feelings.

*   *   *

At the back of his mam's house was a stretch of rough grass, which then, in early summer, was full of golden buttercups. It was flanked at both sides by the backs of the other houses that made up the estate from which his mam's house was situated. He had long since stopped thinking of that house as his home, or his family's home. He felt too separated from them to feel any kinship towards them, or the house. He felt, actually, that he was homeless. There was a place where he was supposed to be but he would never view it as anything even remotely resembling a home.

He lay there, in the grass, and contemplated what to do next. He had run away again but hadn't decided what to do as yet. God only knows why he always ran back to his old neighbourhood before he went anywhere else. If anybody had been around, Billy could easily have been seen. But there was no one.

On the spur of the moment, Billy decided to run through the gully that ran *between the houses on the right side. It wasn't even dark yet so he was taking a risk, although, if he was truthful with himself, he would have admitted that perhaps he secretly hoped he would be seen. Once around the front of his mam's house, he ran into the big sloping field that was directly opposite. He climbed up into one of the trees that sat along the left side, and gazed down the hill, to the river below. Beyond the river, across the other side, was a wood.*

It was to the woods that Billy instinctively then ran. It was a friend to him. Whenever he felt upset or frustrated, he would run to any wood he could find and hide himself in its dense green depths. Just as other little boys ran to their mothers, and poured out their troubles, Billy climbed trees, gaining comfort from their branches folding round him, taking the place of a parent's embrace. To Billy, the big, solid trees were like protectors who were always ready to grant him comfort.

That night, he found the woods much darker than usual. His friend, the moon, was hiding behind a thick layer of clouds. But he wasn't afraid. There was nothing he feared from the outdoors, especially at night. Billy was undecided as to what to do next, when, out of a dark patch of shadows, came a movement. Something came trundling along in his direction. The light was far too dim for him to see distinctly. Then the newcomer lifted its head and began sniffing the air. It was a badger.

Billy could see the strange white-and-black face moving from side to side before it went across to the big oak tree, put up its two front feet and rubbed its neck lazily against the rough trunk. It began to snuffle around the tree, in the hope of finding food. Billy watched it for hours, during which the badger moved closer and closer towards him. As dawn began to make its appearance, the badger slowed down its scavenging, for its day began with the evening twilight and finished a little before sunrise.

Despite Billy's troubled situation, and the constant vigilance that came along with it, he began to feel drowsy. Watching the badger had kept Billy from dwelling on the uncomfortable side of things but, as the new day began, he involuntarily started to become so dreadfully tired he could scarcely think clearly of anything. The day had been a long one – what with the escaping and then travelling several miles on foot – and then with the contrast of the peacefulness of the woods and the soft sighing of the faint breeze through the tree-tops, a strange dreamy feeling began to steal over him. The sun was beginning its rise and the darkness was failing. His eyelids quite ached from watching the badger with fully opened eyes, especially straining through the weak, shadowy light.

Both Billy and the badger were asleep as daylight began to filter, quite strongly, through the trees.

★   ★   ★

It was also during that time, because the abuse had been revealed, that Billy finally got referred to a centre that offered counselling specifically for survivors of childhood sexual abuse. There he was introduced to an amazing support network which also must have helped him to open up and verbalise more effectively. His counsellor's name was Amanda and he felt comfortable with her right from the start.

One of the first things Billy learned was the benefit of using 'safe places' in your mind. The idea was that, whenever he got anxious or had a panic attack, he could think of somewhere that he felt safe in an effort to relax.

'What's your safe place, babes?' I asked, knowing instantly mine would be tucked up in my cosy bed wearing flannel jim-jams, reading a good book by candlelight, while drinking hot chocolate – and expecting something similar from Billy.

'In a field in the dark.'

Bloody hell, I thought, that's brutal.

'Amanda said maybe I should pick somewhere that I think is nice, maybe somewhere I like to go instead,' he continued. 'I told her we love to go to Ruth Lake camping, but that I don't feel safe there, but she thinks that the lake is a better thing to picture when I'm stressed.'

Too bloody right. Ruth Lake is nicer than a field at night, I thought. 'Ruth Lake is a perfect place to remember,' is what I said, though. I shivered as I imagined being in a dark field all alone.

His progress was slow but it was progress nonetheless. There were still many times that Billy was very withdrawn and, as with the months after his breakdown, I again had to try to negotiate the best way to support him. Somehow, I had to try to figure out when it was best just to leave him be, when he needed me just to listen to him, or when to offer my support in a more subtle way. Sometimes, we went days without even mentioning it at all; I was always aware, though, that it never left him, and, just like when I was trying to help him cope after his mum's death, I again left it up to him to decide my level of involvement. I could stand back and do that because I knew that he knew I was willing to do whatever it took to make things bearable for him.

I knew that dredging it all up was awakening things long buried and it was obvious he was being plagued with flashbacks. He had been having flashbacks for years, even though he had been working hard at suppressing his memories, but once he *allowed* them to be properly awoken his flashbacks occurred tenfold – the actual act of admitting to himself that the abuse did happen somehow causing continual bombardment. And, as had been the case his whole life, there was still no rhyme or reason behind the things that caused him to experience the flashbacks.

One summer morning about two months after the initial phone call from Liam, I asked Billy to hang some washing on the line. I was busy doing something else. About an hour later, I noticed just a few items of clothing were on the line, the rest still in a pile in the washing basket, with Billy nowhere to be seen. I found him sitting on the couch. My initial reaction was one of anger but, luckily, something made me stop myself before I lashed out at him. I hesitated before I spoke, although my instinct *was* to snap, but I knew that would get me nowhere.

*   *   *

Billy heard the faint jingle of coins becoming louder as the footsteps came nearer. With eyes glued to the line of light under the door, Billy's breath caught in his throat. The familiar shadow stopped in the middle of it. Billy could feel the pounding of his pulse in his neck. He lay frozen – unable to move, blink or even breathe.

A distant voice called out from somewhere beyond the door, and the voice of the shadow made a muffled reply. The quieter voice came closer as the louder voice moved away, until they met somewhere down the corridor. A conversation ensued but the voices were too far away for any words to be distinguishable.

Billy recognised the reprieve for what it was. A chance to escape. He had only a few minutes to get away and he began to rush as he heard the two voices advancing towards the closed door. One of the voices sent a thrill of fear through his heart. With the swiftness and stealth of an experienced cat burglar, Billy dressed and crawled out of the highest window – the only window that wasn't locked – by first climbing up the curtain, squeezing through the tiny window and then dangerously shimmying down the drainpipe.

His first task was to negotiate the quickest means of escape. The home was in the country so there was little chance of coming across a pushbike that he could steal. A horse... that would do. There were plenty of them around.

★　　★　　★

'Why didn't you finish hanging out the washing?' I asked coolly, determined not to sound acerbic.

'Oh... sorry, I forgot,' he answered distractedly.

'You forgot? How could you forget? You stopped right in the middle of doing it?'

'I just forgot, all right! Bloody hell, Alix, stop going on, will you! Sod the washing!' he snapped.

I took a deep breath in, at the same time fighting the urge to scream. I wondered what it would be like just to lose control and actually let my frustration take its desired course – to yell, throw things, vent. Of course, I didn't; instead, I chose my words carefully, so as not to antagonise him. 'I don't care about the washing, Billy. I'm more concerned about you. You don't have to bottle things up any more. Obviously, something has upset you. You're acting all weird again... I just wish you would let me in.' I stopped talking, aware that I was close to tears, any display of which I felt would not help my cause. Fuck the washing, I thought to myself. I was so sick of it all. I wanted to be supportive but I also just wanted a normal bloody life.

I went out into the garden, deciding I might as well tackle the sodding weeds. It was at times like that when I could almost feel the insidious strands of bitterness tightening around me. I could cope with all the stuff around Billy's issues but I thought it was totally unfair that I had my infertility to endure as well. I so much didn't want to be bitter but sometimes I simply couldn't control it. I knew I would feel better after gardening.

An hour later I came back inside and found that Billy had run me a bath. Sweet of him, but I wanted him to open up, not to try to be nice to me. I didn't like how it made me feel. I lay in the bath and fantasised about feeling nothing, not caring.

It wasn't until quite a few days later, just as I was getting to the point where I was not obsessing over what had caused Billy to withdraw, when he explained what had happened.

'It was very strange,' he said. 'And yet it wasn't strange at all.' He sounded slightly surprised.

'Go on.'

'One minute I was pegging out a towel on the line and, the next thing I knew, I was sitting down on the couch. I shouted at you because I couldn't remember what I was doing... at least not at first.'

'What do you mean?' I tried to speak lightly but it wasn't working very well, not really understanding what he was getting at.

'I don't really know, or rather I do, but I can't think quite how to say it.' He seemed tired. He looked up; his eyes lingered on my face, his clothes bringing out the colour of them. That day, the vivid green gave him a certain brightness, although the shadow in his eyes never lessened. His strange expression was one almost of curiosity, as though he hadn't seen me before. 'I guess I just started remembering bits and I couldn't think straight. I got all confused. So I must have gone and sat down.'

'What were you remembering?' I asked. 'Things from your childhood?'

'I wasn't sure at first but, after a while, I could see myself. Christ, Alix, it was so clear.'

'In what way?' I asked, trying to sound everything I wasn't feeling. I was terrified he was going to divulge something I wasn't ready to hear. I was desperately trying to appear calm on the outside while inside I was bracing myself for the unthinkable. I can't have done a very good job, or perhaps it was just a coincidence, because Billy added, 'It's just a silly memory about a clothes line.'

'About a clothes line?' I questioned, with relieved surprise. I let out a small chuckle, more a release of tension than because the comment was amusing.

He continued to talk and I began staring into space.

What followed was a touching tale about Billy stealing a clothes line from a nearby farmyard, while on the run from one of the many children's homes that he had attended. He had taken it in an effort to make a sort of bridle that he could use on one of the horses in a nearby field. He needed to get out of the area quickly and, as he hadn't seen any pushbikes he could pinch, he figured riding off on a horse would be the next best thing, and kind of cool into the bargain.

He recounted how he had waited until all the lights in the farmhouse were turned off, and had then cut the clothes line down while standing on an upturned bin. I sat listening to Billy's tale. In my mind's eye, I pictured a scene very different from the reality of the situation, that is until Billy's description of himself as dirty, hungry and cold quickly dispelled my initial image. That he ended up taking the horse back to its field after realising he couldn't bring himself just to abandon it when he had arrived at his destination not only proved that his horse-napping was in no way premeditated, but also that he obviously was an empathetic little thing.

I told Billy it was good to remember things and to talk about them. A look of something crossed his face. Was it incredulity, or was I reading too much into everything? My initial assumption was probably pretty close, though, as Billy added, 'Good for who? Every memory is really about something bad.'

I became aware that there was more lurking behind the horse-napping scene than had been conjured up in my mind. Even those seemingly harmless memories must have made Billy on edge. One memory inevitably led to another and, with each one, he was being led closer to the dark side. Why he had run away didn't come up and, to be truthful, I knew that it wasn't the time to ask questions. The point was that Billy was finally sharing a memory. Even if he was still clearly holding back, I told myself he was at least making headway.

Many more times little memories came out. Sometimes, it was just a little something that didn't necessarily have a negative effect. But he always, to some degree, behaved as though he was keeping his memory on a short leash – as if he was aware that if he gave them free reign he would be out of control with the onslaught. He was still keeping a lid on his demons, but I knew that he was constantly bombarded with his flashbacks – he couldn't keep a lid on those. Whether that was something he consciously did or whether it was his brain yet again protecting him, I wasn't to know. I suppose the latter was probably the case, and a good thing, too, for he was getting it all out but in a somewhat protective manner. That's not to say that when a particularly painful memory made itself known he was shielded from the trauma, because that certainly wasn't the case. However, he seemed to experience the more painful memories when he was in a better position to handle them.

The phone calls with DC Liam Harris continued and, after each one, I could see the inner turmoil etched on his face. Billy would become withdrawn all over again. He sat for ages in the darkened basement, obviously going over things in his mind. I knew the signs. I knew to leave him be.

As I had long since believed, it was during those seclusions that all Billy knew to be the worst came rushing back to him. Fragments of memories, memories that had been prodigiously beaten into submission, carefully boxed and buried, then thankfully forgotten, were suddenly resurrected. They would come flailing at him, free-falling into his consciousness and, as they did, he found himself, each time, confronted with how he was made to feel – all the different emotions intruding, bringing him to his knees; anger that his mum hadn't saved him; anger that he had been taken away from home; guilt that he was angry at his mum; guilt that he hadn't stopped the men from doing such horrible things to him; disgust with himself; shame; rage. Once all those feelings invaded his psyche, he obviously needed time alone not only to come to terms with the memories of abuse, but also to sort out the feelings that were evoked.

One stormy night, after a particularly difficult telephone conversation, Billy broke down. It was a combination of revealing some particularly painful facts to Liam, as well as the stress of it all, that culminated in a mentally exhausted Billy falling apart. We sat in our cosy living room sheltered from the actual storm, but not the symbolic one. He was so upset. I knew I had to be brave and listen to whatever it was he had to say, if indeed he wanted to talk about it. As it turned out, he ended up mainly venting about many different things, a lot of which were directed at the police for bringing it all up. He went off on many different tangents.

I wasn't required to comment at all and it actually was most probably better that I didn't. I just listened. He was talking as if I wasn't even there, which, in a way, I think probably made it easier for him. My imagination painted him as very small against the enormity of his harsh reality. So strong were my sympathies, I even imagined I heard, in the howling wind outside our window, the sobs of the little boy who lived that life. I wished he could continue to dream about nice things and forget all the bad stuff but I knew that was impossible. Billy knew it, too, and it scared us both.

It seemed that Billy had been asked by Liam if he had told anyone about the abuse and that was a bone of contention with Billy. It was at the root of all his bad feelings towards his mother. He felt that he *had* told her, very early on, about his first experiences but, since nothing changed, he came to the conclusion that either she didn't believe him or, worse, she didn't care enough to make it stop. He then flipped on to another issue and then another, talking himself out of steam. By the time he was finished, I had been exposed to supplementary bits of information that helped me to understand all the more what he was dealing with – in his head as well as with the police inquiry.

Even before the whole investigation started, Billy talked quite openly about the physical abuse. I think most likely because he knew that I had known, right from the early days of our relationship, that he had experienced physical abuse in the children's homes. Also, I sensed that he wasn't as ashamed of the physical abuse in the way that he was about the sexual abuse. I found that in itself upsetting. It told me that he obviously had either been witness to physical acts of violence against other children, or had been the victim of such attacks on so many occasions that he viewed it as normal. There had been so many comments over the years about how one care-giver or other had frequently hit, kicked or pushed him. Receiving back-handers and slaps about the head were commonplace. He spoke about angry men, cruel men and vindictive men, but he never really spoke about these experiences as if they were in any way inappropriate or out of the ordinary. He was simply stating fact. He knew that those experiences caused him to feel bad, but he thought they were par for the course, that everyone got treated that way. A lot probably did, but it wasn't until the investigation was under way that he realised that any abuse, be it mental, verbal, physical or sexual, was not OK.

At the beginning of the investigation, when Liam was first talking with Billy on the telephone, he didn't elaborate on the physical abuse specifically because he didn't think it was significant. The sad reality was that physical abuse alone would not have received the same importance as far as the investigation was concerned. Of course, that doesn't diminish the awfulness of physical abuse but, bearing in mind that caning was allowed back then, it makes it much less likely that it would have been treated with the same degree of seriousness.

Obviously, the sexual abuse had the most severe impact on the way Billy's psyche developed, but the physical abuse had serious ramifications attached to it also. Because the sexual abuse was so prevalent, and happened with multiple adults, the ones who were physically abusive were then seen as 'all right' because they hadn't become sexually active. But, in many ways, it was the physical abuse that led to the insidious self-worth issues. It was partly because the sexual abuse was so bad, and abnormal, that the physical abuse then became more 'normal' and 'less' bad in Billy's eyes. Which then led to it becoming acceptable in a way. And when physical attacks and mental degradation become acceptable, any self-esteem or sense of self-worth that may have been present inevitably becomes extinct.

It was also true that merely talking about the physical abuse made Billy more angry about it than he had been before it was dredged up. He despised the nasty care-givers but he wasn't exactly angry with them – he was more resigned to their nastiness. Once I started asking him questions about the physical abuse, he became much angrier.

I suppose I asked him about the physical abuse because I couldn't ask him about the sexual abuse. It was selfish of me, really, because I think it served me more than him. I got to feel as though I was supporting him, while he just became increasingly more and more angry. It's hard to know if talking about it was beneficial. I mean, he got stuff out, but I don't know whether it was worth it. I suppose it's better out than in, but it certainly was worse in the short term.

Billy became very annoyed when he remembered one of the worst incidences and I think he shocked even himself when he realised the intensity of his feelings, especially since he still has the scars. It had all happened when he was caught running away from an approved school. He was sent to a remand centre to be held until someone from the approved school could come and pick him up and, while there, he was 'punished' for running away. He knew right away that it wasn't like any of the other times that he had received a caning. This man went mad. He struck him over and over with such intensity that he quickly became out of breath and sweaty. Worst of all, Billy sensed that this man was actually enjoying it.

When he was finally returned to the approved school, he was sent to the head who informed him that he would need to be caned for running away. Billy told them that he already had been caned, but they didn't believe him. He was to return to the office at the end of the day for his punishment. Billy felt sick at the thought; he didn't think he could bear it again. As he left the room, the head noticed him flinch as he walked away from him. Even though Billy had had his clothes on during his caning at the remand home, the severe blows had left painful welts criss-crossing his back and the slight touch of his jumper brushing against his burning skin left him in terrible pain.

The head walked over to him and lifted his jumper up. The shock of the air hitting his raw skin was enough to make Billy feel faint. Parts of his jumper stuck to his back on the broken, weeping skin and he bit his lip to control the cry as it was pulled off. He was promptly taken to sit down on a chair and told that he would need to see the nurse.

As he sat waiting, he heard raised voices behind the door of the head's office. He couldn't make it all out, but he heard someone say, 'They had no business taking it into their own hands... he isn't their responsibility...' and he hoped that the nasty man at the remand home would get into trouble.

Shortly afterwards, he was taken down to see the nurse. She gasped as she lifted up the jumper and then she just washed the wounded area with a flannel and put some cream on the worst of the injuries before putting on some bandages, barely speaking a word. Billy wondered if she thought he deserved it. He hoped not, but he was never to know. Other than having his bandage changed, he never heard anything about it again. It was just another thing that was shut away somewhere in the deeper recesses of his mind.

Of course, if he thought that physical abuse was low on the list of importance, then mental and verbal abuse was even further down that list. He is so blasé about the latter that even now I don't think he acknowledges how much being called 'brainless', 'a useless little shite', 'good for nothing little sod', 'pathetic whinger' and so on affected him. Of course it has.

The sexual abuse was something altogether different. He reacted differently to that form of abuse, mainly because he was so ashamed. It seemed to me that he had thought that silence and acquiescence were the only viable weapons that he could use to defend himself – or at least not to make it become even worse. Billy told me that, as a young boy, he had thought that, if he could just shut up, then, eventually, the bad men would stop and leave him alone. As an adult, that silence haunted him, for he felt that he should have screamed it from the rafters, and questioned why he hadn't.

I don't know where we thought it was all leading. I suppose we just sort of hoped Billy would tell Liam all he knew and that would be it. It wasn't until we heard from Liam that he and another detective, DC Mark Barnes, were coming to Canada to obtain our official statements that we realised what a big deal it was. I mean, for us it was, and had always been, a big deal, but it came as a shock to both of us to realise just how serious the investigation must be if they were sending two detectives all the way to Canada just to get our statements.

Of course, their impending visit stressed Billy out even more. It was bad enough talking about it all over the telephone, but when they came he would have to do it face to face. Inevitably, there were times when Billy strongly regretted agreeing to help them with their enquiries but, deep down, I still thanked God that it had all come about. It was incredibly stressful but I couldn't forget that, because of their phone call, we had been saved, so to speak. I had had my suspicions validated and we began to get the support we so desperately needed – Billy by being referred to a fantastic support centre and me by finally understanding the root of Billy's mental illness and finally having the acknowledgement from doctors, family and friends that I was right – Billy needed and deserved help.

So many things became clear. All the pieces of the puzzle slotted into place and everything made sense. There obviously was a lot of hard work yet to be done, but things were so much easier because I was no longer fighting alone. Billy was back.

11

UNDERNEATH A PAPER MOON

I see the way you face
This cruel, cruel descent
But it wouldn't take a miracle
To change the way things are today
Maybe just a sign

'It Wouldn't Take a Miracle' by Dirk McCray

I love looking at the moon. Crescent, half, full – it doesn't make a difference, I find them all mesmerising. It's a weird concept to think that the moon shines down on all of us. It sees everything. Looking up, on a clear night, always makes me feel important and insignificant at the same time – as if I am kind of privileged to see it but, at the same time, I am acutely aware that the speck of energy that is me is just a minuscule ingredient of all that the lunar rays preside over.

There was a time when I was frightened of it, or so I am told. Apparently, while standing in my cot and pointing at the crack in the curtains, I would cry, quite hysterically, 'Moodle… moodle…' The story goes that I cried for quite a few nights before my parents figured out I was pointing at the moon. From then on, a big nappy pin kept the curtains together. I have no memory of that, I was far too young to remember. Obviously, I didn't carry the fear with me as I grew.

I find it very strange to think that, at the very time I was eighteen months old and scared of the moon, that same moon was shining down on the nine-year-old Billy, illuminating his nocturnal journeys and providing comfort. That very same moon. For some reason, my moon-gazing always seemed to be most prolific when life was carefree. Needless to say, I had hardly even noticed it at all in the autumn of 2000. Come to think of it, my moon had been barely noticeable for way too long. Could it really have been years? I guess I had been far too preoccupied with everything.

In the few months before the two Welsh detectives came, we had been treated to a break from all the upset that the phone calls had generated; our stress levels hadn't lessened to any acceptable degree, though, as we were constantly aware of their impending visit. That concern left no room for insouciant observations of the solar system. The moon had become disposable and I hadn't even noticed.

Both Billy and I were worried about the Welsh detectives' arrival, but for very different reasons. Billy was obviously dreading having to speak about the details of his abusive childhood. The prospect of having to reveal such intimate facts face to face with anyone would have been bad enough, but to have to go through it with two male detectives made it all the more difficult.

I was worried about how Billy would respond to them. He was so distrustful of anyone in authority. I prayed they would be genuine and kind. Liam certainly sounded warm and caring on the telephone, but his voice could easily have been deceiving. I knew Billy would form an opinion very quickly and, for everybody's sake, it desperately needed to be favourable. Billy's judgement was more often than not extremely accurate; at least, it was if he didn't form his opinion based solely on appearance. I'm not completely sure how he does it; he just seems to zero in on mannerisms and behaviours that, to him, indicate character flaws and untrustworthiness. He picks up on things that the average person doesn't even notice and his record of character assessment is such that I have to acknowledge his uncanny accuracy. Too many times he has formed an opinion of someone and he gets it spot on, although sometimes it is months before he is proved right.

The problem is, though, he is also prone to pass judgements that come from the abused child's perspective. That makes it difficult to know whether he is using the skills he learned as a child to make an accurate assessment or if the chip on his shoulder is dragging him down. However, it seemed that, over the years, his inaccuracies were always the ones that were to do with him personally. If I asked him his opinion about someone he had met – say a work colleague, for instance – he could have him or her pegged almost instantly. Someone whom he was involved with, especially someone in a position requiring trust, could almost always cause his insecurities and mistrust to surface. Hence my concern over the detectives' visit.

All children have excellent bullshit detectors but Billy had had such intensive training on the subject he'd managed to hone the skill. I just had to hope that he wouldn't let his prejudice overrule his head. I felt sure they would be, if nothing else, dedicated. The problem would be, however, if they were arrogant with it. Billy doesn't do arrogant. I suppose that is what worried me the most, because very often when people are particularly good at what they do, they can come across as arrogant. That's generally not a bad thing, I don't think; it just would be in that situation. If they had walked in all full of themselves, the whole thing would have gone pear-shaped.

As the time drew nearer, I tried to impress upon Billy that he should just take them at face value and not to assess them too much, but I knew it was falling on deaf ears. He was even a bit bugged at me and responded with a rather pissed-off: 'What do you take me for? If they are polite to me, I'll be polite to them. If they are fuckers to me, then I will be a fucker back!'

'Of course they won't be! They are on your side,' I added.

'Aye, whatever,' he replied disbelievingly. He seemed to be on a different page and I was quite puzzled by his increasing hostility. 'If they don't believe me, then…'

'Billy!' I cut him off. 'Of course they believe you.'

'What the fuck do you know?' he snapped, before retreating downstairs, once again leaving me baffled.

*　　*　　*

The policeman grabbed him by the scruff of the neck.

'Let me go!' Billy was immediately resisting, partly because he hadn't seen the policeman, so was shocked at being apprehended, and partly because he knew what would happen next.

'What are you doing hanging about at this time of night? What are you up to, lad?'

'I ain't sayin' nuffin'!' Billy was still squirming to get loose.

"Right, me laddo. Are you from the Children's Home?'

'No!'

'Right, well, let's just go there, shall we, and see if they know who you are?'

'No, no! Please don't take me back there! Please, sir. Aaah, sir!' Billy started to cry and become more aggressive.

The older policeman threw him roughly into the car.

'He seems right scared, like, ya know. What do ya think's up wi' him?' the younger officer asked.

'Nowt! He's playin' us, lad! Don't take no notice!'

'I think we should at least ask him… have you seen the look in his eyes? He's scared of somethin', I reckon.'

'Jesus Christ, man! Will ya listen to it! Don't be so soft, he's bleeding played you for a right mug, ennit!' The older policeman laughed.

Billy could see them laughing and his anger towards them trebled.

'I still reckon we should ask him.'

'For fuck's sake, Dio, you tryin' to tell me how to do me job now, are ye? First bloody month on the force and you think you know it all. You're fucking wet behind the ears, lad!' They just stood there looking at each other for a moment or two.

Even from the back of the car, Billy could see the younger officer's flushed cheeks. Billy thought it was from the cold. The other one just looked angry.

'All right, then, if it will make you happy, I'll ask him!' He stomped off to the car, slung the door open and asked, 'Why you creatin' so much? You scared or somethin'?'

Billy paused; he so much wanted to tell him, but he was also scared. After all, he'd been warned, 'Keep your bloody mouth shut, if you know what's good for you…'

'Well? If you've got somethin' to say, say it!'

'They hurt me,' Billy replied quietly.

'Oh, they do, do they?' the officer said mockingly. 'Give you a clip round the ear, do they? I bet you deserve it an' all, aye.'

'They do bad things.'

'Aye, aye, boyo. And you don't, I suppose?' The officer shut the door forcibly and strode over to his partner.

'Just as I suspected… the lad's trouble!'
Billy knew they didn't believe him.

★   ★   ★

Christ, he is so complex, I thought to myself. I felt, at times, that I needed a bloody degree in psychology to make any sense of him. I sat down, experiencing an odd sense of déjà vu – which wasn't really all that odd, considering we had had many conversations that ended with Billy leaving the room in a huff and me totally baffled. What *was* odd, though, was how I always had the same feeling come over me when I was in these situations. The *feeling* was the déjà vu.

With a sense of lucid detachment, every detail of my immediate surroundings seemed unnaturally vivid, even though they were of no importance. Everything was quiet, the room slightly chilly. The colours in the rug by the fireplace seemed brighter somehow. The horse statue on the mantelpiece seemed almost real, as if its hooves were going to come down from the rearing-up position and it was going to gallop away. The sun shone brightly into the living room, enveloping it with an ethereal glow, while casting shadows and colour on the picture above the mantelpiece. The picture, an engraving of a painting from 1862, *The Maid and the Magpie*, took on the same lifelike quality. I looked at it, half-expecting the Catherine Cookson-like scene to come to life.

Some trace of peace remained deep within the over-riding confusion and frustration. I remember thinking how peculiar it was that nothing whatsoever had happened. I hadn't meditated or even really had a chance to question Billy's behaviour and, in fact, the entire experience had felt quite ordinary at the time – nothing particularly otherworldly or supernatural about it, at least not like other times. And yet, I felt it. Without any bidding, answers once again appeared to me. I hadn't even had time to think about why Billy had responded the way he had or why he was so hostile. I'm sure if I had spent time going over it in my head, like I always do, I would have come up with the same, or at least similar, conclusions – it was just strange the way the thoughts just appeared in my head. As if someone was answering a question that I hadn't asked yet.

At any rate, within minutes of Billy going downstairs, I was no longer confused by his attitude. I saw that he was *expecting* the detectives to act in the same way as all the policemen he had ever encountered in his past. He was so totally unprepared for them to be on his side that he hadn't even realised yet that they actually were.

The adults in Billy's childhood have a lot to answer for. No one saw past the façade to the child underneath. No one bothered to find out why he was so angry, or why there was no light in his eyes. Not a teacher, a social worker, a care worker, or even just one of the many policemen he encountered. I didn't want to believe that there had been no one, but the fact is there really hadn't been, and that has to have had a serious impact. I know he had awful things happen to him at the hands of his abusers, and it goes without saying that those experiences were horrendous. I wish with all my heart that he hadn't been subjected to any of it, but I actually think it is almost sadder that not a single person saw past his behaviour. No one saved him. The thought of him being scared, fending for himself, alone and misunderstood is what I find particularly heartbreaking. Maybe that's because I don't actually let myself think of the actual abuse, but it is *because* of the fact that no one was there for him as a child that made him so unable to accept that someone, somewhere, might actually care for him, and have his interests at heart.

I realised he would just have to find out for himself that they were on his side. Obviously, they were going to be respectful and courteous towards him; it was just so far removed from his experience that his brain wasn't registering the possibility. Also, the very fact that he had grown up being assessed by social workers, care workers, policemen, psychiatrists and many other 'professionals' ensured that he would, and probably always will, assess other people. The echoes of destruction emanating from the battlefield of Billy's mind could once again be seen in his actions.

I don't think Billy realises that he assesses people and makes judgements. Even if he did, it wouldn't make any difference, because he can't help seeing things through his child's eye view of the world.

★   ★   ★

'Well done, Billy! That is a tremendous effort!'

Billy really liked Mr Andrews. He was always so nice to him. He wasn't like any of the other adults. What is more, he was nicer to Billy than to any of the other boys. Billy felt special for the first time in his life. Whenever he was in need of comfort, encouragement, praise or help, Mr Andrews always seemed to be there, ready, and very much willing, to lend a hand. It was as if he knew, even before Billy knew himself, when he was feeling particularly lonely, scared or upset.

It took a while for Billy to adjust to the attention. He had been fending for himself for months before Mr Andrews came on the scene and had absolutely no experience of affection from any quarter.

Initially, Mr Andrews started to single Billy out with the odd word of praise maybe once or twice a day. Then there began the occasional ruffle of hair or pat on the back, progressing to small, quick hugs, which became longer embraces. It was done in such a way that Billy began to crave the attention, especially if Mr Andrews cooled it down a bit, which he did now and again.

Over a period of time, it went from never having any positive physical contact to being hugged, patted and embraced almost continually. After about three months, Mr Andrews initiated contact on a daily basis and it progressed to whenever the opportunity arose. Sometimes, the opportunities were even manufactured.

It got to the point where it was even noticeable to the other boys, who began teasing Billy about it. It was hardly surprising that the other lads became jealous of their frequent displays of playful messing about. All the boys missed their fathers – even if they hadn't known them before going into the homes – there, they were all fatherless.

Billy particularly loved it when the attention was given specifically to him, in front of the others. It made him feel even more special somehow. He had never felt worthy of even a nod in his direction, so, understandably, he lapped it up. Billy didn't particularly enjoy the time when they were alone, even if they just went for a walk in the grounds or something, but that didn't happen often and it was a small price to pay.

During that time, Billy was also being treated very poorly indeed by other staff members. Mr Henry especially put the fear of God into Billy, which only increased his bond with Mr Andrews, and led him to feel as if it was them against the world.

One day, Mr Andrews told Billy that he was taking him to a football match to see Cardiff City play the following Saturday. At first, Billy wasn't too keen on the idea. He wasn't sure why, he just didn't particularly fancy going. Mr Andrews noticed and asked him why he didn't seem excited about it. He seemed disappointed and Billy didn't want to be the cause of it. He was just about to lie, and say that he was excited, when Mr Andrews suggested that they take his twin brother with them. Billy liked the idea; he missed Jon and very much wanted to see him. He also thought he might get to see his mam.

It didn't work out that way. The afternoon highlighted how separate Billy and Jon had become. They had come from a shared experience from womb, through poverty and occasional violence at home, to an unnatural division that was to be the beginning of a lifelong barrier. Jon's world wasn't Billy's any more. Billy knew it, and a seedling of resentment was sown. He mentally moved away from Jon —effectively starting his disconnection with the rest of the family – and toward Mr Andrews. He only saw his mam for a moment when she dropped Jon off, and then not at all when they dropped Jon back off at the house, which only served to heighten Billy's feeling of detachment.

That Saturday was also the day that smashed Billy's new-found self-worth to smithereens, shot his belief that Mr Andrews was different from the others completely out of the water, and expelled the idea that he had ever been special to him at all. Only half-an-hour after he had mentally turned away from his family and toward Mr Andrews, his relationship with him blew up in his face. Mr Andrews ripped it all away and went from comrade to predator in the space of 30 minutes, during one autumnal afternoon, on the way back from a Cardiff City Football Match.

*   *   *

Of course, the abuse itself has a huge role to play, too. Children need to be able to distinguish between right and wrong, good and bad – to differentiate the good person from the bad person. When you are just a child and someone you think is good turns out to be the worst kind of bad, it is very damaging in so many ways but, in particular, in the development of perception and trust. It blurs their judgement. Billy may have developed the ability to make accurate character assessments, sometimes even intuitively, although, as I have said, a major problem arises when he makes judgements based on that blurred perception and mistrust.

Before the detectives from South Wales Police arrived, I don't think Billy actually wondered what they would be like, as I did. Well, if he did, he didn't tell me, but I suspect that sort of thinking is a female thing. If he thought about them at all, I think he probably thought he already knew what they would be like. I would even go as far as to say that he wanted not to like them.

I don't think there is a stereotype for Welsh law enforcement. At least, not like there is for other types of policing, or that I am aware of anyway. I considered various possibilities – *Starsky and Hutch*, the Coen brothers' film *Fargo*, *Morse*, *Frost* or even a *Mr Bean*-type detective – I couldn't begin to guess, although a John Nettles character would have done quite nicely.

DCs Harris and Barnes phoned from their hotel the day they arrived in early November 2000. They were staying at what was formerly called The Empress, the nicest hotel in Victoria. Billy thought it was typical that they were staying there… I thought it was nice for them. I knew enough not to vocalise that thought. I gave them directions to our house and they arranged to come the next day. We didn't know what to expect, how they were going to go about taking our statements or how long it would take. I arranged to take the first day off work so I could give my statement first. I was surprised they even wanted one from me.

For the rest of that day, tension hung in the air. They were in Victoria and there was no going back. That night, as we lay in bed, we chatted. Perhaps the darkness had made it easier in some way. I couldn't help but notice that it was like the calm before the storm.

'Why do you stick with me through all this shite?' Billy asked.

'Because I love you.'

'But everything is so awful there is no good stuff.'

'Love itself is what is left over.' I tried to explain what I meant but wasn't doing a very good job. 'When I was a little girl, I used to think that marriage was a great big fairytale. I thought love was all about the big things – the house with the picket fence; the family Labrador; 2.4 children; holidays. I remember when I was only five years old I imagined being married to Desi Arnaz from *I Love Lucy*. I didn't know that was his real name, though; to me he was Ricky Ricardo. You know that old doll I have?'

'Aye, that lovely thing without hair and arms,' he laughed.

'Well, I even called *it* baby Ricky,' I confessed, chuckling.

'You've never told me that before.'

'I haven't thought about it for years. The doll has always been Ricky. I just sort of took it for granted – kind of forgot how it came about, if you know what I mean? Anyway, I used to picture living in a big castle in England, in the most amazing countryside, with my husband Ricky. He loved me more than anything in the world. Everything was perfect. We were always together. Having fun and travelling all over the world. At home, we had a whole floor at the top of the house that was the nursery, full of toys for our lovely cherubic babies. There was a river running through the garden. We had horses, which we rode, side by side through the fields. We were always happy.'

'Exactly! You must be disappointed.'

'That's just it. I reckon love isn't about the big things. It's about the little things – the way you make my birthday cards; the way you call me "sparrow"; the way you know which cup I like my tea in and which cup I like my coffee in; the way you never tease me about *having* specific cups, for God's sake; the look in your eyes… No, I'm not disappointed in the slightest!'

'Next you'll be saying, "The best presents are the ones that cost nothing,"' Billy teased.

'Piss off,' I said, pushing him playfully.

'I want you to have the big things, too.'

'Well, maybe one day we will… they're just not important, that's all.'

'You'll not get me living in a castle!'

'Piss off and go to sleep!' I laughed.

'Night, babes.'

A translucent moment I didn't want to end.

The next morning, right on time, the visitors' rental car pulled into the driveway. I couldn't resist peeking out the window to try to catch a glimpse, much to Billy's disapproval – another female thing, I think.

I couldn't get a good enough view without being seen, though, so I was forced to abandon the mission and wait until they came in.

As soon as I saw them, I was relieved. They were lovely – so nice, thoughtful and polite. They were, of course, completely ordinary. And yet they were not ordinary at all, if only due to the fact that they were Welsh detectives, and they were there in our front room. There was nothing ordinary about that.

Almost straight away, they acknowledged how difficult the whole ordeal must be, for Billy in particular, but also for me. They offered understanding and empathy and assured us that they would proceed at our pace. I knew that was probably said in an effort to placate, as they did have a time limit, although I appreciated the sentiment. Billy was polite but understandably strained.

After meeting them and talking about how they were going to go about taking down our statements, Billy went downstairs. We spent the rest of the first day going over mine, which was a bit of a tedious affair, to say the least. Apparently, they would have taped us if we were in the UK but, as they had to come to Canada, they had to both manually take down what I said. Then Liam put it all together, they went over it again with me and, once I was happy with the outcome, I had to sign each page. It took hours and it left me wondering how the hell they were going to get through Billy's statement. After all, mine was only about the few things that I knew about Billy's childhood and the years since we had met. Billy's would chronicle a lifetime.

While I sat in silence, during which time Mark was working on his laptop and Liam was writing down what I had said, I watched them – trying not to make it obvious but, nonetheless, checking them out. Mark was the nicest, the one I knew we could trust. He reminded me of Inspector Morse's sidekick, the one played by Kevin Whately. He looked like a wholesome family man – in the nicest possible way. Strangely, just as I was thinking that, his mobile phone rang. Being slightly techno-challenged, I didn't realise that mobiles could work so far away, which they obviously could, as he answered the call from his son. It was a very sweet conversation that ended in him telling his son that he missed him and loved him, verifying my initial observation.

Liam was a different kettle of fish altogether. He was younger, I thought, although prematurely grey. He was definitely one of those men, rather Philip Schofield-ish, who looked much more handsome grey – and handsome he most certainly was. He was well dressed and was obviously fashionable and trendy. He, too, revealed he was married with kids but, to me, he wasn't in the same category of 'family man'. He seemed more 'one of the lads'. I knew Billy was going to find him slightly arrogant but, thankfully, I didn't think it would be a problem as he didn't appear to be 'full of himself'. Actually, 'confident' is a better description than 'arrogant', and that had to be a good thing. Either way, as I said before, I think sometimes arrogance comes when one is very good at what one does and I suspected Liam was, indeed, a very good detective.

The combination of the two of them was perfect as far as I was concerned. Mark would make the whole thing easier to bear and help us to feel comfortable and Liam would get the job done. And, at the end of the day, we wanted a result. We wanted justice to be served. We didn't know where the investigation was heading but, ultimately, we were in pursuit of vindication – and healing.

That first night, after they left, Billy was very stressed and, to be honest, he also sounded paranoid. He was still having trouble accepting that he, and they, really were playing for the same team. As I suspected, he thought Liam was a bit of a poncy, cocky 'Jack the lad'. I felt strangely protective of them and that night was the start of a *nightly* session of me sticking up for them but, at the same time, ensuring that Billy never lost sight of the fact that, ultimately, I was on his side. I also had to make sure that Billy stayed calm so I was careful not to stick up for them too much.

It was very hard. And, really, who's to say that my opinion of them was the right one? What was vital was that we had started the whole process and, in order to get through it myself, I had to believe that they were good people.

That fundamental difference in our outlook has come up so many times during our relationship. Billy thinks most people in authority and otherwise are not to be trusted. I think most people are trustworthy. Maybe I am naive and too trusting, but I would rather find out I am wrong than not trust someone who is.

It goes beyond that, though. Billy lives in a world where Paul Burrell didn't actually care about Princess Diana, but just profited from their relationship. I live in a world where he is truthful and genuine and where he cared for her deeply. Billy lives in a world where Catherine Zeta-Jones married Michael Douglas because of his celebrity status. I live in a world where she married him for love. What the truth is is totally irrelevant, but I know which I prefer to believe.

I'm not totally naive, although I know it sounds as if I am. I know that there are doctors and solicitors that are in it for the money; that there are bad policemen and politicians, teachers and priests; but I want to believe that the good outweighs the bad – by a long chalk. I totally understood why Billy saw things the way he did and I didn't for one minute blame him but I had to maintain my view. Actually, sometimes it would have been easier to jump on the cynical bandwagon, especially when I was feeling sorry for myself, but I couldn't let myself do it. I want to live in a world where good prevails and sometimes it boils down to choice; the choice of how you perceive things.

So whether our Welsh visitors were solely acting in their own interests or not, I had to believe that they were doing it because they cared. And, anyway, you can't tell me that someone would accept a job that ensures that they spend more time at work than they do with their families and subject themselves to the misery of investigating serious sex crimes if they didn't want to do their bit to make a difference. Granted, some people do take jobs for the money, but I don't think anyone does work like *that* for the money, or just for the credit of solving the crimes. In my book, they don't get paid enough money or receive enough credit. They *must* care. Certainly, just voicing my views wasn't going to change the education of a lifetime but at least I could try to keep Billy's thoughts from spinning out of control.

On Tuesday morning, they arrived a little later than arranged. A combination of jet-lag and too much socialising the night before ensured both men found it hard to get started. I could tell by the look on Billy's face that he wasn't impressed when they mentioned that they had 'partied' with the local police the night before. I actually thought that it was nice that they got to hang out with Canadian officers, comparing their jobs, relaxing and having a good time. They both couldn't believe how police officers in Victoria thought nothing of eating in restaurants in full uniform, reminding me once again of the different attitudes towards law enforcement.

'It is surprising how two English-speaking countries are still culturally so different, isn't it?' I commented. 'Especially since the Queen is still the Head of State in Canada.'

'Not as different as the US, though,' one of them said.

'No, you're right. They aren't even members of the Commonwealth. I definitely think Canada is somewhere in between,' Billy interjected.

We continued chatting for a bit, then I went off to work, having arranged to start late, and left the others to get down to taking Billy's statement.

The time had come. Liam and Mark told him to take his time, start wherever he felt comfortable, and just to tell them what he remembered. He had been dreading that moment, terrified that, when the time actually came, he wouldn't be able to speak, that the details that were there in his thoughts wouldn't actually come out. At the same time, he was terrified that they would. He hadn't gone into explicit detail on the phone but he couldn't get away with leaving anything out any more. He knew that, once he actually said the worst bits out loud, not only would he not be able to take them back, he wouldn't be able to pretend any more that they hadn't really happened.

He had been spending a great deal of time with his counsellor, Amanda, at the counselling centre, preparing for this moment, but even with her he hadn't said a lot of the worst bits out loud. Those words, the ones that betrayed all, were the hardest to say. Arse. Penis. Penetration. Vagina. Breasts. Oral Sex. Stolen virginity. Sodomy. Semen. Rape.

Once those words were said he felt sure they would look at him differently. He felt sick with humiliation and dirty with shame but, once the time actually came, he was very surprised to realise that he could practically feel the tidy cupboards of his mind begin to unlock, and then open. Thoughts and memories were spilling out and, incredibly, he *wanted* to get them out. He remembered a lot but, as there was so much, even then, all those months later, he was still remembering more elements.

So, the door *did* open – just a crack maybe, but the sights, sounds and smells flooded out. He hadn't had to speak of the details to any great extent before, but the time had come – and he knew it. He also knew that it would all be for nothing if he kept anything back, so he vowed to himself to tell it all, no matter how hard.

There was a tightness in his chest. He cleared his throat hard and coughed, hoping to ease it. 'He… erm, Mr Henry… he was one of the house fathers. He had a beard that was bushy and full around the face, his hair was dark in colour and it was out of control – he had a lot of hair on his head. He also had a lot of bodily hair… it… it w-w-was more prominent on his back. He was of a broad build, 6ft maybe. He never appeared happy. I don't think I ever once saw him laughing – he was more sort of withdrawn. One thing I particularly remember is looking down and seeing that he had big feet… God, ah, that's weird. I don't know why I would have noticed his feet… Oh, ah…' Billy shook his head, as if to shake something away and then cleared his throat. It was an odd movement – nervousness perhaps? 'I found Mr Henry a very stern, cold person. He appeared to be a control freak. I remember he enjoyed walking and took us many times…' Billy then inhaled deeply, realising as he did so that he had barely stopped even to take a breath. 'Sorry, was that too much or too fast?' he asked. 'I haven't even started at the beginning.'

'You're doing fine. Carry on when you are ready.'

It didn't really matter, he was at least talking. Billy paused and cleared his throat again. 'Erm… do you mind if I smoke?' he asked.

'It's your house, mate. Whatever makes it easier for you,' Liam replied.

Billy self-consciously pulled a cigarette from the pack. He flicked the lighter over and over with his hand faintly shaking. The flame finally sparked and he inhaled deeply while lighting the cigarette. Feeling the nicotine hit his bloodstream and with a slightly more relaxed feeling, he continued. 'Right, ah… OK, ah… the first incident involving Mr Henry occurred in the bathroom. The bathroom was situated at the top of the stairs, turn left, walk a few yards and the bathroom is on the left.' Billy paused thinking he should give them time to catch up. DC Harris seemed to be writing so fast, and the other one was typing faster than Billy had ever heard before.

DC Harris looked up and nodded so Billy continued, 'The more I think of it, the more I think that he didn't have much involvement with the day-to-day running of the place. I saw him mostly on weekends and evenings. Anyway, I… I was h-h-having a bath one day. I believe the bathroom had a bath with shower connection and a curtain that could be drawn around it. There was a sink, although I can't recall a toilet in the room. While I was in the bath, it would have probably been around 8.00 or 9.00pm, Mr Henry walked into the bathroom. He sat on the side of the bath. I was lying in the bath facing the bathroom door. Mr Henry started flicking water at me and I started laughing. Mr Henry then started talking about growing up. He used the word "puberty", although at that age I didn't know what it meant. I recall him saying that I would grow body hair. He mentioned facial hair like himself. He continued to flick the water at me every so often. At this time when he was talking about body hair, he would point to the parts of my body where I would grow hair. When he spoke about chest hair he touched my chest. I didn't feel uncomfortable at the time. He then brushed against my lower belly, and flicked some more bath water. I remember laughing together, which was nice, because he was usually so grumpy and mean. I'd never seen him behave like that before. It didn't seem bad at the time because he had seen me naked before. And I had seen him naked before… when we had gone to the Empire Pool.

'A few weeks later, I was in bed in my dormitory and he came and yelled at me for talking after lights out.' Billy knew he should elaborate at that point, but he wasn't ready yet so he just brushed over it and continued. 'There was also Mr Peters. He could be really strict and nasty sometimes. He would hit me… well, all of us really. He was a miserable old git, nobody liked him and he didn't seem to like anyone either. Not even the other teachers or staff members. There were a few dodgy things with him, too, but other stuff was so much worse I didn't pay too much attention to them. I guess I was desensitised by the time he was around. That's what my therapist says anyway… I remember he used to make us get out of bed in the middle of the night and make us go to the toilet and he'd stand and watch us until we went. I hated him for that. He'd keep shouting for us to hold our dicks… it went on for ages because I never needed to go, and even if I did I couldn't do it because he was watching me… he used to yell and hit us before he'd let us go back to bed. To this day, I can't have a slash if someone else is there. I started pissing the bed after that an' all.'

'OK, Billy, you're doing great. Let's go back to that later. We'll take a breather now, if you don't mind, and start again in a bit.' DC Harris smiled and got up. 'Any chance of a cup of tea?' he said while rubbing his hands together.

'Oh, yeah, yeah, no worries.' Billy jumped up, happy to change the subject.

Half-an-hour and three cigarettes later, they started again. 'Then… ah, there… there was Mr … ah, Mr Andrews …' Billy hesitated while saying the name as if he was trying to recall the facts, but it wasn't that. Billy remembered it all too well; he just had trouble saying it out loud. After more throat-clearing and lighting another cigarette, he continued, 'Ah… at… at first, I liked him the most. He was a weird looking bloke. He…' Billy remembered every tiny detail of every one of his abusers and Mr Andrews was no different. He told the detectives everything, all of which he pulled from the crystal clear video that constantly replayed in his head.

'He … ah… he was the only one who paid any attention to me. He would laugh and joke and was generally good company. He praised me to the end of the earth… actually, he would go overboard with praise. I thought he was showing genuine friendship. I thought I was his favourite. In the beginning, I lapped it up… then he changed.'

Billy hardly even paused, reeling it all off, almost as if he had no control over it, but still he was holding back – and he knew it. He just didn't know how to form the worst bits into words. 'It was horrendous and very frightening to me – but I suppose, not altogether actually very bad. Not compared to what happened later, but it was such a shock… then, over time, he became bolder, taking greater risks… but no one noticed. He was very careful for them not to. He became more aggressive. I tried to hold him off, and I never stopped protesting... but he had a way about him that shut me up. He was strong, persistent and threatening. I knew no one would believe me – I was a delinquent after all. My only respite was when I got punished and made to stay in my room.'

'Did you tell anyone?'

'Once I told my mam but she didn't believe me,' he answered gruffly, angry at the question. He felt it implied, because he had pretty much kept quiet about it, that he was lying. He had asked himself countless times why he had never told his head or another teacher. He cleared his throat.

'Did you tell anyone else?'

'How could I? Anyway, who would believe me? I was just the delinquent accusing the adult!' he replied angrily, answering his own question as well as theirs and trying to convince himself, just as much as them. 'No one would have believed a word, my own mother didn't... why would they? I would have been branded a liar.' He paused, and then continued less agitated, 'It happened quite a few times, to varying degrees, and I was in a panic – very upset. Traumatised, I think, looking back. I didn't sleep or eat. That made me the most angry. I guess because I thought he liked me. I felt tricked.'

Billy stopped in order to let them catch up. As he sat staring at the floor, he was remembering things – the routine, with all the chores; table tennis in the common room; the battered couches and mismatched chairs; the teachers' cars – Mr Andrews' car was especially easy to remember as the make and model was very distinctive.

Billy spoke for hours. It would have been easy for them to become confused. His leapfrogging from past to present often leaves me hazy, just from the effort of trying to understand him. It is as if, with the influx of memory, the past and the present intermingle – seemingly without context. A moment 35 years ago is as all-consuming and vivid as the worries of yesterday and tomorrow.

He spoke quite quietly, which I wouldn't have thought made it any easier, and it wasn't all in order, but he was getting it out. He flipped from one abuser to another and jumped from one home to the next, but it was a start. He elaborated when he needed to, and said *those* words – the explicit ones that he couldn't ever have imagined saying out loud. He had been omitting them, he knew, sort of brushing over them. Leaving blanks here and there but, by omitting them, he couldn't be sure if they were getting the gist of how bad it was. They were being so understanding, he felt he could risk it… after all, they must have heard it all before.

When he finally stopped on the first day, the room was quiet, save for the clicking of Mark's fingers on his laptop and the faint scratch of Liam's pen as he wrote *those* words down. Billy realised with a start that they would be there for always, down in print. He hadn't thought of it like that before. He took another drag and exhaled a torrent of smoke into the air to mingle, close to the ceiling, with his painful reminiscences. It was as if the words seemed to be floating about over their heads, enforcing a momentary silence. Billy was very relieved to see that they didn't appear shocked at what they had heard. Even so, Billy continued to feel as though he was holding his breath.

The day that followed was more of the same. And the one after. And the one after that. 'I cried a lot… I was silent a lot… I was angry all the time. I always felt ashamed…' On and on he continued. 'He made me scrub the toilet floor with a toothbrush…'; 'She said I was a nice-looking boy…'; 'She told me to keep it our secret…'; 'She locked the kitchen door…'; 'She asked me if I liked it…'; 'He forced me into another room. I tried to resist but he was too strong. He was acting weird. I was very scared, but he kept on and on. I passed out…'; 'He came and got me at night and took me back to his room. He would make it seem, in front of the other lads, that he was taking me out of the dorm for talking after lights out, but I was never talking…'; 'I ran away…'; 'I got caught…'; Billy carried on with great attention to detail. All of it was extremely hard to think about, and it was most definitely hard to tell, but he didn't 'sugar coat' anything. 'I got caned…'; 'I got beaten…'; 'He came in again, while I had a bath…'; 'I could hear his footsteps. I was holding on to a cushion and everything around me was just a whirl. I felt like I was outside of my body, looking in like … ah, I dunno how to explain it…' There were many pauses over the days but still he continued with more. 'When I went to my room I hid, curled up in a ball – I fell asleep. And then woke up and saw that it was light out and then the next time I woke up it was dark. I must have slept all day – I dunno how… from the shock I suppose…' Again he paused, and then continued, on and on, the similarities of each incident now apparent, in that *those* words were used – just different abuser, different place.

The days ran into each other. They had many breaks, trying to relieve the pressure for them all. It was almost as hard for them to hear it as it was for Billy to vocalise it. The unthinkable.

After each break, Billy would inhale deeply and then force himself to continue. There were many examples of a little lad being extraordinarily protected by his amazing mind. When he talked of his head 'being somewhere else', or that he had been 'on the outside looking in', or that he was 'floating' – all were examples of such protection. Details of the utmost depravity were interspersed with innocent observations. Details of horrendous events were mingled with the layout of rooms and the look of the furniture. Billy the adult often spoke with the innocence and style of a very young child. His memories were seen via the eyes of that little boy, not the 40-year-old man. All of which made it all the more touching to hear.

After each session, Billy was emotionally drained. Sometimes, he couldn't believe he was that same boy, as if it had all happened to someone else. He felt sorry for that Billy and cried tears for him, as if he was crying over someone else. On other occasions, he was only too aware that it had been him, and remembered all too well. He often involuntarily shuddered just out of the sheer enormity of it all.

He had to reconcile himself with many truths – some made his memories easier to come to terms with, others made him even angrier. His feelings about himself were mostly very harsh and derogatory. His adult self had a lot of trouble forgiving his younger self. It was going to take a long time for him to allow himself to forgive Billy. For so long, he had blamed the young Billy for allowing it to happen.

Ironically, one of the things that caused him to be the most angry at himself was not realising that the first bath-time incident had been a grooming situation. He was enraged with himself for laughing with Mr Henry when he splashed him – even though he couldn't possibly have known. He also thought a lot about the very first time, the time he had been taken from his bed. Just because it was the first time. It wasn't even the worst. It was just the first. Probably, he had obsessed over it because he knew that the moments leading up to it had been lost for ever, as well as the opportunity to change something, anything, that might have led to a different outcome.

He knew that, before the very first time, he couldn't have been frightened because he didn't know what was about to happen. To this day, he remembers every detail of the moments of that day – the ones leading up to, and straight after, because that was when his innocence was taken, never to return. He mourned for those days – forgetting that, actually, they had been entirely filled with physical and mental abuse. He has more trouble getting over the memory of that first 'morning after' than he does of any other. Even more than the morning when he was nine years old, when he sat on the toilet and felt liquid coming out of his arse.

The days following that first incident didn't include the horrendous pain or the blood, but he had still been in a terrible state. It had been the shock, then waiting for it to happen again, being frozen with fear and immobilised by the knowledge of what could happen, that had done it. That, and the fact that he realised he couldn't trust anyone. Wondering if it was going to happen and then anticipating the horror ensured he never relaxed and never had a good night's sleep. In some ways, it was worse because he hadn't yet become an expert at flying away. Maybe that was why it held so much more pain for him.

On the first day of taking down Billy's statement, I asked him to ring me when the detectives left to let me know how they'd got on and was quite surprised to have not heard anything before I left work. I drove home feeling slightly sick, worrying that things had gone wrong and Billy had either run away or was too worked up to ring me. It was at times like that when I realised just how much Billy's behaviour over the last few years had really affected me. Simply not receiving a prearranged phone call sent me on a roller-coaster of emotion – I imagined all sorts of scenarios. Before all the upset, I would have just thought that he'd either forgotten or was just busy, and that would have been that. However, after all the upset, my mind raced and my tummy churned whenever things didn't go according to plan.

When I arrived home that night, it was with great relief that I saw the rental car still parked in the driveway as I pulled into our street. Relieved, yet surprised, I parked on the street and went into the house. As soon as I opened the door, I smelled and saw the evidence of anxiety. A layer of smoke hung near the ceiling, the lack of fresh air ensuring a pub-like staleness – not a good sign. I vowed not to comment – he deserved to be able to smoke in the house while he was going through this process and not to get criticised for it, even though I hated it. They had said they would be another hour or so, so I decided to go shopping.

I wandered around Thrifty's, randomly putting things in my trolley that I neither needed nor wanted, my mind unable to concentrate or focus on groceries. I recalled that all three of them looked exhausted but Billy looked OK, all things considered. After aimlessly walking up and down the aisles and then paying for my unwanted purchases, I returned home.

They were still there but they said they were just finishing and it was OK for me to be around at that point. I pottered in the kitchen putting the shopping away and generally trying to appear busy. I could hear them chatting and I was so pleased to hear Billy talking to them and actually even laughing with them. I suppose all three of them were trying to lighten the mood, endeavouring to wipe the nastiness away for the time being. I'm sure it would have been much easier for them to try to put the day's accounts out of their heads for the night if they ended on a happier note. They both thanked Billy for his openness and bravery and added that he had done brilliantly.

They both came into the kitchen to say goodnight to me and to chat a bit and then they left. It was evident that both of them had shown a level of kindness and understanding that gave Billy the courage to start to expunge the details of his past. If either of them experienced any feelings of shock or horror, Billy said they didn't show it, which obviously made it easier for him. Undoubtedly, they would have found listening to such things very difficult to stomach and they revealed as much to me in the kitchen before they left. I very much appreciated that they hadn't shown their feelings to Billy.

That night, we developed a sort of pattern. They left, we went through the motions of talking about how the day went, we ate dinner – well, at least I did; Billy usually just moved the food around his plate while only actually eating one or two bites – and then Billy went downstairs, to be alone.

My attempts at talking things over weren't very successful. We never got very far and it usually consisted of me refereeing. I repeatedly found myself explaining why Liam was, according to Billy, acting harshly at times. I wasn't there so I could only go by Billy's interpretation of things, but I rather doubted that Liam had been harsh. I had witnessed many times Billy's habit of over-reaction and his tendency to misread other people's reactions and emotions. He certainly did it to me often enough, so I doubted that Billy's version was accurate.

I suggested that perhaps Liam was coming across as insensitive because he was concerned at getting it all down correctly. 'You will have to get past seeing them through such cynical eyes. Yes, they *need you* to get them the result they want but we need them, too. We want the same thing,' I said on one such occasion.

'He keeps asking me to repeat myself. I don't think he believes me.'

'I know you aren't used to people believing you – it must be hard to trust them – but you've got to realise that they *do* believe you.' I was desperately trying not to show my frustration. I was getting sick of repeating that, of course, they did believe him, over and over again. Obviously I understood, but my reassurances always seemed to land on deaf ears. I took a deep breath, calming myself deliberately. 'Do you trust me?' I asked.

'You know I do,' he answered in a detached sort of voice.

'Well, *I* trust *them*. So please *trust* me, to trust them.' I hesitated but he hadn't seemed to have shut off yet, so I continued. 'When Liam goes over and over things, he is just getting a clear picture himself and also ensuring that he has tied up any loose ends. He is also being a bit of a devil's advocate. If one tiny thing can be proved wrong by the defence or if something doesn't add up, your whole account will be worthless.'

It took a moment for him to answer, although he didn't look particularly hesitant. It was more as though he was looking for the right explanation. 'Hang about.' He paused, again seemingly trying to

215

formulate his next words. 'Today, I was telling them about a time when one of the men pulled me into a toilet cubicle. I said that he shut the door a certain way. Liam got me describing it over and over and he even got me to demonstrate. You know, sort of act it out. Anyway, I realised I had described it arse about tit. The way I explained it the door couldn't have closed… I guess Liam was doing what you said.'

'Exactly… you remembered the incident. You just had the little detail of how the door got closed the opposite way round in your head. Ultimately, he isn't disputing the big stuff. He *knows* that all happened. He just has to make sure the small, seemingly insignificant details don't screw it up if they don't make sense. You remember the bad stuff in total detail but remembering the little things 30–35 years later must be much harder. You can't expect to remember it exactly as it was.'

'Aye, but that's just it… I do. I remember every tiny, sodding thing.'

'Well, maybe they find that hard to understand and they just think it is better to be safe, by going over it all again and again, than sorry. Try to think of them as being thorough, rather than critical.'

'I get you now, aye.'

I wasn't sure if he did really get what I was trying to say or if he just wanted to end our conversation. He did that often – agreeing, just so that he didn't have to talk any more. I could really only hope that some of it would sink in.

I knew going downstairs to be on his own was how he coped and I wouldn't let it hurt my feelings. I wanted him to need me but, obviously, all those years he had to cope all by himself meant that coping on his own was all he knew. He wouldn't even let me 'look after' him when he had the 'flu, so he certainly wasn't going to let me now. He didn't know how. I didn't know how not to.

On that first night, I felt sure the one thing he would have loved to have had while being down there on his own was a beer – or six – but he never asked me to get him some. Actually, if he had, I probably would have. I was that eager to help him relax and somehow shut off his mind because I knew that all that he had talked about during the day, and even more stuff for good measure, would be cruelly replayed over and over. As irresponsible and inappropriate as it sounds, if I could have got my hands on some drugs, I would have given him some. I was

216

that willing to give him the respite but I was pleasantly surprised to find that Billy actually slept a great deal that first night. I could hear his snores very soon after he went downstairs and lay on the couch.

Later, when I went to bed, I barely slept at all – getting up every half-an-hour or so to check on him. His slumber was by no means restful. It was very fitful and I stood there imagining him reliving his horrors. His sleep had something unsettling about it, as though he sought unconsciousness with a relentless, feral desire and, once achieved, clung to it. I hoped the deeper, less disturbed sleep was more comfortable. He normally was quite an insomniac when very stressed, so I was grateful that his body was looking after him.

That ability to sleep became a pattern for the rest of that week – or not sleep, as was the case with me. I once again marvelled at his brain's ability. I was so stressed I really wasn't able to 'be there' for Billy in the way that I had been in the previous months. His brain then took over where I'd left off and shut down every night, allowing him to get the sleep he so desperately needed – and me the temporary respite.

My lack of sleep was surely contributing to my lack of ability to focus on Billy. Yes, I talked to him and reassured him every night, but I was not giving as much as I had. I was aware of the change but I was powerless to alter it. I even looked forward to him going downstairs. I was just too tired and so very overwhelmed.

Throughout all of that, I was still going through all my health issues. During that past year, I was constantly experiencing pelvic pain and had progressed to having to take painkillers round the clock – the large amounts of codeine keeping a rein on the pain for the most part. I had been able to continue working and being strong for Billy, but only if I had at least ten hours of sleep each night. My body was fighting the disease, the pain, the medication and all the stress, so I needed more sleep than the average bear. Even with ten hours a night during the week, I would 'catch up' on the weekends, sleeping twelve hours a night and napping in the afternoons. Hence, the insomnia I was experiencing while Liam and Mark were in Victoria was taking its toll. I had to go to work so it was my time with Billy that suffered. I really just wanted to zone out in the evenings, so Billy going downstairs and flaking out suited us both.

It became evident during that time that Billy was having nightmares a lot. Perhaps he had been all along and I hadn't realised; then, when sleep eluded me, I was able to hear him frequently shouting out during the night. I thought it unfair that even asleep he wasn't free of the torment. Flashbacks while awake, nightmares while asleep – it was a wonder he'd remained as in touch with reality as he had.

I couldn't imagine which were worse – the flashbacks or the nightmares. Both were completely out of his control. In the mornings, I would ask him if he had slept OK. If he said no, I would then invariably ask if he had had a bad dream. It was silly of me to ask the question really. I mean, I was no closer to the truth with or without his response – if he said that he didn't remember having a bad dream, he probably did but just didn't want to tell me. Also, if someone says they've had a bad dream, one is almost obliged to ask what it was about and, at the end of the day, I didn't want to hear what it was about. I wasn't ready yet, so why did I even ask? The urge to nurture I suppose, another legacy of the barren woman. It has got to go somewhere and, hopefully, without causing too much irritation.

Billy wasn't irritated by the 'motherly' questions. He didn't *know* how mothers mothered or how wives treated husbands. He had had no experience of either. There had been no role models of either in his childhood, so how could he know? He was used to me and that is what I did – mothered.

One morning, while Billy sat drinking his tea in a moody silence after a particularly bad night, I asked, 'You were very restless last night, babes. Did you sleep OK… did you have a nightmare?' I hadn't even really intended to ask him. It just sort of came out automatically.

'You what? No. I slept fine!' he barked.

I wasn't to know but it wasn't that I had asked that was the problem, although it was probably irritating that I had. No, it was that he had been reminded – annoyingly reminded – of nightmares that he was desperately trying to keep down, but they kept pushing their way up like beach balls in a swimming pool. There he was trying to push the ball under the water and my question caused him to lose concentration, just for a second, and the ball exploded through the surface.

★　　★　　★

'I'm going to the footie today,' Billy announced to one of the lads while they were cleaning the toilets.

'Piss off… you're not going anywhere,' the lad, also called Billy, replied.

'I am.'

'Fuck off,' Billy number two spat. They both used language that, coming from ones so young, should have been shocking, but had, in fact, become their normal vocabulary.

'You fuck off. I am.'

'All right then… who ya goin' with?'

'Mr Andrews. He's picking me up out the front.'

'Fuck me. You serious?'

'I'm not messing, honest.'

'Well, how come you get to go?'

'I dunno… I don't even like football but at least it gets me outta this place.'

At first, being told he was going to the match had made Billy feel unsure and he thought it was a bit strange that he was getting taken out on a Saturday, although he had to admit it did make him feel rather special, especially since he was the only one from the home who was going. On top of that, he was excited because Mr Andrews had told him that they were going to take his twin brother, Jon, as well. What was even nicer was that he would get to see his mam when she dropped Jon at the match. He began to look forward to it and, when the day came, Billy couldn't help himself from getting excited, although he wasn't even thinking about the match. All his thoughts were on seeing his mam.

But she didn't linger.

She simply dropped Jon off and left. She had said hello, and she asked if he was all right, but it was the kind of statement to which a response wasn't sought, and Billy knew it. Impersonal. That's what the exchange had been: impersonal. She seemed annoyed and Billy was convinced it was his fault, which made him feel annoyed as well – with himself.

The match itself was uneventful. A couple of times the crowd got quite excited but Billy didn't even know what was going on – his lack of concentration on the match seemed to anger Mr Andrews, but he didn't say anything. Billy often sensed that he was a bit annoyed with him, even though he didn't think he had done anything wrong. He wanted Mr Andrews to like him and tried his best to keep him happy. He was the only one who bothered with Billy at the home and had always been so nice to him. Sometimes, Billy was sure he caught a glimpse of something on his face but then he would act all nicey-nicey with him and it always left Billy feeling slightly confused.

Billy had enjoyed seeing his brother but it felt different with him somehow and it made him feel at odds with himself. Mr Andrews kept putting his arm around them, but Jon didn't seem to like that. Billy told Jon that that was just how Mr Andrews always was, but Jon kept his distance. The Bluebirds won but Billy wasn't even bothered.

They dropped Jon off on the way back to the home. It was very hard on Billy. He would have given anything to be able to go home with Jon. Instead, he had to stay in the car while Jon went running up the front path. Billy didn't even get to see his mam before Mr Andrews sped off down the road. Of course, Billy was hurt – and angry, come to that – but nevertheless he decided quickly, even before they drove out of Llanellog Hill Crescent, that he didn't need them.

By the time they were driving past Cardiff Castle, Billy had come to realise that Mr Andrews was the only one who cared. Two minutes later, Mr Andrews slowed down as they approached Cathedral Road, then pulled into a car park by Sophia Gardens. Billy looked at him, wondering why they had stopped. He dared to think that maybe he was going to get him an ice cream. He seemed different. He looked at Billy with a weird look on his face. He put his arm round Billy's shoulder and drew him closer to him. Billy could feel his breath on the side of his face – it smelled faintly of cigarettes, but mostly stale. He was made uncomfortable by Mr Andrews's manner, but it was the closeness of his body and the way his hot breath felt on his cheek that made Billy feel queasy and apprehensive. Billy wasn't at all sure why he felt uncomfortable.

Then, strangely, everything seemed to start moving in slow motion. It started to rain, the drops sounding unusually loud as they hit the roof of the car – which, as it happened, was a good thing as it drowned out the sound of Mr Andrews's heavy breathing. Billy stared straight ahead, unsure of what was happening or what he should do. Leaves fluttering down from the swaying trees overhead were haphazardly deposited on the windscreen. Billy focused on one in particular and began staring at it, the bright-red colour of which was being imprinted in his memory at the same time as his hand was forcibly put in the man's crotch, and made to move back and forth.

Billy just kept staring at the windscreen. Staring. And staring. Until Billy found out that sometimes, if you stare at something long enough, you can make bad things go away. Kind of like sleeping with your eyes open.

★　　★　　★

I felt bad that my question had caused him anxiety. I could tell he was even more preoccupied after my enquiry and I chastised myself for it. I couldn't deny that, if he had pampered me the way I pampered him, it would have driven me mad. I hated that I had to think about everything so much and wondered what it would be like to have a husband whom I didn't feel the need to look after. Everything was getting blurred.

Was I this way because of Billy's breakdown? Certainly, without a doubt. Was I like this because of a need to nurture? Definitely. Was it bad or good to be this way? Most likely a bit of both, but probably more bad for our relationship than it was good for Billy. I just wanted it all to be over. I was so tired with second-guessing my reactions to things, pre-planning my responses and analysing everything.

On about the third day, when I arrived home from work, Liam said he needed to go over something with me before they left for the day. Billy said his goodbyes and then took Ben for a walk. I made us all a cup of tea and we sat down at the kitchen table. Liam started by saying that they needed to clarify two things that I had said when I gave my statement a few days earlier. The first was to do with what Billy had said when I asked him if he had been abused. 'What exactly did you ask Billy?' Liam asked.

'I asked him if he had been abused when he was in care,' I replied.

'Did you specifically ask if he had been *sexually* abused?' he persevered.

'No… I just said abused.'

'Did he clarify that the abuse had been sexual?'

'No… well, no, he didn't, but I know he knew what I meant… and I know his affirmation was referring to sexual abuse,' I stammered. I did that sometimes when I was trying to vocalise my thoughts. I hoped it didn't make me sound unsure.

'How did you know?' Liam keep on.

'Well, obviously, I didn't mean physical abuse because I have always known he was physically abused so why would I be asking if he had been *physically* abused?' I was beginning to feel frustrated because I wasn't sure if I was explaining myself very well.

'How do you know that he didn't think you meant mental or verbal abuse?'

'Because he doesn't even consider them to be abuse.' By that point,

I wished I *had* told him that I had originally said 'sexual'. I wouldn't have considered it lying, not really, it was just a silly formality.

'Right then.' He reached over and handed me a piece of folded paper. 'Do you recognise this?' he asked.

I opened it and began reading. I was a bit taken aback and it took a few moments to register. 'Oh, um… yeah, yeah… ah, it's a letter I sent to Billy's sister, Lauren.'

'Yes,' Liam agreed. 'It shows that you did indeed wonder whether Billy had been sexually abused but also that you couldn't broach the subject with him. Also the date proves that you wrote it before we contacted you. Were you in any way aware of the investigation, or did you hear anything about it from friends or family back in Wales *before* we contacted you?' he then asked.

'No, not at all. I had no idea.' I worried that I didn't sound genuine, mainly because I was thinking about the fact that they had read a personal letter that I had written to Lauren. I didn't get a chance to read it all and I couldn't remember all that was in it so I just had to hope that there wasn't anything too personal in it. I was then preoccupied with my embarrassment and it made me a bit slow in my response. But then I realised that you couldn't get any *more* personal than what we were already talking about, which immediately made me feel silly, and the letter promptly became insignificant.

'It's a really nice letter… it shows you think a lot of her.' Liam stated, as if on cue.

'I really do,' I replied. 'She's like Billy in a lot of her ways.'

'Have you ever discussed sexual abuse with Billy at all?' he asked, getting back on track.

'No, not directly… well, I guess, yeah, yeah, I have, sort of. But not to do with this investigation. Well, actually, I suppose it is related to it but it wasn't at the time… I mean, it was years ago. I already told you about it. It was back when I asked him about when he had first had sex.' I was talking quickly. Most likely out of nervousness and frustration.

'Right, well, that brings us to our next point that we need to clarify,' Liam said.

'Oh, right.' I didn't really see where he was going with that line of enquiry.

'You did say in your statement that you had asked Billy about when he had first had sex and that, at the end of that conversation, you said that you told him that what he had described was sexual abuse. But, you also stated that, prior to us contacting you, you hadn't ever discussed sexual abuse with Billy. Which is what we need to clarify. So, do you remember saying both those things?' Liam asked.

'Yes, yes, that's right. But I don't really consider them to be the same thing. The first time wasn't really a discussion. I just made a statement, and then it was never acknowledged again,' I explained.

'Right, well, can you just go over that first discussion again?'

'OK. Well, it was soon after we met. We were talking about first relationships... well, at least, that was what I thought we were talking about. Billy said he was eleven. I remember I was shocked but I assumed he was referring to exploratory fumbling with a girl at school... you know, behind the bike shed or something...' I giggled nervously. 'I asked him who she was and he said that she was employed by one of the homes when he was in care. I remember I was totally shocked and had said something like "that's totally sexual abuse". Billy was obviously uncomfortable and he completely clammed up and quickly changed the subject. That was it really... we never mentioned it again.

'It's strange because I remember being absolutely appalled at the time but I must not have wanted to acknowledge it then because I forgot all about it... I mean, I must have been in denial or something. I honestly didn't think about it again until just recently.'

I paused, grabbed my mug of cold tea and swigged it back. My throat and mouth were terribly dry. I then continued, 'I absolutely never imagined in a million years that she was the last in a very long line. Or that it had started years and years before he was eleven. In fact, I think he probably thought he was a man at eleven because he had already been through so much, which I guess would be why he didn't feel too embarrassed to tell me.'

Liam then asked, 'So Billy only told you about her at that point?'

'Yes, that's right. We didn't discuss anything about any kind of abuse at all until just after you contacted me,' I reiterated.

Liam continued writing for a bit, then added, 'OK, I think that's all.' I was surprised that it ended so abruptly. I really couldn't tell whether my input had been helpful or not. They really didn't give any indication one way or the other. After a few minutes, they packed up and Liam said I could read through what he had recorded and initial it the next day. And then they left.

I thought about it after they left and I could see they must have wanted to clarify how I knew we both had been referring to sexual abuse and that we hadn't talked about it in detail before they contacted me. It was like I had said to Billy, they were just being thorough. I hoped I had explained myself well enough.

Then, after five long days, each as stressful and exhausting as the one before, they were finished. Billy's statement ended up being 58 pages long. They had been particularly interested in Billy's accounts of the abuse suffered at the hands of Mr Henry, as he was one of the men they were investigating. We hadn't known that other boys had already named Mr Henry. The other abusers that Billy named would, of course, lead them in yet other directions, but for now the focus was Mr Henry.

We were told that they would be in touch regarding a possible court date and the arrangements for our attendance. As illogical as it sounds, we both found ourselves experiencing a certain sense of shock. Well, at least that is what I experienced on hearing the news, and I assumed that Billy was feeling the same, as his expression seemed to me to portray exactly what I was feeling. Why we were surprised, I don't know. We, of course, should have seen it coming and, I suppose, in some way we did. How could we not? But, to be honest, I think we had had so much to concentrate on we simply hadn't thought about that side of things. I mean, obviously it stood to reason that there was a chance it would go to trial. Liam and Mark had been working towards that end. We just hadn't thought about our part in that. Our minds just hadn't taken us there. One step at a time and all that.

Then they were gone, just like that. Within a few days, the drama of their visit wore off. In fact, sometimes it even felt like it had all been a figment of our imagination, that they hadn't actually been in Victoria at all. Of course, the telling had brought some semblance of relief, mainly because all secrets are a weight. Obviously, the larger the secret, the bigger the burden; shame carried a pretty heavy one.

Billy had become such a different man to the one he would have been, on so many levels, but it was all made so much worse because of the years and years of trying to keep it all a secret. The secret itself was horrendous enough, but it was the shame he felt that spurred him to keep it all such a guarded secret in the first place.

Because *he* felt shame. How sad is that? The perpetrators of those horrific crimes were the ones who should have felt shame, but they never do. It is always the victims who feel the shame. It was that shame that he had been marked by, probably most of all, and it was the fear of exposing the shame that led to the monumental task of suppressing it all.

In some respects, it is the keeping of secrets that perpetuates the misery and prevents healing. The act of protecting, guarding and omitting became so convoluted until it morphed into something that took on a life of its own – ironically, it almost succeeded in taking *Billy's* life.

The telling had also brought to the fore one of his main concerns, the worry that he might be perceived differently if the truth ever came out – as if me knowing the real him would have somehow tainted my view of him, changed my perception, altered my love.

I thought back to the look on his tortured face before he answered my question about whether he had been abused; it had held such a pleading expression. I remembered that I had felt as if I had read his mind, when a voice in my head said, 'Hear of my shame, but love me still. Please.' Then, after he'd said that he had been abused, the comfort he seemed to find when he realised that it didn't make a difference had been immediately evident.

I like to think that it was me whom he elected to unveil himself to, that I got to be the chosen one who learned of the secret first. But I'm not, not really, because I just happened to be the one who asked *the* question at the right time. Nor was it Liam or Mark, who had been privy to the very first details uttered out loud. They just happened to be the ones who heard it all first. Really, the liberation was his alone. With himself.

Soon, our lives had once again settled into a deceptively normal routine. The 'normal' being the new normal, the one we had created since the breakdown, the one where we subconsciously cocooned ourselves. The safe world of Billy, Ben and I doing our thing – night-time walks, watching videos, drives in the country, with the odd breakfast out, although dining in a restaurant could only ever be considered if there weren't many cars in the car park – busy restaurants were strictly out.

During the week, I would go to work and Billy had a routine. Taking his medication, having breakfast (something which he had never done), hanging out with Ben or playing with him in the garden, weight-training in the gym that we had set up in the garage, 'side-effect' napping in the afternoon, then preparing our evening meal. He made chillies and stews, shepherd's pies and pasties – and found that, actually, he really enjoyed it. His only variation to this routine was his weekly appointments with Amanda.

At weekends, if Billy wouldn't even go for a drive, I often gardened or did jigsaw puzzles while Billy pretty much replayed the same routine as the weekdays. I am sure I turned to such worthwhile pastimes as they allowed me to immerse myself fully in them with the minimum amount of thinking, thus providing a break of sorts. Obviously, doing puzzles – especially the 5,000-piece ones – required concentration, but the concentration of searching for a specific piece freed my mind of any other thoughts – which I both loved and needed. Also, adopting the technique of scanning served me well. Other methods may have achieved faster results, but I needed to take up as much time as possible. Fellow puzzlers will understand the appeal and, as dramatic as it sounds, I owe my sanity to jigsaws.

In the past, I have always been able to immerse myself in the hundreds of books I read, but that method of escapism had to be abandoned once the stress increased. Reading the same line over and over didn't cut it and nor did getting through a chapter with none of it sinking in.

Somehow, we had orchestrated an acceptable lifestyle. We knew we were in limbo but we still needed to be comfortable in that limbo. We were coping, at least in a certain fashion, as long as nothing came along to upset the apple cart.

12

PAIN IS THE ONLY WAY

Shaking with fear
And the fright of the nightmares
And the ghosts that haunt his dreams
He stares into the darkness
With sweat pouring from his brow
Is he dreaming still
Or is this madness as real as it seems

'Nightmares' by Damien McCarthy

Time passed slowly and quickly simultaneously. Christmas came and went once again and, by the beginning of 2001, we had settled into a relatively cushioned state of limbo. Although it has to be said, in a lot of ways, it felt like we were on a train – the trouble being, we had no idea where it was heading.

Intellectually, we knew we had hard times ahead, whether the case actually went to court or not. If it were to go to court, obviously it would be very stressful for Billy to stand up as a witness; but if the Crown Prosecution Service decided not to continue, then it would all have been for nothing. I wasn't sure which I dreaded more. I couldn't imagine Billy actually standing up in court and telling it all in front of a judge, the jury and a courtroom full of people, but I also knew he would be gutted if it didn't get that far. Regardless of the reasons why, he would take it to mean he wasn't important enough to warrant it and it would be yet another kick in the teeth.

In spite of all that, though, we somehow managed to position ourselves emotionally in a sort of deluded bubble, even though we knew it was far from over. It was as if we had shrouded ourselves, subconsciously yet indisputably, in cotton wool.

Billy carried on seeing Amanda once a week and pretty much continued with his daily routine. I, possibly even more than him, was in denial – and, being so desperate for them to be so, pretended things were fine. When we talked, it was of mundane things. My mind seemed to be recoiling from the important stuff and clutching desperately to the non-essentials. We got to a place where I could just about forget but, inevitably, concerns and worries would worm their way into my head in the quiet, dark moments – sometimes hours before falling asleep.

During the weekdays, at 3.00pm, between his nap and preparing our evening meal, Billy watched *Coronation Street*. We were both *Corrie* addicts and I also watched it whenever I could, but it was an awkward time for me so I usually had to wait until the omnibus edition on a Sunday morning. Billy would ring me at work during each commercial break, teasing me with titbits of gossip. One day in April, right on cue, the telephone rang. 'It's all happening on the *Street*, babes,' Billy's voice taunted down the phone.

'Shut up, shut up, shut up… I'm not watching it yet,' I pleaded.

'OK, but it's good, you've gotta watch it. I'll phone you in the next one.'

I got all the children eating their snack and stole a few minutes to watch the last bit. As the credits rolled up the screen, I expected the phone to ring, but it didn't. Thinking it strange, I dialled our number instead. It was engaged, and it stayed engaged for well over an hour.

Finally I got through, but the answer machine kicked in on the sixth ring.

'Billy, are you there?'

He didn't pick up – not a good sign. I redialled immediately. It rang five times before he picked up. I counted.

'What?' he snapped.

'What's going on?' I replied, faking insouciance.

'What do you mean?'

Oh great, he's gone all moody. He knows full well what I mean, he's just being awkward, I thought to myself. 'The phone was engaged for ages… who called?' I asked.

'Liam.'

'Oh.' I was monosyllabic with surprise. It was, after all, later than he usually called. 'It's midnight, UK time,' I added, typically focusing on the unimportant stuff – delaying tactic, I suppose.

'He's on night shift.'

'Oh.'

'They've got a court date… we've got to go… I'll see you when you get home.'

'OK, babes,' I replied to the dial tone, realising that he had hung up already. I sat down and wondered how it was that some of the most important things people had to say were often relayed as addendums or postscripts to a conversation. 'Bloody, bloody hell… here we go again,' I said out loud to myself.

Billy didn't take the news well. I can't say I was all that surprised. For me, I think it was more the impact of being jolted back into reality that left me somewhat shell-shocked. The knowledge that it really was going to go to court and the realisation that we would, of course, have to attend brought a whole other set of concerns and worries – not the least of which was that we actually had to *get* there. It seems strange but it really wasn't until Billy was faced with the reality of going back to Wales that we both realised how our lives, and Billy's in particular, had become so isolated.

He became very anxious at the thought of travelling to the UK and spent a lot of time discussing it all with Amanda. Billy was still on stress leave from work and, except for his appointments with Amanda, there wasn't any need for him to go out anywhere, so his anxiety over going out hadn't become apparent. He had been in the habit of avoiding situations or experiences that made him feel uncomfortable in such an elaborate way since childhood that he didn't even realise he was doing it. His brain had been conditioned to cope in that way for so long he had become powerless to it. Add to that the behaviour adopted since the breakdown and the result was that he was left with a myriad of habits and phobias, all from anticipating being in situations that could trigger flashbacks, predicting the anxiety and adapting through avoidance. We had been living a life that others did not see – and nor did we.

It quickly became apparent to me that he obviously had a problem and, after talking it over with our GP and encouraging Billy to talk about it with Amanda, he was eventually diagnosed with post-traumatic stress disorder and agoraphobia. It was amazing how so many of his idiosyncrasies were explained away solely due to these diagnoses. I could see that all of it was related to his earlier abuse and, in a roundabout way, I also realised that I had been correct in thinking that his view of the police and other authority figures was due to his childhood trauma. It was all interconnected.

I could recall countless times when his behaviour had baffled me, and now, finally, it all made sense. I even found myself thinking about things that Billy had said or done years before and then, suddenly, understanding would dawn, as the light went on in my head – everything making sense and falling into place. He hated to be surprised in any way, always wanting to know where he was going and what to expect. No wonder he had said, all those years ago, that my organising made him feel safe! He had always adhered to routines in everything he did – going to the same shop to buy cigarettes, for example, even if it meant driving across town; filling up on gas at the same station, even if we were closer to another one; insisting on driving to places using the same route, even if it meant he was going out of his way. All those things showed a pattern that, up until then, I hadn't even noticed. So many times I had joked about him always driving along Bay Street – to be truthful, it used to drive me crazy. We would often take much longer to get somewhere just because he had to get there by going down *that* road, the one that, for some inexplicable reason, he felt comfortable driving along. Even a detour, due to road works or something, would throw him into turmoil and cause him to panic. It seems so strange to me that I hadn't questioned such peculiar habits. Now they seemed to be so indicative, but, hindsight being 20/20 and that, I guess it wasn't all that strange.

I guess individually his foibles didn't add up to much but, by looking at our past as a whole, and with the acquired knowledge of his abuse, it all seemed so obvious. I hadn't thought it particularly strange that he could never bear to be touched without prior knowledge and would visibly flinch if taken unawares. I could never walk up behind him and give him an unannounced cuddle and I had to be ready for him physically lashing out if I dared to cuddle up to him in bed if he was already asleep. Even my hands on his back could trigger the swing of a clenched fist. I had become accustomed and simply wouldn't have ever thought that my hand lovingly placed on his back, or indeed any of my demonstrations of affection, would cause his brain subconsciously to register a potential threat. He had developed, as a survival mechanism, an ability to be hyper-vigilant so that still, as an adult, when someone approaches him or takes him by surprise, he can become super-aware – his body wired instantly to accelerate from a state of resting to peak fight-or-flight mode. He often reacted so quickly it was as if he had known something was going to happen even before it did. Of course, now it is obvious that such reactions were totally understandable when you took into account his terrible experiences as a young boy, but back then, God, I didn't even question it!

The years after the breakdown, before I found out about the abuse, had been so hard. It had all been so confusing but, once I had found out about it, it made everything else make sense. Sometimes, I thought about what would have happened if Billy hadn't hit rock bottom when he did. What if the timing hadn't been right and I had given in before he'd been ready for help? But then I reminded myself that it wasn't a coincidence that he'd come to his senses at that time. My *genuine* reaction was what had turned it. I really believe that. The interesting thing is that I couldn't have faked that feeling of numbness. If I had faked it, Billy would have known, and the power would have been taken out of it. It was just as though his psyche knew that my psyche had shifted – so subconsciously that I hadn't even appreciated it – and he felt threatened by it. I can't help but see the connection between Billy losing my support and deciding to fight.

I also thought about all the attempts he had made to shut me out. I couldn't really blame his mind for convincing him to try to push me away. His mind had been protecting him by pushing away any threat.

I was thankful that his mind had possessed the ability to protect him throughout his turbulent childhood so I couldn't, and shouldn't, have ever turned my back on that same function that made Billy run from me and push me away. His mind had done a stellar job of protecting him for so long, and from such a young age, it was hardly surprising that it tried to accomplish the same result again. That reaction was entrenched. Wired in. He needed something like a psycho-electrician.

I have to say, I am actually quite surprised that I didn't lose patience with him in the early days of our relationship. However, I was only nineteen when we first met so I can't take credit for any patience, understanding or insight. I was as egocentric as the next teenager – and certainly naive in some ways – so at least at the beginning I can say that I *am* surprised, but obviously I am glad.

I can remember, even all the way back to when we first met, that he had many quirks and behaviours that, at the very least, were slightly odd but perhaps might have warned of the trouble that lay ahead. The obvious signs like mood swings, low self-esteem, self-deprecation and so forth had been evident, but I suppose I thought that 'my love' would change that. The 'eccentricities', like never going into restaurants unless they were practically empty – and that was on a good day; on a bad day, he wouldn't go full stop – were just seen as quirks and, to be honest, I can't actually remember what I really thought about them, other than that they were funny personality traits. I must have been irritated sometimes, but I guess I didn't really think they were that peculiar, and certainly not sufficiently outlandish to leave an impression.

I guess because he had always been that way, I never really questioned his oddities or, if I had, I must have found his explanations entirely satisfactory. I really hadn't fully appreciated all of this until he was diagnosed with agoraphobia. I'm sure also that the fact that I was rather unsociable myself and quite the homebody made Billy's behaviour less apparent than perhaps it would have been if I had been more outgoing. In any case, I was glad I had never pressed the matter *and* I was glad I finally understood.

After we got all the details from the witness support worker about where the trial was being held, which hotel they would book us into and what our travel arrangements were, the rest was a waiting game.

The trial was scheduled to start at the end of April; however, as they didn't know when Billy would be called to take the stand, they couldn't tell us when our flight would be. They couldn't even guarantee the end of April, so it was all up in the air – which certainly didn't do much for Billy's state of mind.

One afternoon, totally out of the blue, Billy blurted out, 'I don't know what it will be like to be in Wales after all these years. I don't know if I will bottle it.' His admission proved to me once again that I really had no idea what was going on in his head. He appeared relaxed, intent on watching something on the telly, when actually he had been thinking of anything but the TV programme.

'Try not to worry about it, babes. Just take it one step at a time.'

What a load of crap, my inner voice interjected, as vocally I portrayed the opposite of what I was feeling. There I was, shitting myself, and I was actually telling Billy not to worry. My tummy churned every time I pictured Billy actually in Cardiff. Probably because I couldn't actually imagine him going through with it and the mere thought of that possibility made me nervous. I really could see him getting all the way there, losing the plot and going on a bender and not even turning up at the court. Then again, maybe when the time actually came, he wouldn't even go to the airport. He hadn't even gone to his mum's funeral after all, so that was a distinct possibility. The thought of having to tell Liam that Billy wouldn't get on the plane or that he had gone missing in Cardiff made me feel sick.

He then stood up, and added in a slightly agitated way, 'I just don't know how to be. Everything is whirling around in my head and I can't think.' He paused as though for breath, as if that slight intake of air would summon up even an extra ounce of strength. Strength enough for admissions. With his shoulders squared bravely, he continued, 'I'm scared. I don't know how to be *that* boy any more. I don't want to be him again… and I will be when I see *that man*…' He broke off, his lips trembling and his rigid spine beginning to bend under the weight of emotions.

My voice failed me and I gulped for air, trying to force back the tears. Oh, good God, I said to myself. I hadn't thought about that part of it… of course *he* would be there. Jesus, how old would he be?

Billy didn't seem to notice that I hadn't said anything and, after recovering himself, he continued, 'I didn't know how to be like the other lads – how to be normal, whatever the fuck normal was, so I invented myself. I looked at the other boys, and even some girls, and watched how they acted… I tried on their lives for size. Sometimes, after school, I pretended I was going home to their houses, as if I was part of their families. I sometimes even hid in their gardens and watched them through the window. I made things up and told so many lies… I just didn't want to be me. The more lies I told and the more trouble I got into, I sort of backed myself into a corner. I was a nutter and I couldn't have got out of it even if I wanted to. I was hard and I didn't let anything get to me.' He paused again for a moment, but I could tell he wasn't finished. 'I don't want to be *him* again, but what if going there makes *him* come back… or, worse, what if I can't hack it now that I've changed?'

'You haven't changed that much, you know. You're still that little boy in so many ways,' I replied, thankful that I had found my voice.

'Will you do something for me?' he asked sheepishly.

'What?'

'Will you get me some beer? I just want to relax.'

I didn't know what to say. Part of me was mad that he had put me in such a position but, on the other hand, I totally understood the need to relax and forget about it all – even just for one night. I knew it wasn't the right thing to do, but I also felt sorry for him. I knew it was risky but I listened to my heart and not my head and went to the liquor store. I hated how it made me feel, driving to buy the shit I vowed I would never buy for him again. I so didn't want to be an enabler, but I did acknowledge that Billy deserved some relief. I told myself that I would ask our GP if there was anything he could take to help him relax, just until the court case was over. That was enough to give myself the permission to do that, for the last time.

Billy drank all six bottles of beer and fell into a deep sleep on the couch downstairs. I tried to justify my part in his drinking by telling myself that he hadn't actually drunk that much and at least it wasn't hard liquor – totally ignoring the fact that he shouldn't have had any alcohol at all with the tablets he was on. Deep down, I knew that, if a person is drinking for the sole purpose of forgetting their problems, then that is where the slope starts getting very slippery.

The next afternoon, Billy appeared somewhat subdued. The conversation the day before, that told of his concerns about the boy he had been and how he had behaved back in his childhood, had obviously unsettled him. He had unsuccessfully been trying to push that younger Billy away, but the pattern of the previous few days had made it difficult and had surely contributed to his reflective state of mind.

Coupled with those thoughts, he had also been trying to pinpoint accurately the exact timing of the incidents that had occurred in his childhood – trying to figure out the wheres and whens of it all. Months before, he had come up with a sort of timeline with Liam but it had been done in a somewhat generalistic fashion. He had known which children's home he had been sent to first, and then the others just sort of slotted into place with the use of phrases like, 'I must have been at such and such a place in that year because I went to so and so school at that age…' It all made sense but, nonetheless, he still tried obsessively to remember the corroborative details that he knew were in his memory somewhere.

That night, we went over to my parents' house for dinner. It was while we were just about to eat that one such memory was triggered. On the drive home, Billy told me that, when he had looked at the joint of beef, he felt a tiny seismic jolt of a memory. He said he knew exactly when he had been at a certain children's home because it was from that home that he had come when he had been taken to his mum's house for a particular visit. Billy remembered that because Mr Andrews, who was from that home, had dropped him off. He knew it was Mr Andrews because he knew the car – the car that was so distinctive. The window on the driver's side had been wound down and Billy remembered thinking how silly it was to have it open on such a cold, windy day. It was November. He said he knew that because it was his sister's birthday, and that's what had made that particular visit special.

As that was going on in Billy's head, my dad had started to carve the beef. I remembered that I had looked over at Billy and noticed the blank, yet vaguely perplexed look on his face. It confirmed to me that he wasn't with us. I thought how odd he looked, just staring at the meat. He looked confused, although he should have been used to seemingly random memories suddenly appearing in the forefront of his mind. But I knew he never was. He said that seeing the roast beef had reminded him of looking through a window at the vicarage and seeing the vicar and his family sitting down to Sunday lunch. Maybe talking about looking through windows the day before had played a part in retrieving that memory.

Again, he remembered what a cold day it had been because he could recollect how much he had been shivering while standing outside, jealously looking in on the cosy scene before him. He also recalled hungrily eyeing up the delicious-looking joint. He said that looking through the window at the vicarage happened on the same day as his sister's birthday because that morning he had gone to the shops to buy sweets for her. The idea had been to buy a birthday surprise that he could get with the money that Mr Andrews had given him. He didn't elaborate, but I secretly had my own thoughts as to why he had been given the money. I watched him squashing that memory. I knew he wouldn't let his mind take himself *there*.

Billy said a further seismic jolt had reminded him that the vicarage day came about when he had run off after being accused of stealing the money he had used to buy the sweets. He knew he had meant to tell his mum about seeing her purse down the side of the settee, and he knew he hadn't got round to it because the idea to go and buy the sweets for Lauren had happened before he had got the chance. I imagined that getting the blame for something he hadn't done fuelled the feelings of anger and frustration that must have constantly been swimming around inside him.

He said that that blame had precipitated the bolt that had brought him to the vicarage, and the roast beef. He said that it was as if seeing the roast beef had caused things to be pulled out of his memory file, all at exactly the same time. I agreed, but I thought that he had retrieved them a bit out of order. Right after noticing the roast beef, he remembered when he had been at a particular children's home because it was on Lauren's birthday. It would have made more sense if seeing the meat had reminded him of looking through the window of the vicarage. But, regardless of the order, he had been reminded of a chronology of memories – the details of which corroborated what he had already worked out with Liam. Putting all the bits together had somehow validated what he already knew in a way that pleased and excited him but the feelings were short-lived because he was soon reliving an overwhelming feeling of hurt. It was the exact feeling he had felt when no apology had been given following the recovery of the intact purse, all those years ago. He said that he remembered that he hadn't stuck up for himself. He said there really was no point. He didn't seem to blame himself for that decision, probably because he knew that there really *had been* no point.

The unfairness, the hopelessness… it had all come back, right there at my parents' dining-room table. As always, all his emotions travelled along the seams of other hurts, especially the old unacknowledged feelings from an abusive upbringing. Under my watchful eye, Billy had left the table. I knew that the familiar sensations of an impending panic attack were making themselves known.

It was a long time before Billy ate a meal at my parents' again. As tends to happen with panic attacks, he associated that panic attack with the act of eating there.

By the next night, it had become obvious that my decision to relent and buy the beer when my head had warned against it had been the wrong one. I shouldn't have been surprised. Billy obviously liked the effect the alcohol had had so much he rang a shop that brings alcohol to your door which, needless to say, resulted in him being pretty drunk by the time I got home. I never even knew such places existed.

Luckily, he promptly passed out which was the best thing because I don't think I would have been able to stop myself from exploding. I knew by the next day I would have calmed down enough not to get into an argument with him, which was just the way it had to be then. I couldn't give him an excuse to freak out and pull out of the court case. Not that he could have, really, because I suppose by that stage they could subpoena him or something but, at the end of the day, they couldn't make him go if they couldn't find him. Christ, he'd run away enough as a kid so I was sure he was more than capable if he put his mind to it. My mission was to ensure he kept his emotions as stable as possible and not to add any fuel. I often wondered if Liam and the rest of them realised how close he came to bailing out and how much I had to pussy-foot around him in order to secure his attendance.

I ended up taking a few days off work – that was how agitated and concerned I'd become. I was doing my best to keep him close, to keep him from returning to the gathering depression, but it was clear to me that I was losing the battle. I was so determined to cope, yet so clearly unable to fix it all on my own. I didn't know if I was doing the right thing and I lay awake in the dark of night hating having to be the one who always had to hold it all together.

I knew Billy was passively mad at me while I was home those days. He knew full well what I was doing, although I didn't admit to him that my reason for staying home was to ensure he didn't drink. He was sulking around in a bad mood the whole time, but at least he wasn't drinking. I encouraged him to go to the centre and talk it all out with either Amanda or one of the other women who had been a great help to him. I knew it would help. I also got some medication from the doctor to help him relax.

Thank God, he did agree to go and see Amanda. She, as always, helped a great deal. I really don't think he would have coped through it all if it hadn't been for the support from the centre.

My method of coping was quite different. For the first time, I was easily overwhelmed so my brain dealt with things individually. It was the only way I could cope. In effect, I compartmentalised all the things I had to deal with. I couldn't just avoid dealing with something purely because I was so stressed, otherwise everything would unravel. My work, Ben, the house, my chronic pain and my infertility were all individually boxed up and took up half of my brain space. Billy took up the other half, and that box was always open. There was no room for anything or anyone else.

The box of work was opened and dealt with at work. Once I left at the end of the day, it was completely out of my head. I had to have Post-Its everywhere to remind me of early drop-offs, meetings and upcoming activities. One day, a child came bearing a bunch of roses and a box of chocolates. 'Happy Valentine's Day!' he shouted excitedly, prompted by his mum hovering in the background. I hadn't even realised it was February, let alone Valentine's Day.

'Thank you so much. They are lovely!' I swallowed hard, suppressing the lump in my throat. 'We have so much planned for today,' I continued, while frantically reeling off a mental checklist. Glitter… check; stickers… check; red paint… check… I'll have to cut out some heart shapes… shit, Naomie's birthday… I'll have to ask Mum to cover over nap time while I rush to the mall… 'Let's say goodbye to Mummy and then how about you help me put these lovely flowers in a vase?' I held the little boy's hand and waved to his mum – a smile painted on my face, my head in a whirl.

The box containing my health issues remained closed until I couldn't control the pain with my regular pill management. One night I was forced to take action and go to the ER after a day when my neglected, worsening pain became unbearable. I was admitted into hospital and was forced into confronting the truth.

The box containing my infertility issues was locked. However, the truth that I had to face while in hospital prised it open. When I went to the ER, I was asked the usual questions. I had been countless times before and I knew exactly what was wrong – the symptoms were always the same. What I hadn't realised was that the computer didn't show that every time I had gone to the ER I hadn't just been admitted, but I had also required surgery. It only showed how many times I had presented at the ER with pelvic pain.

I also hadn't realised that every other time I had been in, my gynaecologist had been contacted and he had given his instructions for me to be admitted. This time, though, he was out of the country and couldn't be contacted. The ER doctor suggested that I saw the gynaecologist on call, but I wouldn't. I had seen so many incompetent ones and had the scars to prove it. I had finally found the best guy in Victoria, and had been told I shouldn't see anyone else – and that I had the right to refuse. He knew my case and I trusted him.

The ER doctor was cocky, arrogant and very patronising. He didn't seem to like that I said I knew what was wrong with me and I knew what drugs I wanted. In hindsight, I can see that he probably thought I was either a drug-user or a nutcase but, at the time, I was in a lot of pain and he really irritated me. He sent me for X-rays and tests that I knew were a complete waste of time, not to mention taxpayers' money. I kept on telling him what was causing the pain. It was exactly the same as every other time, yet he prattled on about all the other things that could be causing it.

When all the tests he had ordered came back negative, as I knew they would, he started saying that maybe I didn't understand the pain scale. I wanted to throttle him but, even though the morphine had done nothing for the reduction of my pain, it had chilled me out enough so that I couldn't be bothered to carry out the attack. I explained that I had been told that I needed to have a hysterectomy, but that I didn't think the pain warranted such drastic action yet. He actually said that I was in danger of becoming a martyr! I calmly, thanks again to the morphine, told him that I lived with a '3' pain all the time. When it went up to '5', I took Tylenol with codeine to get it back down to a '3'. When it got to the point where the pain rose to '7' or '8' and I couldn't control it any more, I would come to the hospital for pain management and any necessary surgery. I told him that it was my understanding that it was also the adhesions I had that were causing the trouble as much as the endometriosis, as my bowel was attached to the pelvic wall, and also that I experienced regular haemorrhagic cysts.

He clearly wanted me to shut up but the drugs had significantly loosened my tongue by this point, so I continued to babble on. I told him that, once I got treatment, I would go back to living with a '3' and I found that acceptable. I even admitted that, if I had to live with a '5' all the time, perhaps I would agree to a hysterectomy, but I just didn't think a '3' was bad enough. So, yes, I told him, I do understand the pain scale… and, if I get to the point where living with a '3' is too much, then I will make the decision, but for now the answer is still no.

I was surprised that he hadn't interrupted me but, to be truthful, I don't think I gave him much of a chance. I hoped I had finally said enough to get him off my back – or not too much, depending on how you looked at it.

I actually didn't see him again but, over the twelve or so hours that I waited in the cubicle in the ER for a bed to become available, at least four different nurses came in and put in their two cents' worth regarding the benefits of hysterectomies. 'I've never felt better…'; 'Best thing I ever did…'; 'New lease on life…'; 'Pain free…' It seemed everyone had something to say. That had never happened before, so I was sure that the charming ER doc was behind it all. I needed the pretence that things were OK and his interference was threatening it. It was ridiculous, but essential, to have that stiff upper lip and the nurses' attention was making it quiver. I also felt that their comments were betrayals, even though intellectually I knew otherwise. I just wanted someone to say I was right – right to put my baby girl before my pain. Lying there by myself, I allowed my mind to shift from the physical to the philosophical and realised I wouldn't do it. With that decision came the acceptance of what was happening to me and the realisation that it still was *my* choice. Nothing had been taken out of my control. Yet.

I finally fell into a drug-induced sleep and awoke some hours later on the ward. To my complete disbelief, I was on the maternity ward. There were pictures on the wall of smiling mums holding their babies; leaflets on the bedside table about breastfeeding; in the distance, I could hear crying. That lovely newborn-baby cry, which, on just hearing it, was producing a physical pain that almost surpassed the one in my abdomen. I was aware of my throat constricting, making it hard to breathe.

Behind the curtain, in the next bed, I could hear a woman's voice. She was talking softly, the way mums do to their precious offspring. Almost on cue, in walked 'the daddy', weighed down with flowers and balloons.

Was this some kind of sick joke? I started to cry. I couldn't control myself. Conveniently, just at the right time, Sophie arrived for a visit and immediately said, 'What the fuck are you doing in here, for Christ's sake?'

I couldn't even answer, I was crying so much, seriously in threat of hyper-ventilating by this stage. Sophie left the room and I found out later that she complained at the nurses' station. Of course, it wasn't their fault; they didn't allocate beds. I had seen on the news about the bed shortages so it was probably just a cruel coincidence. You just had to take what you could get, but I thought that they should at least check to see what people were in for before sending them to the maternity ward.

I was told that they would do what they could to change me and, in the meantime, a lovely nurse came in and covered up all the photos. The lady beside me was going home that day and they said that they wouldn't put a pregnant patient or new mum in that bed, which they didn't have to do. Sophie phoned Billy and got him to bring in a personal CD player and I listened to Enya instead of the noises of a happy maternity ward.

That evening, I got the news that a bed had become available in another ward. A porter came to wheel me down. As we waited for the elevator, a woman came and stood alongside us. I had my bag on my knee, hiding my belly. 'When are you due?' she asked.

'Not for a while yet,' I lied, more concerned about her potential embarrassment if I said what I wanted to say. It was merely an innocent presumption. But it hurt like hell.

The very next day, as I was lying in bed in my private room – oh, thank heavens for small mercies – I got a surprise visitor. A social worker! I was appalled. 'What the fuck does she want?' I asked myself. 'People like me don't have social workers.' She sat at the end of my bed and I immediately took offence. I was quite rude, which is unlike me but, after the events of the previous day, it was hardly surprising.

After a while, I relaxed and decided I may as well just accept that she was there and talk to her. She asked me a few questions about my health and my home situation and got me talking in the way that 'they' seem able to do. In for a penny, in for a pound, I thought, and started to tell her about my infertility and the situation with Billy. After a time, her questions became more and more personal and she also started acting a bit strangely. She had been fine up until I started talking about Billy. I was beginning to think she was a bit of a bitch.

Then, just as I was starting to think it was getting a bit weird, she apologised for being unprofessional and said that she had experienced a very similar situation in her own marriage. She put her notes down and we chatted 'off the record'. She asked me a lot of questions and it was obvious that she was asking for her own benefit. I was sure I noticed tears in her eyes and then she revealed to me that her husband had also been abused as a child and he had had a breakdown. She was clearly upset and admitted that she didn't have the strength to stick by him and they'd got divorced.

'I'm sure you did the best you could at the time. It takes a level of reception on their part as well. Maybe he just wasn't ready for your help,' I said with a strange, yet not altogether uncommon feeling of role reversal. I felt bad that, because I had talked about supporting Billy, I had made her feel guilty for not doing the same for her own husband. It just goes to show, you never know what is going on in the lives of the people you encounter. I thought she was being bitchy when, in fact, I had hit a raw nerve. The grumpy bank teller; the frosty shop attendant; even the moody ER doctor I saw – who knew what was going on in their lives?

The social worker stood up abruptly and concentrated on picking up her things, I think in an effort to compose herself. She began fiddling with her briefcase. 'Well, Alix…' She paused awkwardly. 'I enjoyed talking to you.' She spoke without looking at me. Then she looked down at me. 'Don't waste your time or money going to a therapist or counsellor. You have the gift of self-counsel.'

She placed her hand over mine for a second then turned away. She seemed slightly embarrassed as she made to leave. She pulled the curtain around, behind herself, as she walked through it and then, almost immediately she poked her head back. 'How did you know that standing by your husband was the right thing to do?' she asked, as if she had had to summon up the courage to ask the question rather than it being an afterthought.

'I don't know, really. I can't actually explain it. I just feel things sometimes.'

'Do you feel the same about the hysterectomy?'

'Yeah, I do. It's not the right time yet. I know that. I may never have a biological child but now is not the right time to kill my chances.'

'Don't let anyone try to convince you, Alix. You'll know when the time is right, I'm certain of that!'

She turned and was gone. It was so surreal. I was left wondering if I had imagined it all – just like I felt after Liam and Mark had gone back to Wales. Her comment about not wasting my money going into therapy left me feeling rather pleased. It's normally what everyone suggests when stressful things happen, isn't it? 'Maybe you should see someone… it will help you to get closure…' I never could see how the mere verbal divulgence of 'my issues' would lessen them to any degree, or to grant me closure, whatever closure is. It will never truly be closed, or over.

I really don't think there is any closure to be found in the truly tragic. You just have to learn to live with things in some acceptable way; or, if you are blessed with faith and circumstances permit, you forgive. It's like saying, 'Move on'; some things are so bad you will never move on. Again, you just learn to live with them.

Billy will never just move on. Even when he has worked through his issues, something as severe as the abuse he went through will always be there.

The following day, my gynaecologist finally made it in to see me. I asked about why the social worker had appeared. He said he had never recommended the visit and, according to the notes, nor had my GP. He figured that the ER doctor must have arranged it, either because he thought I was a drug-user, or that I wasn't capable of making an informed decision about the hysterectomy. I also realised my hysterics in the maternity ward may have played a part as well. Whatever it was, at least I got to hear someone finally tell me I was making the right decision. It kind of made the time spent in the ER and the maternity ward worthwhile after all.

Before I left the hospital, after another surgery to clear out all the adhesions and to laser away any endometriosis, I was told yet again that a hysterectomy was my best option. My gynaecologist also said that, if we planned on having another go at IVF, we needed to do it sooner rather than later.

I couldn't tell Billy what he had said. I didn't want him to have to cope with that on top of everything else. I knew IVF was out of the question; Billy was no way stable enough emotionally and we couldn't afford it. I just had to bide my time. I did have the option of taking a drug that put me into an induced state of menopause but, as it wasn't covered by MSP (Medical Services Plan), the $1,065.30 that we would have to pay for a three-month injection was more than we could afford.

My gynaecologist once again proved his brilliance and got me a free sample, so it looked as though I had at least been given some breathing space, although I knew I wouldn't be able to put it on the back burner for much longer.

The box containing household issues and the dog was probably the most neglected. Ben had some health issues himself. He had changed quite dramatically and I feared the worst. Coincidentally, this all manifested itself not long after Billy's breakdown, which meant that Billy hadn't even seemed to notice. I regularly took him to the vet, on my own, and never discussed it with Billy. He simply wasn't available, mentally or physically. After voicing all my concerns to the vet about Ben, he diagnosed him as having canine cognitive dysfunction, a condition in which dogs show symptoms that could be interpreted as a dementia. I highlighted the strange behaviours – standing and staring at a blank wall; going outside and then seeming not to know why he did; his complete isolation from us (he no longer slept either on our bed or on the floor beside the couch); his lack of appetite; his lethargy; and countless other concerns. It was strange, but I could see the similarities between him and some elderly people I knew who had dementia. He was vacant a lot of the time and he had lost his sparkle. Sometimes, he didn't even seem to recognise me, which broke my heart. However, over the previous few years, after his initial diagnosis, his dementia hadn't seemed to get worse. The vet thought this was strange as it is a progressive disease. I was just relieved and didn't ask too many questions.

Apart from the dementia, Ben also had problems with his ears and had to have a few minor ops to drain fluid from both the earflap and the ear canal. It wasn't too serious, although it looked as though he was going to need a total ear ablation, which would have left him deaf. It sounds awful, I know, but I wouldn't, or couldn't, accept that and refused even to think about it. I religiously gave him all the meds, which thankfully I managed to administer properly and I never let myself think that he wouldn't be fine.

Actually, the whole medication thing was a bit of a comedy sketch. I managed to make him lie down, always in the kitchen so I could clean up more effectively, and I would proceed to clean out his ears; with cotton wool, cotton buds, a bowl of warm water, his medicated ear wash and his ear drops at the ready, I would tackle the job. I don't actually know how I managed to hold down a 100lb dog with one hand and administer ear drops with the other, but somehow I did. Then he would scramble up and shake himself as I stood by cringing, droplets of ear goo and medication being flicked *everywhere*. Somehow, the hefty vet bills were paid on time, as were all the other household bills, but I honestly don't remember writing the cheques or balancing my chequebook. It was just all done on autopilot, I suppose. And the cleaning… well, that was therapy.

Even though everything was crumbling around me, the organising, the cleaning, the nurturing… doing those fundamental 'female' things was how I stayed in control. I would go as I always did, into the kitchen. I cleaned with the kind of ritualised dedication that is comforting when other areas of life seem to be slipping out of control. I routinely washed and tidied the dishes away and swept the kitchen floor. Work that women had done for centuries. Ironically, I turned to it precisely because I didn't want to think about being a woman or of the inability to achieve the epitome of all that being female is. A tidy house makes for a tidy mind… isn't that what they say? For me, it was almost a mantra.

The fierce and feral beast of yearning, frustration, misery and injustice had to be dealt with in a disciplined fashion. Contained. Packaged. But, even then, I somehow knew that it was my expectations, my version of the story that I create around my reality, that makes what is happening seem fair or not fair, good or bad, better or worse. I could decide how I was going to tackle it. I had to stay sane and, for the most part, I did. However, it was not so much any of the other issues that appalled me but the childlessness. I could deal with the 'Billy' stuff and live with whatever the outcome turned out to be because I knew that I was doing all I could possibly do. But the baby thing? That was different. Was putting off another IVF cycle the wrong or right thing to do?

I thought about my infertility all the time, as well as constantly thinking about going to the court case… and Billy's mental health… and work… and Ben… and my health… and the bills… among other things. One afternoon, as I sat in the living room thinking, Billy came in and implored, 'Can't you just stop?'

'Stop what?' I asked.

'Stop thinking. You've got that crinkled-eyebrow thing happening. Just relax, for God's sake.'

'I *am* relaxed. *Thinking* relaxes me.'

'What are you thinking about?' he persisted.

'Everything.'

And it really was 'everything'. It's the only word I could use that encompassed what was really going on. What that was was something I couldn't put into words. But strangely, that in itself kind of explained it. It, simply, was everything.

'That's what I mean… sounds stressful.'

For the millionth time, I thought, you just don't get it and, for the millionth time, I accepted the fact that most people didn't. I wasn't really bothered; I was just frustrated. Why is it that thinking and analysing is perceived as negative? I rather prefer to say I 'philosophise', if only to give it the positive connotation it deserves. I am a head-dweller, that's all there is to it. I have to look for meaning and comfort. Perhaps I am forced to think and look deeper because I can't find it on the surface of things. But, at the end of the day, I have to look because I don't know what else to do.

This life is unsustainable without thought. I had to work out what was right and what was wrong. I couldn't always work it out, but I had to try because just trying helped me to survive it all. I have to admit, I spent a lot of time thinking. But I reassured Billy that thinking is a good thing, for me at least. It actually kept me from falling apart. Which was just as well because I certainly didn't have the luxury of falling apart. I so wanted to indulge in the unfairness, take to my *chaise-longue* and eat bon-bons. I wanted to bawl. But I knew that, if I did, I wouldn't be able to stop. So, with the aid of thinking and analysing, I boxed it back up. I even put a ribbon on it, in the manner of a smile – to disguise it, I suppose. I would never be OK with the infertility but, when asked, I nodded. It was the easiest thing to do. I said all the right things to people to prove that I was fine… but who was I kidding? It was all bullshit. Behind the coping exterior, I was suppressing a howl so basic and so loud in its primeval harshness it was deafening.

Of course, the mask was well in place. I went on. I knew partly because I was so used to coping it had become, if not exactly a reflex, a point of honour to do so. Partly because I felt that no one could entirely understand how it felt. And partly because I found comfort patronising. On my bad days, I'm ashamed to say, I also felt a kind of jealousy towards people who could opt out and succumb to their stress. It would have been so much easier just to stay in bed all day. I wanted to fall apart. But I couldn't. It wasn't my choice to cope. I didn't want to cope. But I had no idea how not to. I craved my bed during the day and couldn't wait to crawl into its flannelled safety each night.

Then, bit by bit, as the date got closer and closer, the bad days outweighed the good and it became harder. On the face of it, those last days when we were just endlessly waiting to go to court appeared to be affecting me more than Billy, even though I was supposed to be the one who was mentally healthier. Ironically, Billy was calming down — perhaps resignedly, or in a giving-up kind of way, but nonetheless he was still definitely less agitated. It was nice to see him calmer, if not all the time, at least some of the time. But I knew not to let myself become lulled into a false sense of security. I remained aware that his calmer demeanour wasn't a salutary development, it was just another coping mechanism. Nevertheless, compared to other behaviours, it was much more acceptable.

Even so, I was still half-expecting him to do a runner, which I guess was at the root of my stress. I knew he was still the wounded one, no matter what his calmer demeanour suggested. And, despite his superficial manner, I continued seeing signs of torment lurking just beneath the surface, and I was still privy to the fleeting nakedness of that look. Also, due to my extensive training in all that was Billy, I still detected the not so obvious signs of concentration that spoke of a determination to control his mind into making a calculated effort to conceal. He orchestrated within himself a deliberate manoeuvre which enabled the retrieval of the necessary protocols needed for dodging pain and avoiding sadness — or hurt, or shame, or whatever uncomfortable emotion rose within him. The experiences gained from his troubled past had trained him well and had prepared him for the upcoming court case.

Of course, looks can be deceiving. Billy wasn't actually any healthier mentally than he had been, he was just walking on familiar ground. The whole court scene, standing up in front of a judge and everything related to it – that was his territory, not mine. And it showed. I had no idea what to expect, but Billy did, or thought he did. I was a bag of nerves, but Billy appeared not to be. I prayed for justice, but Billy expected nothing. And, actually, I guess the fact that he expected nothing meant that he was in a better position than me. He was obdurate, and had always been so, but only because he had trained himself to be; mainly for reasons of self-preservation. He couldn't possibly have allowed himself to be easily moved by *any* feelings.

I suppose there had been some sort of denial that had gone on, again for self-preservation, even though underneath his obduracy there had always been a smidgen of admission. All of it helped him to weather that particular storm better than me.

Throughout the previous months and months of upheaval, I had maintained the tenacity of the controlled Alix – the resolute one of our little family. But something had happened when her back was turned. Even when I was doing other things, a piece of my mind held steady to the Billy-ness of my life and the babyless-ness of my world, which contributed to the fact that my resolve was waning. I was strangely glad of this. Not because I wanted it to, but because I felt dangerously under pressure and, somehow, because of my waning resolve, the pressure had inexplicably been taken off. We continued waiting, both in our own way. What choice did we have?

13

A WEIGHT ON
HIS BACK

I can't explain what you're feeling
In life I've learnt that we must try
You're lying open, still broken
And now I know things are gonna change

'House of Cards' by Lahayna

The days went by amid an endless fog of dread. And through them all, we waited. Thinking, anticipating, predicting and, of course, worrying. I really don't know how we got through those weeks before we actually left, except to say that you kind of automatically just take things one day at a time. You sort of have to, you really don't have much of a choice. It felt like the cogs of my brain were constantly turning round and round and I'm sure Billy felt the same.

It was during that time of such introspected brain activity that I was given a warning. Well, more than that really. It was a premonition. Plain and simple. I was never going to give birth. I don't know how or why it came to me then but I suspect my subconscious needed to get used to the idea during a time when so much other stuff was prevalent *and* taking precedence. It was actually a good time to become aware of my fate because I couldn't dwell on it. I couldn't pay attention to it. Not really. I told no one. They would have said I was just too stressed and I was most likely becoming paranoid or something. I couldn't bear to hear that, even though I knew it did look that way. And, of course, I couldn't vocalise it because it was still in a locked room at the back of my crowded mind. I may have known it was there but it was nowhere near the part of my brain that controlled speech.

The tragedy of it left me breathless. My mind wandered to it, then off it, and paused on odd thoughts here and there. For some reason, I remember that I had thought about how earthquakes, tornados and tsunamis are called natural disasters. They are forces of nature that ravage the earth, leaving a path of destruction in their wake, right? Well, then, what about disasters that are *against* the force of nature? What are they called?

The premonition episode happened on a night when I had allowed myself to think of our non-baby, which, I guess, brought on the pictures of her in my mind's eye. You know how when a person is about to die they supposedly see their life flash before their eyes? Well, lying in bed that night *before* I went to sleep, miraculously not thinking about going to court, our dark-haired cherub flashed before my eyes. I saw her on a swing, being pushed by Billy – a happier Billy, who had put weight on and looked healthy. I saw her running through a pile of leaves, the colour of her hair blending perfectly with the autumnal splendour. I saw her smiling at me cheekily with a milk moustache. I *saw* her.

As I lay there, frightened to blink in case it stopped, I heard a rushing in my ears. The crescendo of sound reminded me of water spraying out of a hose with increasing intensity, or of water gushing out of the hot water tap when the immersion had been left on too long. Then, with an audible f-f-floop, just like an air bubble travelling down the hot water pipe, the projector stopped and the slide show was over. Dark. Cold. Quiet. Nothingness.

Looking back, I know it was at that moment that I knew, in the deepest part of my soul, that my chance of ever getting to meet that gorgeous girl had gone for ever. I'm sure I was awake. Well, OK, maybe I was asleep, but, even if it had just been a dream, I had still been given a message. And it wasn't a very nice message. I would never get to touch her skin; I would never get to feel her breath on my neck as I held her; I would never get to endure sleepless nights, get to feel guilty for the millions of things that mums get to feel guilty over, or get to feel frustrated through endless temper tantrums. There would be no runny noses; no bedtime arguments; no teenager yelling, 'I hate you,' or staying out past her curfew. It broke my heart. Molly was gone.

I'd had it all planned – I was going to read her stories, sing her lullabies and take her on walks. I was going to brush her hair, wash her little clothes and cut her tiny toenails. I was going to make her Hallowe'en costumes, teach her the alphabet and prepare her for her life. I was going to love her. So how could that be? It just didn't seem right.

It was an unnatural disaster.

A tsunami had washed her out to sea; an earthquake destroyed our foundation; a tornado had blown her up to the moon – the moon that I had been too preoccupied to notice. That's what it was. An Unnatural Disaster.

I didn't completely admit it to myself, at least not in any concrete way. I suppose I tried to convince myself that I was wrong, that it was all a big mistake.

*   *   *

I knew Mr Drew didn't like me but I couldn't really figure out why. It wasn't something I was used to. I mean, teachers had always liked me. I always did my homework on time, I was never late for class, and I never played truant. I was polite, respectful and well-behaved. There was no reason that I could come up with, nothing that I could figure out, that would explain his negative view. All I could guess was that he'd simply made a mistake – misjudged me in some way. He couldn't have been very perceptive because, if he had spent any time 'seeing' me, it would have been quite obvious. I was not the kind of girl whom teachers didn't like.

Inside, in my head, I didn't have much respect for him. Of course, I didn't show it, but I simply couldn't think much of him because, when it came down to it, he wasn't even smart enough to figure out what type of girl I was. And it really wouldn't have taken much.

He had his favourites – but then most teachers did – and I didn't mind that because I had been 'the favourite' on one or two occasions, so I knew what that was like. It was just strange that he never called on me when I raised my hand to answer a question. He scowled at me a lot. He even gave me a few detentions – punishments that I never deserved. And he graded my papers harshly.

After a series of bad marks on reports that I'd spent a lot of time on, I was determined to try to figure out what it was all about. I thought about it from all angles and, finally, decided to try to see me through his eyes. I knew that most judgements that were made about people were due to the friends one hangs around with – and nowhere was that more true than in high school. I soon realised that, if he had just judged me on my friends in that particular class, it would have been easy to come to a misconception. Not one of my close friends was in that class and the two students whom I teamed up with for lab experiments and the like were not of my usual clique. The girl who sat behind me and the boy who sat beside me were friends from all the way back to my Willows Elementary School days. In fact, I quite liked the boy. I had always thought him cute, but, of course, I had never told anyone because we were from different crowds. My friends were not his, and his friends were not mine. We moved in completely different circles but there, in that classroom, we were friends. We got on well and laughed together a lot… which probably gave Mr Drew the wrong impression. That was really all I could come up with.

I wasn't prepared to turn my back on my friends, though, to achieve a better opinion from Mr Drew. We continued being friends and Mr Drew continued only calling on the 'good kids'. But it didn't bug me any more.

Towards the end of term, I received a C- grade on a paper and I was very upset. He usually gave me a C+, which was still lower than I thought I deserved, but a C- was going too far. I cried when I got home. The next day, he asked me to resubmit it, which I did. I was pleasantly surprised to get upgraded to a B+. He simply said he had made a mistake. I wasn't sure if he meant a mistake with my grade or a mistake with his opinion of me. Maybe my mum or dad complained, or he had seen my disappointment. I didn't know. But what I did know was that, after that, he started to like me.

It made me believe that, when things don't feel right, maybe a mistake has been made.

*   *   *

I was somewhat comforted by the knowledge that, even if it wasn't a mistake, even if it was true, I *would* still get to see my little Molly. I was confident that I would. And I have, many times. You know how it is – crowded space, sea of bodies, one familiar face looks your way – or maybe you don't.

These days, whenever I think about seeing her, I intellectually realise it is just daydreaming and wishful thinking. However, every once in a while, I see a child who looks just like the little girl in my dreams and I get the familiar cold-prickly skin feeling. Obviously, I never take it beyond a casual glance. Of course, I know that, whoever she is, she is not mine and Billy's... but if she looks back at me, then I feel like our Molly is saying hello to us through that little girl. Lots of times, out and about on the street or in the grocery store, a child will look at me and then, when she is walking ahead holding her mum's hand, she will turn and look back at me, as if she recognises me, too. It's enough. Because it *has* to be enough.

Now, whenever I hear James Blunt singing 'You're Beautiful', I relate to the words. I know that what the song means to me isn't what it really means, but all the words just fit so well. I'm sure Molly is an angel; I constantly see her face, and it too, is usually in a crowded place; she always smiles at me; I will always feel like I don't know what to do... because now I really do know that I will never be with her; and unfortunately it's time, and I must learn how, to face the truth. No other song has lyrics that mirror my thoughts so eloquently. I really only change one word so that it is a song about what I want it to be about. Everybody does that. In my version, my angel isn't with another man... she is with another mum.

Just before the court appearance, I wasn't as upset about my childlessness as you might think. At least, not consciously. Looking back, there were many, many times when I was so obviously sad. Inwardly, of course. And just for me. But still sad. I just didn't acknowledge those times.

I remember, in particular, one morning at the nursery, when I had been close to tears as we were all outside getting organised to go to the park or somewhere. As was our normal routine that day, I had strapped the youngest kids into the triple stroller while the older kids lined up against the outside wall. Well, I say older, but they were still only three. As usual, as soon as I told them to line up, they clambered to the wall and shimmied their bottoms back against it, just as they always did. It was a strict rule as it goes – the lining-up bit – for I needed to know that, while I was concentrating on the younger ones, the others were in one place, and stationary. And it was a good rule, one of many that they all mastered.

They were so cute. No matter where we were, whatever the circumstances, I only had to say 'line up' and they'd find the nearest wall. Sometimes, I asked them to do it just so I could watch them. 'Good listening,' I would say, and I was always met with beaming faces gazing up at me. All so proud.

Anyway, that day, as I was concentrating on tying buckets and sand toys on to the stroller, one of the little ones dropped their spade. I noticed one of the older girls standing against the wall with her arm held up. She looked so adorable, especially since I could tell she wanted to move but she knew she wasn't supposed to. I had no idea how she knew to hold her hand up to get my attention, but I asked what she wanted and she said, 'Can I get the spade?'

'Yes, honey,' I replied. I watched her lean down, her chubby, sun-kissed legs bending, and her hair spilling forward as she picked it up. She gently handed the spade to the child in the front seat. She spoke so softly and was acting with such maternal care I couldn't take my eyes off her. It was as if everything else stood still, frozen in time, except for the bubble of energy around her. A butterfly fluttered round her face, so close it tickled her skin, causing her to crinkle her little freckly nose as she squinted in the bright sun.

I could taste her tropical sunscreen, hear her innocence, see her throaty, velvet voice and smell her angelic-ness — my senses were momentarily thrown out of kilter, heightening the sense of suspension. Time was brought to a halt. 'You lovely thing…' I found myself saying out loud.

She peered up at me. And, after what seemed quite a delay, she said, in a feathery, silken voice that was entirely three-year-old, 'I not a thing, silly. I be a girl.'

'You're a honey bunny,' I said, ruffling her hair and bringing myself back. I was near tears, but I didn't know why… even though it was obvious.

It's funny how you can be more than one person living in the same head, at the same time. And even more so that one can protect the other. Of course, I know now what I was protecting myself from. Part of me wishes I could have stayed protected for ever.

Certainly, the stress of going back to Wales, and the whole court thing, buffered my sadness quite a lot. Especially since, just a few days after the premonition, we got the phone call we had been anxiously waiting for. We literally only got a few days' notice of our flight date and then I had to scramble around organising cover for the nursery and care for Ben.

So you see, I shoved that heartache way, way back. It was as if my brain took it upon itself to make an almost muscular effort to push it down, and to sweep it under. To think that was what Billy had had to endure for over 35 years! My thoughts just then, all my thoughts, were telescoped on Billy and the trial; any other issues simply fell out of its realm and so weren't acknowledged.

The nursery parents were very supportive. Well, at least all but one family. I had agonised over whether or not I should tell them why I had to take time off. I wanted to protect Billy's privacy, but I took my business very seriously and I didn't want it to look as though I was traipsing off on holiday without any thought for the nursery. So I told them individually. I still haven't forgotten any of the heartfelt and empathetic displays of sympathy and emotion.

One family, in particular, was great. Their six-month-old son had only just started the month before and I felt terrible leaving him so soon after he had finally settled into a routine with me. Obviously, him starting nursery was a huge adjustment for both mum and baby and I was loath to make her transition back to work any harder then it already was. I had just got him to a point where he was no longer crying when he was left in the morning and I felt incredibly guilty being the cause of his having to go through another adjustment. Both his mum and dad were wonderful and very understanding, insisting that I wasn't to feel guilty and that the baby would be fine. I had trouble adjusting to the role reversal but I was, nonetheless, extremely grateful.

Only one family reacted badly and took their child out of my care. I must admit, I was shocked at their reaction. They weren't unpleasant in any way and were insistent that their decision wasn't because of me. But I knew it was because of Billy.

It was my first, but certainly not my only, display of prejudice. In hindsight, I guess I can see that, ultimately, they were just trying to ensure their child's safety, but it makes me furious to know that people hold such a misguided opinion of victims of child abuse, especially sexual. I hadn't realised until then that people were going to view Billy differently... and judge him. I didn't, and it didn't occur to me that anybody else would.

The fact is that some people see the statistic that a high percentage of paedophiles were sexually abused in childhood, but they fail to realise that actually the percentage of victims becoming paedophiles is very low. They are two different statistics and the truth is clear when you examine the facts. I was fiercely protective of Billy and I hated even one person making such an unfair judgement. However, I guess encountering only one family's bad reaction, out of the thirteen families that I had registered, was pretty good going. I had always been honoured that I had been entrusted with the care of their most precious gift, but, for the twelve families that stuck by me, that honour was multiplied tenfold. I was proud of their trust and incredibly grateful for it.

It wasn't until I had begun the ritual, systematic preparations that I realised how out of sorts I had been over the previous weeks. The absence of my usual spirit had only been detected when I gathered strength back up again. Almost as soon as I started organising and putting things in order, ready for our departure, I began to gather my wits, increase my resolve and come into my own. It was so obvious to me that I had been derailed simply because I hadn't been able to prepare. Getting ready to go, precisely and methodically, ensured I was at my best and *that* calmed me.

That calmness, which I experienced often and which always came when I was particularly enjoying my orderliness, always gave me an added element to my consciousness. It was a heightened or accelerated quality that gave me the awareness of being both a receptor and a transmitter, as though enveloped by some pedagogic enchantment. Maybe the calmness allowed me to be more spiritually conscious, or maybe the act of organising made me more in tune spiritually which, in turn, led me to feel calm.

But, regardless of how it came about, I often experienced 'stuff' in that state. Actually, the day after we got word of our flight arrangements, I read an article in a magazine about something or other, I can't remember what exactly, and I came across the word 'halcyon'. I had never seen nor heard of it before, so I looked it up in my dictionary and found that the first entry said it meant peaceful, gentle and calm. I remember thinking it was a good word, and that I must remember it. I also marvelled at how fitting it was, especially due to my efforts of late to remain just that.

Then, that night, I picked up the novel I was reading at the time, ready to read a chapter before going to sleep, and I opened it up. My bookmark slipped out – which never happens because it's a magnetic one – so I proceeded to skim through, further along than I had read up to, trying to find my place. The very first word I saw was 'halcyon', and then I felt the familiar, cold-prickly feeling.

It wasn't a coincidence – at least, I didn't see it as such – and I couldn't help thinking that using the word 'halcyon' to get my attention was used to spotlight the meaning of that word, which I felt was a message in itself. I was being told to stay calm.

Things like that happen often and, when they do, I take them as a little hello. A cosmic kiss that, just for a minute, half a minute, leaves me feeling something not unlike elation with an overtone of privileged exclusivity. I felt ready to tackle anything.

Through all of the preparations, I was conscious of not creating a palaver or making too much fuss in front of Billy. I had to keep him calm and, for Billy, too much going on wasn't conducive to calmness at all. We didn't talk about it at all. We couldn't. Secretly, I think we were both shitting ourselves. I know I was. Even the packing was done under a veil of secrecy once Billy had gone downstairs. I'm not sure why. I suppose I didn't want Billy to have to confront it until the last possible moment. Looking back, I know that was ridiculous, as I'm sure he was thinking about nothing else. I was just terrified of breaking his seemingly apparent calmness and sending him over the edge.

★   ★   ★

'Approved School.'

He knew what the ruling would be. And really, as far as he was concerned, what hope did he have anyway? Social workers, police, judges – they only saw what they wanted to see. He knew that they thought he was a bad 'un and that they looked down their noses at him. They always believed the worst and they never, ever believed what he had to say. So what was the point? Of course he was being sent to Approved School.

He sat kicking the leg of the chair in front of him, feeling absolutely without hope, and almost certainly giving all those around him exactly the impression that he had accused them of having. It wasn't the first time he had had to appear in Magistrate's Court and experience told him to expect the worst.

When it was time for the magistrate to hear from Billy's social worker, a man – who turned out to be the social worker's father – approached the bench with a written statement from him. The magistrate read from it aloud.

Just hearing part of the first sentence, just a few words really, had Billy shutting down – 'out of control'… 'delinquent'. Billy had only ever seen that particular social worker on one occasion, so he was completely baffled as to how he could come out with all the things he'd written. The letter made it sound as though he had known him for years.

'What a bastard,' Billy raged inwardly, 'what a fucking, suit-wearing, tie-wearing bastard. He didn't even have the decency to be there in person. He'd rather be away on holiday sunning himself on some fucking beach than to be there, where he was being paid to be. He had sent his father, for fuck's sake! There's fucking social workers for you!'

Billy wasn't listening anyway but, as usual, there was no mention of what had been happening to him. No mention of why he had been running away at every chance. They weren't interested. They didn't ask any of the important questions. They weren't interested. End of story.

Billy was so frustrated and angry he got up and kicked his chair over.

Job done.

Approved School.

★   ★   ★

The morning before we left, I got the first indication that he was actually going to go. He asked me if I had packed his best shoes. I replied as nonchalantly as I could that I had, but inside I was so relieved I could have fainted. I knew we had a long way to go before we were actually at the court, figuratively as well as literally, but at least at that point he intended to go through with it. Not only that, but he even wanted to wear his best shoes! His question may have been a tiny indication, but I knew him well enough for it to speak volumes.

Maybe I wasn't giving him enough credit, but I didn't sleep at all the night before we flew. I had a terrible notion that he might leave in the night. I even went as far as hiding the van keys. I was determined to do all I could to get him to the court. I really believed it was a necessary step in his recovery. I didn't dare think about the possibility of that abuser getting off. I really couldn't go there. Billy simply had to get that bit of justice.

I didn't know it at the time, but Billy had talked himself in and out of going countless times throughout that night. His bailing out was really that close.

We were dropped off at the airport and caught the plane to Vancouver, where we then had to catch our connecting flight to Heathrow. By the time we were in the departure lounge, my nerves were shot. I didn't even go to the toilet, even though I needed to, and watched Billy like a hawk when he went into the men's toilets to make sure he didn't take off.

Once seated beside me again, Billy waited, impressively patient. I found it very difficult to stay still. Then, out of nowhere, our names were called over the loudspeaker, asking us to go to the front. I had no idea why we had been called and I practically had to drag Billy to the desk.

The woman behind the desk said that, since we had paid so much for the tickets, they were going to upgrade us to first class. I gratefully accepted their offer even though we hadn't been the ones who had paid for the tickets. It hadn't occurred to me to look on the tickets to see how much they had cost. I assumed they would be around the $800 mark, but my curiosity was pricked so I pulled them out of my bag to have a look. I was utterly shocked to see that they had actually cost $3,665 each! No wonder we were being upgraded! I thought it was so ridiculous that the Crown Prosecution Service had waited until they knew the exact day Billy would be called before they booked our tickets, so that they wouldn't have to pay our hotel bill for more nights than necessary. And then they ended up paying so much more. What a waste!

The excitement of being upgraded allowed me to forget about things but I was still very wound up. I remember allowing myself to relax once the aircraft had taken off. At least for the next ten hours Billy couldn't get off. It really was one step at a time. Of course, lying back in the big roomy seats and drinking a large glass of champagne that the stewardess brought round helped no end.

Upon arrival at Heathrow, we had so much to concentrate on Billy thankfully didn't have a chance to change his mind. He was so caught up in the culture shock of being around so many people and focusing on the breathing techniques he had been taught to help him through his anxiety that he was a bit of a zombie following me around. I had also given him an Ativan tablet in the hope of calming him, which certainly contributed to his state.

We went through Customs, retrieved our baggage and found the rental car all without a hitch. Thank Christ, I was a seasoned traveller and nothing went wrong, otherwise we would have been up the proverbial creek.

Initially, it was going to be arranged that we went by train to Newport. However, I contacted the person who had been organising all our travel arrangements and asked if we could hire a car instead. Not only was it cheaper, it was a much more acceptable mode of travel for Billy as he became very anxious on public transport – hence the need to drug him in order to get him on the aircraft. I didn't really understand the 'car' preference because I would have thought he would have been more likely to become stressed out driving without knowing the exact directions, but it soon became obvious that it was a matter of one being less stressful than the other. He was very tense when driving, but he would have been more uncomfortable in a confined area with people he didn't know.

The weather conditions couldn't have been worse. The rain was lashing down, restricting vision so much it was nearly impossible to read the road signs, making the drive particularly stressful. I kept reassuring Billy that I wouldn't get lost. It was just the M25 and the M4, so it really was straightforward, but Billy's prediction anxiety went into overdrive. 'We're not going to see the goddamn sign! We'll miss the turning!' Billy muttered angrily.

'We won't miss it but, even if we do, I'll be able to put us right again. Just relax!'

Jesus Christ, was nothing simple? I thought. Then it dawned on me that, if Billy was obsessing about getting lost, at least it was taking his mind off the trial. I decided to let him rant if he needed to and just tried as best I could to zone it out, saying the right things at the right time to keep a lid on it.

We eventually arrived at the Newport Hilton almost exactly 24 hours after leaving Victoria. We, of course, were shattered. I couldn't wait to get to our room, unpack before having a bath, and then bed. At the front desk, we were given a message to ring one of the witness support workers from the major crime support unit as soon as we settled in, which Billy did. The man told Billy that he and a colleague would meet us downstairs in the hotel bar at 8.00am the next morning. They would then go over everything with us and answer any questions either of us had before escorting us to the courts.

As soon as Billy hung up the phone, his ranting was once again redirected. Now he was all worked up about how inconsiderate and insensitive 'they' were at arranging our flight the day before he was due in court – especially since we had arrived at 9.00pm and we were getting picked up eleven hours later. Billy called them everything under the sun and was convinced that all they cared about was paying the least amount on hotel bills as was possible. Secretly, I doubted his theory, thinking that they did care but were actually not very smart when it came to their expenditure.

Actually, I was relieved that we didn't have time to dwell on what being in court would really be like. It was all so rushed Billy didn't have time to think too much, which, I was convinced, could only be a good thing.

'Total bastards!' I dishonestly agreed. Under normal circumstances, I would not agree just for the sake of it and actually enjoyed arguing my point, but at that moment I knew the easiest way to placate him was to agree. I didn't feel bad at not sticking up for 'them', whoever 'they' were, because I knew that I was doing it all for the sole purpose of getting him to court. Which is what 'they' wanted. I knew I was manipulating him, and had been since the beginning, but I concluded that the end justified the means. I was so tired and jet-lagged that I was having more than a little trouble keeping my opinions to myself. I was having a significant problem just thinking straight, never mind anything else.

Much to my relief, Billy agreed to take another Ativan and crashed out on the bed, which enabled me to have a long hot bath – water that wouldn't lather properly, I might add. It was something to do with hard and soft water but I could never remember which was which. I lay there and thanked my lucky stars that there was a bathtub. A shower would not have cut it.

The sound of Billy's snoring was as relaxing as my usual choice of Enya. I knew all was safe as long as Billy slept. If he had not gone to sleep, I wouldn't have dared to get in the bath, fearing that he would grab the opportunity to escape. I even kept all our money in a money belt that I kept with me at all times. Looking back, I can see that my logic wasn't actually very logical at all, for, let's be honest, if he had wanted to leave, I couldn't have stopped him.

Billy slept all night. I had trouble getting to sleep, most likely a combination of nerves and jet-lag, and I knew I needed to sleep otherwise I seriously ran the risk of getting a migraine. Stress was a trigger as well as lack of sleep, so I was worried I would end up having to endure the ritual vomiting in the toilets at the court on top of everything else. Just the thought of getting a migraine was enough to give me one, so I seriously had to get some sleep and stop my head.

As a rule, I never slept for more than three hours at a time, partly because I woke up to go to the toilet at least once a night, but also because I would always wake up whenever I moved or tried to turn over, due to my chronic pain.

Miraculously, that night I slept right through until just moments before the wake-up call. For a nanosecond, I forgot where we were. Then the telltale British ring tone shattered the silence, reminding my befuddled brain instantly. I had taken a bit more of my codeine to try to stave off my pelvic pain as best I could, as well as thinking it might stop a migraine, but, because of the caffeine content in the tablets, usually the more I took, the worse I slept. Thankfully, that hadn't been the case.

Billy was up. Sitting by the window, drinking his tea, he stared out at the trees. Not a particularly pleasant view, but I doubted he was even seeing it. I didn't want to bring him out of his trance, so I went into the bathroom instead. I tried to drag out the rituals of hygiene. I didn't want to face the day any more than I knew Billy did. We didn't speak. We both just got ready on autopilot, orchestrated smoothly, as if we were mechanical. We moved back and forth, washing and dressing without getting in each other's way.

Unlike machines, though, we both were full of emotion. Our silence wasn't awkward. If anything, it was comforting. We knew, without vocalising, when we were both ready to go. There were none of the usual questions – 'Are you ready to go? Have you got the room key?' We just sort of knew what the other would do.

I took a last scan of the room . Whatever the trial's result, Billy's part in it would be over by the time I saw myself there again. Then we just left the room and walked slowly side by side down the hallway. I saw Billy breathe deeply. He was shutting himself off *and* switching himself on. Preparing.

We met up with the witness support workers and went to sit at a table. After all our introductions, one of them went to get us all a coffee. I knew I wouldn't be able to swallow anything, but I couldn't even bring myself to decline the offer. Once we were all seated, they carefully went over what would be happening upon our arrival at the court. I was relieved to hear that a counsellor, specifically assigned to Billy, would be there to meet him at 9.30am. I was so glad that there would be someone available to him other than the detectives and support workers who were directly involved with the investigation. I knew he still didn't trust them 100 per cent but, hopefully, a proper counsellor would help.

I sat there, and I could feel myself zoning out, so disinclined was I to talk. My mind began wandering to the ridiculously trivial. I noticed crumbs on our supposedly cleaned table. I listened to the ridiculous laugh of the woman next to us. I wondered what could have possessed the man at another table to choose *that* shirt. I struggled to focus and pull myself together. They were talking with Billy, going over his statement and reassuring him. I could hear their voices but they started to sound weird – just like the teacher from *Charlie Brown*. I realised, with horror, that I was about to faint. The thought momentarily paralysed me. I then concentrated on gathering my thoughts to the mental rhythm of 'focus… breathe… focus… breathe…'

I looked up and noticed, with great relief, a ladies' toilet. I knew I had to splash cold water on my face quickly. I don't know how I did it, but somehow I managed to excuse myself and actually walk across the room. How I felt on the inside can't have been noticeable as nobody looked at me strangely.

Once in the bathroom, I splashed my face with icy water and felt marginally better. I was still shaky and faint and realised I hadn't eaten since the plane the day before – my concern for Billy's wellbeing transcending my personal needs. The last thing I felt like was food, but I knew my blood sugar had plummeted and, if I didn't eat something sweet soon, I would start throwing up. And, if I started throwing up, it would continue for ten to twelve hours with the usual intervals of thirty minutes to an hour. I couldn't risk that.

I had been lucky enough not to get a migraine, so it was stupid to let lack of food be the cause of any further problems. I remembered I still had a bar of chocolate in my bag, along with a packet of boiled sweets and a roll of mints that I had bought for the plane.

I was just about to retrieve the Mars Bar from the depths of my bag – it really was carrying everything but the kitchen sink – when two women came into the bathroom. I went into a cubicle. I couldn't stand there, in front of them, stuffing food in my mouth, in there of all places! I flushed the toilet to mask the sound of the wrapper being ripped open. Although why I bothered I don't know because, even if they had heard, they would have assumed it to be a tampon or something. I stood there in the tiny cubicle, appalled that I was actually going to *eat* in there. I was already feeling sick and the thought of the toilet right behind me didn't help much. I rarely ever use public toilets for their proper purpose, and then only when I'm desperate, so that whole scenario was ridiculous.

I carefully held the chocolate in its wrapper. I'd touched the door after all. The first bite was hell. I was sure I was going to be sick. My mouth was dry and I could barely swallow. I grabbed my water bottle out of my bag and took a big swig, washing it down. Somehow, I ate the whole thing. I drank some more water to rinse my mouth and then decided to suck on a mint in an effort to settle my tummy. I also decided to take an Ativan tablet. I had been prescribed them before when we were going through IVF, so I knew that I would be OK. During IVF, you take one before egg retrieval to relax you and the procedure had been a piece of cake, so I assumed the tablet worked. Finally, I quickly splashed water on my face once more, thankfully alone again, and hurried back to the table.

No one seemed to notice how long I had been gone, and perhaps it really had been only five or ten minutes or so. They were still talking, which was a relief, as I didn't want to keep them waiting. I sat down and decided to do my best to drink the cold coffee, hoping the caffeine would perk me up a bit.

Billy seemed OK. I sat, focusing on relaxing, and purposefully not listening to what they were talking about. After a while, I felt quite a bit better. I was no longer shaky and I was definitely less tense. Even when they all stood up and made to leave, my tummy didn't turn over.

On the way to the court, we followed the witness support workers to the car-hire place. Conveniently, it was on the way to the court so we were able to drop the car off on the way. Once we were all together in the car, we drove the rest of the way engaged in small-talk. I would have preferred to not talk at all, as I know Billy would have preferred. I knew they were only trying their best to alleviate our anxiety, but that would have been too tall an order. As we sat closely beside each other on the back seat of the small Fiesta, both of us nervous beyond description, I could feel the tension in Billy's body – a static current running out of him, causing a physical reaction of my own.

Almost as soon as we arrived, Billy went off to talk with the counsellor. I kissed him and hugged him, but he didn't reciprocate. I knew he couldn't. And then he was gone. It all happened so fast and, for the most part, all I felt was relief. I was still worried about him but I knew it was all out of my hands. We were there and his staying was not my responsibility any more. That alone felt great.

I didn't actually want to go in to the courtroom, so I waited in an area just outside the door. Other members of the Operation

Goldfinch team surrounded me. I was introduced to the Senior Crown Prosecutor, who was very friendly and empathetic. His choice of words made me feel validated in a way I hadn't before. I can't actually remember what he said exactly but, once again, it was the feeling that is remembered. It was the only time that anyone had spoken only to me, without it being about Billy. Well, it was, obviously, but Billy wasn't there and he was thanking *me* for being there and sympathised how hard it must have been for *me*. I hadn't expected it and I must admit it was rather nice. It was one of those times when something can mean so much to you but, at the same time, you just know that the other person won't remember it in quite the same way.

I looked up and saw Liam walking towards me. 'Hiya, love… y'all right?' he asked as he greeted me with a kiss on each cheek.

I smiled – as much for seeing a familiar face as it was a result of reminding myself of our family 'left side first' joke.

We exchanged pleasantries. He was clearly excited and maybe a tad nervous. I realised how much today meant to him, too. All his years of hard work had been propelling him to that point. Obviously, this wasn't his only trial during the course of the operation, but I knew he took them all to heart. We stood for a while. Lots of people were talking and there was a distinct air of excitement. I was glad Billy wasn't there to see or feel that; I knew he would take it the wrong way. I couldn't help but see it from their side, though. They had all worked so hard for so long. I didn't expect them to see it from Billy's side or vice versa. All I cared about was that we all wanted the same thing, even if it was for different reasons.

Someone came out and told us things would be commencing soon. My heart lurched. I sat down on a chair by the window. Liam came and sat beside me. I remembered that he and Mark had gone to Whistler for a quick visit after they left us, so, thankfully, I had something to talk to him about. Someone else came to sit by us. I smiled and spoke a few words, mindless small-talk really, but I was trying to make an effort. I wanted to create the right impression, even though I didn't know what that was. I was still obsessively worried about how Billy was coping; how the defence would treat him; how they would make him feel; how he was getting on with the counsellor.

As we sat in the hallway, surrounded by all the others, my eyes were drawn to an old man limping down the hallway. It was a case of sight and subconscious being quicker on the uptake than conscious thought, for my eye followed that man for a few seconds before my brain registered why it was doing so. I realised, just as Liam nudged me and pointed to him. It was *him*.

I watched as he continued down the hall. I guess all the descriptions I had heard were in my head and seeing him triggered a subliminal recognition of sorts. I was surprised that he was allowed to walk by us, just like that. Surely he could have been kept separate. I was glad Billy had already been taken away. Liam said something but I was too shocked to register his words, or to reply.

Some short time later, someone came out and told us that Billy was on the stand. Again, my tummy lurched. It was time. Billy finally had the chance to stand up and speak for the child he was. To stand up and be counted.

An immense feeling of pride overtook my anxiety. He was actually in there, at that exact moment, facing the hardest challenge of his life. But he had ammunition. He had his memory and that memory could save him. It had power and was really his only weapon. It is the only true recourse of the powerless, the oppressed or the brutalised. I prayed it was enough.

What felt like ages later, Liam came back. I hadn't even realised that he had gone, so focused I was on my thoughts. 'He was fantastic,' he excitedly commented. 'He did really, really well.'

'He did?' was all I managed to squeak out.

'He did.'

'Thank you.' I said this quietly, acknowledging an answered prayer. I could feel my eyes fill with tears and my throat become tight. I expelled a huge lungful of air.

The door opened and Billy was there. I rushed up to him. 'Are you OK?'

'I'm fine,' he answered in a way that suggested he did not recognise me as his wife. I was just a person standing there, like all the rest. He was shaking. I could see he was looking at me but I was conscious of him concentrating on the thoughts whirling around in his head. A world I couldn't be part of. The look in his eyes made me feel like he was looking at me truly from behind his face. Like his face was only a means to hide behind. Something he had placed between us.

The counsellor came and ushered him away. Someone told me she would help him debrief. Someone else spoke to me. I don't remember what they said. All that mattered at that moment was that it was over. He had *done* it. My Billy was amazing. I fought back the tears.

The Senior Crown Prosecutor came out and came straight to me. He shook my hand so strongly and emotionally that I knew it was heartfelt. 'He did brilliantly,' he beamed.

'Thank you,' I croaked, before taking a deep breath in. It felt like a long, long time since I had drawn a proper breath. Every inhalation of that day had been a shallow, anxious little intake that had brought no relief.

I may have been mistaken, but I was certain that, when the Senior Crown Prosecutor shook my hand and spoke to me, he had had tears in his eyes. The thought touched me deeply. By then, everyone had become very animated. The atmosphere was vibrant and exhilarated, and I suppose I was, too – although, for me, I think a sort of post-excitement daze somewhat overrode everything else. The relief and excitement were making me feel quite heady. Everyone was chattering and the atmosphere was positive and light-hearted. They obviously thought it was going well. Inside, I couldn't help thinking that they shouldn't count their chickens. My optimistic self had taken an uncharacteristic sabbatical.

Comments were whirling around from many different sources. 'Result!' 'Brilliant!' 'The judge was a good bloke!' 'We could get lucky!' 'Maybe double digits!'

It killed me that we wouldn't be there for the result. I knew Liam would let us know the outcome, but I worried that he wouldn't phone us immediately and I really didn't want to have to wait, even for one more second than we had to. However, the fact that it would be horrible if it wasn't a good result meant that I knew Billy would be glad to be leaving straight away. He was so pessimistic about everything that I knew that this outcome wouldn't be any different. He wouldn't believe it was going well until the verdict was read. For once, I felt the same. The pessimist and the optimist joined in anxiety.

About half-an-hour later, the counsellor came out and said she'd take me to see Billy.

'Is he OK?'

'He's holding up. He's been very brave.'

She led me down a dark hallway and in through a door into a small room. There Billy sat, completely motionless.

'You have done really well, Billy. You should be proud of what you have achieved,' she said.

Billy didn't appear to be very convinced as to the success of his testimony but nor did he seem resigned to its failure.

'Give me a ring if I can help in any way before you return to Canada. I'll leave you to it. Bye-bye.' She nodded once, smiled and left through the open door.

Billy sat forward on the edge of the chair with his head cradled in his hands so I couldn't see his face. I could hear him breathing. There was a slight catch in his breath now and then. He looked up at me, blinking. There were tears in his eyes and he wore the most remarkable expression, in which shock, bewilderment and relief were all mingled. Out of the three, relief was perhaps the most apparent.

'Oh, God,' he said. He sniffed and wiped his eyes on the back of his hand. 'I did it.'

'You most certainly did, babes. They all said you did brilliantly.'

Someone came and knocked on the door and asked if we were ready to be driven back to the hotel. Billy looked at me. I could tell it had just hit him. We were leaving.

We were then driven back to the hotel where we ordered room service, had a few drinks each from the mini-bar and crashed. Still jet-lagged, we both woke up in the middle of the night and were unable to get back to sleep. We ordered some soup from room service, watched a bit of television and finally went back to bed. We were exhausted and overcome with the after-effects of such prolonged, profound stress. I don't think, mentally, it had truly sunk in for either of us that we could actually relax. But, physically, our bodies took over. We both shut down and fell into a deep sleep.

The next morning, we checked out and went to Cardiff to stay a few days with Lauren. Billy was nervous about going but we couldn't come all that way and not see Lauren. At first, I thought that Billy was only nervous of going because he felt guilty for not going over for his mum's funeral and I felt sure that all those feelings would disappear once he was there – but they didn't. Of course, he was made up to see Lauren but he was very anxious and refused to go out. We were there for three days and he didn't once leave the house. I didn't want to acknowledge what was staring me in the face.

While we were at Lauren's, Liam came down to see us and to fill us in on what was happening. He was animated, celebratory and seemingly proud of the victory that hadn't actually come to fruition yet. I couldn't fault him. He told us that, because of something Billy had said while on the stand, he had corroborated four other men's testimonies. He didn't tell us what it was that had been so crucial, but it was awesome for Billy to know that, by taking the stand, not only had he helped himself, but he had also helped four other people. It made what he went through all the more worthwhile.

Liam gave us his mobile-phone number and told us to ring him the following Friday afternoon so he could give us an update. He didn't know for sure if he would be in a position to say too much, but he thought he would at least be able to tell us something about how the trial was progressing.

Just as he was about to take his leave, he also asked us if we would take a policeman's helmet back to Victoria for one of the police officers he had met while in Victoria, and with whom he had stayed in contact. I couldn't believe it when I heard the name. It was the same policeman who had attended both of the call-outs when Billy was at his worst. How ironic was that? Quite strange, really, that Liam had kept in touch with that particular officer. And there we were taking a helmet all the way back to him!

After visiting Lauren, and before flying back to Canada, we went up to Newcastle-upon-Tyne to visit my sister, Kate. We enjoyed our visit with her and thought the Northeast of England was so beautiful. The coastline at South Shields was fantastic, as was the scenery in County Durham, but we couldn't really relax and enjoy it.

The following Friday morning dawned fittingly dark and oppressive. Come the afternoon, we would hear some news. I knew it and Billy knew it, but neither of us spoke of it all morning. I knew Billy had remembered, because he kept wandering around as if he couldn't decide what to do with himself. He looked at me when he thought I hadn't realised. I did the same to him. I sensed he wanted to say something. I did, too, but I was unsure of quite how to begin.

At 2.00pm, Billy rang Liam, as arranged. I was standing in the dining room and I saw Billy out in the garden, phoning from outside as he needed a cigarette to make the call. I don't think I really took on board how important the phone call actually was. I was so preoccupied in my relief that Billy had got through the trial, and was so nervous about hearing whether the trial was going well, that I hadn't paid much thought to the fact that Liam might actually have news of the verdict. I could see by Billy's body language that he was extremely anxious. I could see his mouth moving, but I couldn't tell by the look on his face if the news he was receiving was good or bad. The wait was agonising.

He rang off and came inside, but didn't actually say anything for a good few minutes. The pretence was killing me, but I couldn't bring myself to ask him, almost eager to keep it unsaid in case it was bad, and so not wanting that to be true. Still, his expression gave nothing away. The look he gave me was so exposed, so naked, I felt as though I was invading his privacy just by witnessing it. Finally, Billy croaked, 'It's over.'

He sounded very emotional but not completely distraught. When he didn't continue speaking, I felt like shaking it out of him but, of course, I just stood there, motionless, barely breathing. I felt an omnipresent sense of dread. I tried to read his face, but it was impossible. Alarm began to gnaw away in my stomach. I couldn't stand the suspense any longer and was about to speak, but I hesitated because with his taut silence came a new daunting quality – a subtle reticence that couldn't help but trigger a feeling of trepidation.

The absence of an anguished response, though, was – I couldn't help hoping – promising. It was probably only a matter of seconds but the silence made it seem much, much longer. I was struck by how well I knew that tense silence. All the non-verbal nuances that spoke of our respective fears, hopes and desires – making it not all that silent after all. My thoughts were gluey and unconstructive, clogged with apprehension.

'Liam got a commendation,' he finally said. 'He was really chuffed.'

'Wow, good for him.' I didn't know if one could get a commendation if the case was lost, so I still didn't know the important bit. I waited and looked at him beseechingly and a tad tremulously. Then, with a slight flicker in his eyes and a twitch of his mouth, really in just a fraction of a second, a very intimate exchange passed between us. I then realised, with astonishment, that I *had* understood what had been conveyed. Incredibly, despite the absence of speech, the message had been sent and received. I smiled, just as Billy murmured, 'He was found guilty… he got ten years.'

1

EPILOGUE

(After)

County Durham, England 2005

You know I've found you now
And I will not let you go
You know that time will heal
The wounds that you show
Let the river flow
Let the river flow…

'The River', by James K

It is 'after' the truth came out, but really we are still in the 'during' stage. We are still working at it. Billy still has flashbacks; he still has nightmares; he still feels the need to be alert and very much hyper-vigilant – watching. Forever watching all that is going on, or not going on, around himself. And he still has to work hard at managing and assessing all his wired-in responses to the multitude of triggers that he still experiences.

There are so many triggers that neither of us can predict what they all are, when they are going to attack, or why. Billy knows exactly why some of them are triggers. With some, he thinks he has some idea why they may be significant – a type of shoe someone is wearing perhaps; an accent; the way the sun shines in a room; red leaves; a noise; a voice; a smell… or a combination of any of these, among hundreds of others – literally. There are even some triggers that I can identify but Billy can't. That's how inconspicuous they are. They aren't usually obvious. They aren't even consistent – a blue car seen in a busy street (maybe a particular street) on a rainy day (maybe a Tuesday) might trigger something, somewhere, in the deep recess of his brain. And, really, how in God's name can they be figured out? The answer is – they can't. They *aren't* always understood. In fact, sometimes, we haven't got a clue.

Ever so frustratingly, a lot of his wired-in responses to these persistent triggers actually hinder his path to wellness. In many ways, he is a typical example of how a person could self-destruct when those responses are detrimental. There are too many examples of times when Billy has responded to things with the mindset of a scared seven-year-old running away from an abuser. Even if he can intellectually recognise what he is doing, his brain still responds the 'wrong' way.

Some of his responses will never be rewired. They were entrenched too young, too long ago. But he can learn to manage them better. And it isn't as bad as it sounds. Sometimes, we just have to look at them as the 'responses' that saved him all those years ago. We kind of try to understand them without getting mad at them. They weren't manifested to harm Billy, after all; they were manifested to help him. And they did, very effectively.

To be truthful, Billy still sees his glass as half-empty, but that in itself is an improvement, for he didn't even see the glass before. We don't look at how much further he has to go. We focus on how far he has come.

I have my responses, too. I still hold my breath for a second, just before I open the door, when I return home after being out on my own. Actually, in the years since the worst period of Billy's breakdown, I don't think I have once not had a morbid twinge in the second that I am turning the key in the front door, or not had a quick scan as I enter the house. I still check in the night to make sure he's breathing. Those are responses that are involuntary and beyond my control but, luckily for me, they aren't wired in, they are just habitual. Time will relieve me of them.

Billy is still the pessimist in our family, but that isn't always a bad thing. Sometimes, I wonder why 20 years of hearing my positive take on things hasn't worn off on him a bit more, but mostly I just accept that it hasn't. His cynicism is a cloak donned such a long time ago, and is so heavy, that I doubt he will ever throw it off completely. He is the one, after all, who lives in the skin of the boy who'd grown up learning that people aren't what they seem, that evil is around every corner. He is cynical of others, yet somehow he is genuine. He is the boy who came from a childhood where physical rage was accepted as the common currency – where lying was expected and getting caught was bad. It was a world where communication appeared almost exclusively through acts of casual violence, where innocent touch and random affection were not something that was ever on offer. He was used to quarrels and frustrations being expressed in yelling and blows. He had grown up with it.

He is cynical of others, yet, somehow, and ever so extraordinarily, he is gentle. He is also the boy who was betrayed, in every sense of the word, first from his abusers and then the system. He is cynical of others, yet he is loyal. He *is* cynical, but he has every right to be, and I think it protects him.

It wasn't until 2004 that I actually took the opportunity to read Billy's police statement. Before then, I just couldn't bring myself to do it. Most people have nowhere to file such things. I certainly didn't. Up until 2004, I only had brief glimpses of the severity of the abuse – I witnessed first-hand the damage it had caused to Billy's mental health; I heard a comment from one of the detectives who came to Victoria, who said it had been horrific; and there was the length of sentence that had been imposed by the court. All those things convinced me to shy away from any observations of the details.

When I eventually got to the point where I thought I could handle it, I still had to prepare myself mentally to do so. I can remember feeling nervous and very nauseous when I first held his statement in my hands. It had felt strangely heavy, as if its repugnant content somehow made it weigh more. Obviously, I found it incredibly upsetting and difficult to read for all the obvious reasons, but it was also difficult in a strange, unidentifiable way. I definitely think that, because I'd had a preconceived idea as to the severity of the abuse, I had braced myself sufficiently enough in preparation, so that, when I actually read the details, it was in a detached and disconnected kind of way. However, even then, I wasn't prepared for how much the little details were going to upset me.

One such detail that I read was a comment in which Billy was referring to one of his abusers: 'I really thought I was his favourite. Then he ripped it all away. I never trusted nobody after that.' It was reading things like that – especially the 'favourite' bit – that brought the lump to my throat. You can't detach yourself from those sorts of comments – the unexpected ones – the way you can from the sordid details. Rather, I suppose, the simple remarks highlighted his anguish in a way that one can easily identify with, in a manner that so blatantly trumpeted of his humanness in the face of inhuman acts.

By the time I got through reading the whole statement, I realised straight away how much Billy minimises his abuse, perhaps in an effort to protect us. He often says thing like, 'It wasn't very good' or 'It wasn't very nice.' It frustrates me because I don't think he will be completely at peace until he can acknowledge how really awful it was. But I also know, for sure, that it takes time and lots of baby steps – a great deal of our time is spent going three steps forward, then two steps back.

Sometimes, I try to picture what it must have been like for him but, really, I can't. I don't think any of us, who haven't experienced it, can possibly even begin to. Judging by what I do know of the facts – which isn't everything, because I am sure he didn't tell all to the detectives – it's safe to say it was truly the stuff of nightmares.

Even now, Billy still downplays what he suffered. I'm not really sure why, but I kind of think that maybe he is afraid to admit just how bad it was in case it is too much for him to handle. He at least acknowledges that he was abused, though, and he is committed to working towards wellbeing. When he can actually admit to the severity of what he suffered, I will know that he has faced all his demons.

We live a quiet and simple life now, in a very beautiful and very rural village, in the Northeast of England. It is a village that encapsulates Britain of old. We like that. We are surrounded by all that is pure and wholesome. The homogenised high street is traded for a single shop-cum-post office. The green fields and the trees are the opposite of the urban sprawl and the littered streets. Nature's abundance and spiritual affluence are so far removed from the barren loneliness and the all-encompassing nastiness of Billy's past. It's good for Billy to be here. He is calmer, and I'm sure a lot of it has to do with being here. It is an oasis of all that is good. Billy loves it because it has nothing whatsoever to do with his childhood. And I love it because it produces in me a lovely blanket of spirituality. I think it was Aristotle who said something about a life worth living is one that evokes the feeling of being 'watched over by a good angel'. I feel that here. Definitely. Just that – watched over by a good angel.

This peaceful setting is simply so conducive to improved mental health and stability. Every day, I notice the surrounding beauty, even on the worst winter days. Sometimes, I still have to appreciate the beauty for both of us, on the days when Billy is too preoccupied to see it. But that's OK. It will always be here.

It certainly isn't easy breaking the habits of a lifetime – especially the ones of low self-esteem, inferiority, lack of confidence and zero self-worth, to name but a few. And it is so hard to dispel the bad influences and not allow the damaging memories to take you back to the role of victim. But Billy is having a damn good crack at it. And this wonderful place, with all the lovely people and the community spirit, is the very place to achieve it.

Billy is one of the many walking wounded in our society. But he is walking tall now.

APPENDIX I
INFLUENCES

As children, most of us encounter a few key people who influence our lives – or, at least, impact us in some way. I know for sure that, without having known some of the people I have met throughout my childhood, I would have missed out on some of the most important ingredients that have made me *me*; some were relatives, some were friends, some were neighbours, some were the result of chance meetings that lasted only moments, some were teachers.

I had one teacher when I was about twelve years old who really left an impression on me. He singled me out and, although I may not have been, he made me feel like I was his favourite. Twenty-seven years later, I still remember things he said to me. I'm sure he wouldn't even recall saying any of the little comments he made, or the bits of advice he gave. But I do. Yet it goes even further than that, and the importance is much more far-reaching than just some good memories of some nice things he did or said.

He had an impact on my future. I wasn't the prettiest, smartest, most athletic or the most popular. I was just sort of there, middle-of-the-road. He helped to give me the wonderful sense of self-esteem just from the knowledge that I didn't need to be all those things to be liked. And *that* has stayed with me all these years. It was good to be me. And, as a kid, it made me think that I must be worth it. Which really is how kids think. I don't know if I impacted on his life in any way, but I do know that partly because of him – actually, more than partly, *a lot* because of him – I am who I am.

I've taken it all into my adulthood, as we all do. Just one small gesture or comment can have a huge influence on a child's life. For me, not all the influences were good but none was bad.

For Billy, not all were bad but none was good. When he was at home, his neighbours thought the worst of him, as did his teachers. In the homes, the only care-giver who took him under his wing and showered him with praise and compliments was only gaining his trust, grooming him, waiting for the opportunity to rip it all away by sexually abusing him. The impact of that man – along with the other five abusers and the countless people who, for years, should have noticed and could have helped, but didn't – is the legacy Billy was left with.

After the way Billy was treated, with his lack of proper education, and after all that those things taught him about perception, both of himself and the world, it is hardly surprising that it is taking a lifetime to unlearn and disregard those influences and to make some sort of good, in spite of it all.

He is trying to live in a world where the two Billys co-exist – where his courage and his new 'learned' influences soften the truth and the pain. He is starting to believe that the world is a good place, even though horrible things can happen.

APPENDIX II
MEMORIES

I grew up slowly, leisurely savouring time, experiences and happiness. Despite that, though, or perhaps because of it, I don't actually have many distinct memories – not individually, at any rate. Of course, I have *some* specific memories, but not as many as you might expect. I suppose you could say everything is just sort of one big good memory. A collective memory that ensures I feel safe, secure and warm. Obscure, isolated flashes appear in my mind from time to time, but, although I try very hard for them not to be, most of them are blurred and indistinct.

I definitely remember things: there were my summers in Northern Ireland – going to stay in the caravan with my gentle-natured, fabulous uncle and my lovely aunt – special not only because she is my one and only aunt, but also because she made the best, sugary French toast; walking into Ballywalter, along the sand, with my cousin and my friend to buy choc ices and fruit gums; visits to England, with my other Grama and Granda, having days out all over Derbyshire and Yorkshire, especially playing hide and seek in the huge rhododendron bushes in Clumber Park; camping in the USA; my life in Canada, a happy family, enjoyable school experiences and true friends. But they are very much cumulative, completely inclusive, yet totally non-specific.

Billy grew up fast. Far, far too fast. He hadn't wanted to savour anything. He frantically stumbled through his days, trying to avoid pain and fear, while continually chasing elusive safety. Unlike mine,

Billy's memories are very much distinct, completely individual and totally minute in nature. 'Minute' in the sense that they were detailed and precise, but also in the sense of being singularly diminutive in relation to their collective quantity. Possessing intricate detail, they are cruelly vivid, painfully potent and savagely exposed. They cannot be compared with mine – not characteristically, or in any other way. There were no summertime holidays with grandparents. No uncles to take him on exciting mystery tours. No happy family. No choc ices. No love.

One of life's ironies is that, when memories are bad, they stand out. I often want to retrieve some little detail, yet can't, and Billy never wants to, yet does.

The way I see it, our memories are like threads. My threads are like good-quality, brightly coloured pieces of wool, all woven together to make my security blanket, the thing that keeps me warm. Yes, sometimes it falls, but I only need to wake up and pull it back up. It is always there. Billy's threads are like jumbled bits of scrap, heaped into an overflowing knitting basket. Remnants left over or bits cut from an old unravelling sweater. Dark colours, blacks, browns and greens, all thrown in together.

The thing is, though, even all that mishmash *can* be made into, if not a security blanket, at least some manner of cover. It may be a bit rough and makeshift but it can still be serviceable and capable of producing some warmth. It will be much harder to produce but, sometimes, the harder one works to make something, the more meaningful it becomes. The end result can often be all the more beautiful for it.

I know Billy can do it. He can make it out of his new threads of the memories of *our* life together. Memories that will, hopefully, one day, overshadow the old ones.

APPENDIX III
HOPE

I am not a writer, I am a wife, who first used writing as a way of processing all that had happened to us, in an effort to make some sort of sense out of it all. And then I started to put all the bits together, and it turned into a book.

Also, after reading articles in the newspaper highlighting the complaints of the so-called 'trawling methods' used by the investigators, in this and other operations, I was angry. There seemed to be so much more publicity questioning whether false allegations had been brought about as a result of investigators allegedly enticing people with the potential of hefty compensation payouts. This, we now know, is so far from the reality of the situation it's ridiculous.

Obviously, I can't say what the other operations were like, but it certainly wasn't the case with us. The detectives who dealt with us were totally professional and completely above board at all times. Compensation was never mentioned. No amount could compensate anyway. And, for survivors, going public and fighting for justice is never about the money. I want people to know that. I also want people to know that this kind of abuse did, and does, happen. I want people to know about the devastating effect abuse has on the victims – and, ultimately, society. In the end, we decided to publish our story in an attempt to inform and inspire.

Maybe it will help other wives or husbands to realise that, when problems arise in a marriage, a lot of the time it isn't personal; it is more likely to be due to baggage that their spouse brought into the marriage. Maybe it will help others to support their spouses and to work towards understanding. Maybe it will promote tolerance, or at least make us stop and think. Maybe it will remind care-givers, teachers or parents that even the slightest thing can make a difference. Maybe it will remind parents to cherish their gift. Maybe it will help other survivors of childhood abuse to see that they are not alone. Maybe it will give others hope. We hope so.

My husband is not Billy Connolly or Sheldon Kennedy (the NHL hockey player), or any other famous person who has triumphed over adversity. He is just an ordinary man with an extraordinary psyche, who was somehow able to live through hideous abuse and come out the other side a caring, sensitive person. I don't know anyone who is as thoughtful or considerate of others. As far as I can see, he didn't inherit his spirit from anyone and he certainly didn't benefit from any nurturing in his formative years. I guess he is just one of those people who are the way they are simply because they are who they are. And I am a person who is lucky enough to love and be loved by one of those people.

Acknowledging it and accepting it, that's what sets you free... that's the answer. The rest is up to us. And, whatever happens, I trust that things have a way of working out.

Then something magical
Replaces disarray
Why don't you bring it on
And all that which is beautiful
Will dissipate the pain
And maybe just a little love

It wouldn't take a miracle
Just a little love

'It Wouldn't Take a Miracle' by Dirk McCray

A charity CD, *NAPAC Un-muted*, has been created to accompany this book. The CD incorporates each of the songs that I have quoted at the beginning of each chapter (some of which are original songs written and recorded by survivors). To buy *NAPAC Un-muted* please go to www.alixchapel.co.uk or www.napac.org.uk.